T0304665

*Value in Due Diligence*

# *Value in Due Diligence*

## Contemporary Strategies for Merger and Acquisition Success

Edited by

RONALD GLEICH, GORDANA KIERANS
AND THOMAS HASSELBACH

Routledge
Taylor & Francis Group

LONDON AND NEW YORK

First published 2010 by Gower Publishing

Reissued 2018 by Routledge
2 Park Square, Milton Park, Abingdon, Oxon, OX14 4RN
605 Third Avenue, New York, NY 10017

First issued in paperback 2021

*Routledge is an imprint of the Taylor & Francis Group, an informa business*

ISBN 13: 978-0-815-39886-8 (hbk)
ISBN 13: 978-1-351-14344-8 (ebk)
ISBN 13: 978-1-138-35857-7 (pbk)

DOI: 10.4324/9781351143448

# Contents

# List of Figures

# List of Tables

# Acknowledgments

We are grateful to all the contributing authors for this book and for their efforts to share their expertise. Furthermore, we thank Gower Publishing for the trust they put in us before we had furnished the final version of this book. A special thanks is extended to Jonathan Norman for his patience and support during the process for this publication.

Last but not least, we thank our colleagues at the EBS Business School Wiesbaden, specifically, Ms Luise Sommer and Dr Johanna Schoenrok for their valuable support and feedback.

# *Preface*

The prevailing trend for companies to accomplish growth via mergers and acquisitions (M&A), as opposed to organic growth, continues unabatedly. Despite equally incessant *'breaking news'* headlines about the varied turbulent challenges facing our global economy, most experts acknowledge that this corporate thirst for M&A will continue.

Moreover, taking into consideration that many recent mergers and acquisitions have also become equally newsworthy due to their now legendary failure, there is clearly an ever-increasing imperative for companies to be not only far more meticulous in their due diligence undertakings but to also significantly broaden their due diligence considerations. Herein, lays the rationale for this book.

*Value in Due Diligence* covers the most contemporarily relevant strategies to better assure M&A success. The varied chapters, authored by renowned experts recruited for both their global perspective (the authors come from Germany, the USA, Australia, the UK, Ireland, Ghana, France and China) and for their respective and distinctive expertise in a wide cross-section of M&A issues, are conveniently presented in an 'easy to follow' sequential order paralleling the M&A process.

The authors' credentials result in a book that offers you both a theoretically sound treatise and a comprehensive coverage of the most relevant due diligence concerns (an 'all-inclusive-package' found in only one book!). More significantly, recognising that today's busy managers also desperately need a practical 'how-to', the book's focus on practicality will appeal to all managers, consultants, accountants, controllers, lawyers, professors and students who are committed to understanding, and accomplishing, M&A success.

With respect to the relevancy of the content, the first third of the book, entitled 'Strategy Development and Target Identification', deals with strategic fit, integration and M&A controlling considerations. The middle portion, 'Due Diligence and Results Evaluation' continues covering the critical issues of marketing, innovation capability, IT and also includes a case study on Due Diligence of young companies. In 'Deal Negotiation and Post-Merger Integration', the final third of the book, the subject matter shifts to jump-starting integration, value creation, the role of leadership and the most decisive strategies for post-merger success.

In short, if you are charged with, involved in, or indeed even impacted by, due diligence and M&A activities, be it from either a corporate or academic perspective, *Value in Due Diligence: Contemporary Strategies for Merger and Acquisition Success* will prove to be a compelling and profitable read.

Professor Ronald Gleich,
Dr Gordana Kierans and
Thomas Hasselbach

# About the Editors

## Ronald Gleich

Professor Ronald Gleich started his academic career at the University of Stuttgart in the Department of Accounting in 1991. Paralleling his now accomplished academic career, he has also been active in the private sector as partner at an international consulting company and has assisted international companies with their accounting challenges. In 2003, he joined EBS Business School as Professor for Industrial Management and today is Executive Head of the Strascheg Institute for Innovation and Entrepreneurship.

Professor Ronald Gleich is an accomplished and renowned expert in Innovation and Accounting. He has published numerous books and articles with academics and professionals and is frequently invited to speak at conferences and workshops. Additionally, he is member of several editorial boards.

## Gordana Kierans

Dr Gordana Kierans (née Bjelopetrović) holds her PhD in Business Administration from the University of Kassel, Germany. Subsequent to her university studies, completed in 2001, she has continued her management and academic pursuits at different business schools, wherein she also consulted for small and mid-sized enterprises (SME).

At the Strascheg Institute for Innovation and Entrepreneurship (SIIE), EBS Business School, she is a Research Fellow and heads several projects which are actively engaged with industry partners.

## Thomas Hasselbach

Thomas Hasselbach completed his studies at Johannes Gutenberg University Mainz, Germany in 1995 after which he started his business career with InterCom Group, a consulting company based in Mainz. He was head of several units and led European-wide projects, mainly in Prague and Barcelona. In 2001, he became Member of the Board of InterCom Holding with approximately 150 employees in Mainz, Wolfsburg, Prague and Barcelona. After the acquisition of this company by American Agency Network Bates, Thomas Hasselbach became responsible for the area of Strategic Consulting. In 2003, he started his own business, helping companies like Porsche with its marketing and strategic issues. Furthermore, Thomas Hasselbach is a Managing Director of MikroForum Technology Site near Mainz.

# List of Contributors

## Uwe Bloch

With more than ten years of IT and business consulting experience for banks and telecommunication companies in Germany, Uwe Bloch has played a vital role on IT Due Diligence teams for M&A projects, as well as, developing post-merger scenarios. In addition, he has been part of vendor management teams structuring and restructuring through strategic sourcing and developing new approaches for IT sourcing. In November 2008 he joined Avato Consulting AG as Partner.

## L. Jay Bourgeois

L. Jay Bourgeois, III, is Senior Fellow, Tayloe Murphy International Center, Darden Graduate School of Business, University of Virginia, where he teaches Advanced Strategy and Post-merger Integration. Dr Bourgeois has consulted for more than 50 firms and governments around the world on strategy and post-merger integration. Following five years in international business, Bourgeois received his PhD from The University of Washington in 1978, and taught at Stanford University. Professor Bourgeois has published two books and over 60 scholarly articles and teaching cases. He is listed as among the top 0.5 per cent of the most-cited authors in the field of management.

## Andreas Brokemper

Dr Andreas Brokemper studied Economics and completed his PhD in Controlling on Strategic Cost Management. For more than 10 years, he has worked for the Oetker Group, initially as Department Head of Controlling in Bielefeld, Germany and then for seven years as CFO for the Henkell Group, an international sparkling wine and spirits producer with over €600m in sales and in excess of 2,200 employees. During his career he has joined and led many acquisition projects. As CEO, he also advises many leading companies of the Henkell Group in Romania, Hungary, Italy and the USA.

## Jan Buchmann

Mr Buchmann holds a joint diploma degree in Business Administration and Computer Science from the University of Technology Darmstadt, Germany. After his studies, he worked for two and a half years for an international management consulting company in the strategy and business transformation practice before he joined the doctoral programme at EBS Business School, Germany. He currently works as Project Manager and

Research Assistant at the Strascheg Institute for Innovation & Entrepreneurship at EBS and also advises companies in the fields of innovation and risk management. His research includes the valuation of innovative firms, employee participation in innovation systems and related topics of innovation management.

## Michael N. A. Cobblah

Michael Cobblah is the Country Representative for Ecobank Development Corporation (EDC) in Ghana, the Regional Investment Banking Subsidiary of the Ecobank Group. He oversees the investment banking business of EDC-Ghana covering Stockbrokerage, Asset Management and Corporate Finance. Prior to this, Mr Cobblah worked with various institutions including PricewaterhouseCoopers Ghana, Merchant Bank Ghana Ltd and the Ministry of Finance. He has over 15 years experience in private and public sector financial services in various countries across Africa. Mr Cobblah is a Certified Valuation Analyst (CVA) – International Association of Consultants, Valuers and Analysts (IACVA, Canada) and holds an MBA from the University of Birmingham and a BA (Hons) from The University of Ghana.

## Mehdi Farhadi

Mehdi Farhadi MBA, ADipC is Senior M&A Manager at one of the 'Big Four' transaction consultancies and advises international corporations on transatlantic mergers, acquisitions, divestitures and exit strategies. He was deputy CKO at Arthur Andersen and has extensive consulting experience for more than 15 years. Mr Farhadi is also a Doctor of Business Administration Research Associate at Henley Business School, School of Management, University of Reading in the UK. He publishes regularly in the field of strategy, M&A and growth.

## Timothy J. Galpin

Dr Timothy Galpin is an Associate Professor at the University of Dallas College of Business. He has over 20 years of experience as a management consultant and business manager working with boards and senior management around the world on strategic planning, strategy execution, mergers and acquisitions, divestitures, restructurings, human capital management, business productivity improvement and organizational culture change. Dr Galpin has published three management books: *The Complete Guide to Mergers and Acquisitions*; *Making Strategy Work: Building Sustainable Growth Capability*; and *The Human Side of Change: A Practical Guide to Organization Redesign*.

# Mathias Gerner

Mathias Gerner is a Research Assistant and Doctoral Candidate at EBS Business School, Wiesbaden, Germany. He completed his studies in Industrial Engineering at The University of Karlsruhe (TH) including a semester abroad at the Mathematics and Statistics Department at the Herriot-Watt University of Edinburgh. Between 2006 and 2008 he successfully finished the Management Trainee Program (SGP) of the Siemens AG, Sector Energy. His main research areas are commodity risk management, energy prices and derivatives.

# Michael Graham

Dr Michael Graham is currently a senior lecturer at the School of Economics, Finance, and Marketing at the Royal Melbourne Institute of Technology (RMIT) University, Melbourne, Australia. His research interests include corporate finance, financial markets, and corporate governance. Michael Graham has been published in respectable international journals including the *Journal of Multinational Financial Management*, *Global Finance Journal*, and the *Journal of Economics and Finance*. He has also worked with reputable organizations including The United Nations University, World Institute of Development Economics (UNU/WIDER), and the Australian Competition and Consumer Commission (ACCC). Dr Graham holds a Master of Science Degree in Economics from the University of Tampere, Finland, and a PhD in Finance from the University of Vaasa, Finland.

# Thomas Herrmann

Thomas Herrmann studied Business Administration at the University of Trier, Germany and at the UMIST Manchester School of Management, in the UK. After finishing his studies, he worked at Deloitte as Senior Consultant in the Transaction Services Department, specializing in due diligence projects. For more than five years, he has been working as Acquisition and Group Controller and, currently, as Finance Manager for the Henkell-Group, an international sparkling wine and spirits company, where he assists the Group in many international acquisition and coaching projects.

# Henning Hoeber

Henning Hoeber is a Fellow, Tayloe Murphy International Center, Darden Graduate School of Business, University of Virginia. He was also a visiting researcher at INSEAD, where he formed part of the 'Global Latinas' team, a project group dedicated to the strategic analysis of Latin American multinational companies. His research and teaching interests are in the area of mergers & acquisitions, corporate valuation and strategy, with a special focus on companies from emerging markets. Prior to his studies in Business Administration and Economics in Germany, he spent two years of commercial apprenticeship in Barcelona, working in the shipping and insurance sector.

# Ulrich Hommel

Ulrich Hommel is a Professor of Finance at EBS Business School, Wiesbaden, Germany. He holds a PhD in Economics from The University of Michigan, Ann Arbour, and has completed his Habilitation in Business Administration at the WHU – Otto Beisheim School of Management. He has held visiting positions at the Stephen M. Ross School of Business (University of Michigan), the Krasner School of Management (Purdue University) and the Bordeaux Business School. His main research areas are venture capital contracting, family business finance, real options, and corporate risk management.

# Florian Kissel

Mr Kissel studied Business Administration at EBS Business School, Wiesbaden, Germany and Haskayne School of Business, Calgary, Canada. During his studies, he worked as an intern in the Controlling Department of a German telecommunications provider and as a summer associate with an international consulting company. Florian Kissel currently specializes in corporate finance and valuation in the context of the Master of Science in Finance and Investments Programme at the Rotterdam School of Management.

# Mary Lambkin

Mary Lambkin is Professor of Marketing at the Smurfit Graduate Business School, University College, Dublin. She completed her PhD at The University of Toronto and has been published widely in leading marketing journals. She has also been actively involved in the business world, serving as a non-executive director of several major companies.

# Malcom McDonald

Malcolm, previously Professor of Marketing and Deputy Director Cranfield School of Management, is a graduate in English from Oxford University, in Business Studies from Bradford University Management Centre, has a PhD from Cranfield University, and a D.Litt from Bradford University. His extensive industrial experience includes a number of years as Marketing Director of Canada Dry. Additionally he had authored 43 books. He is Chairman of Brand Finance plc and spends much of his time working globally with the operating boards of the world's biggest multinational companies. He is Visiting Professor at Henley, Warwick, Aston and Bradford Business Schools and Emeritus Professor at Cranfield.

# Laurent Muzellec

Laurent Muzellec is a lecturer at Dublin City University. He holds a PhD from University College Dublin, an MBA from Texas A&M International University and a BA in Political

Science from IEP, France. He has worked as a Trade Attaché for the French Diplomatic Service and as a Business Development Manager for a hi-tech company.

## Brian Smith

Brian Smith is a researcher, author and advisor in the field of marketing and competitive strategy. He is a Visiting Fellow at The Open University Business School. He has authored over 150 papers and books in this field and is Editor of the *Journal of Medical Marketing*. He runs Pragmedic, a specialist strategy advisory firm.

## George Tovstiga

George Tovstiga, a Canadian and German national, is Professor of Strategy and Innovation Management at Henley Business School, University of Reading in the UK. He has extensive international experience as a management educator, industry practitioner, author, and consultant. He has over 15 years industry management experience, notably in the areas of R&D, Innovation and Engineering Management with Xerox Research (Canada) and Bayer AG (Germany) and ABB (Switzerland) AG. His professional experience has been gained in a diverse range of international assignments in the field of Strategic Technology and Innovation Management in both industry and academia.

## Athina Vasilaki

Athina Vasilaki is an Assistant Professor at IESEG School of Management in Lille, France. Her PhD research area was on the role of leadership in enhancing post-acquisition organizational performance. Her research interests include leadership, organizational culture, mergers and acquisitions and performance measurement.

## Keith Ward

Keith Ward studied economics at Cambridge and then qualified as both a Chartered Accountant and Chartered Management Accountant. He has worked both England and abroad as a consultant and has held senior management positions in manufacturing and trading companies. In 1981 Keith joined Cranfield School of Management, where he progressed to become Professor of Financial Strategy, as well as, being Head of the Finance and Accounting Group and Director of the Research Centre in Competitive Performance. He then moved to a Visiting Professorial role at the School until the end of 2008, while continuing with his research and consultancy interests.

## Alfred Yawson

Alfred Yawson is an Associate Professor in Finance at the University of Adelaide Business School. His primary area of research is corporate finance and corporate governance. Alfred's research has been published in leading finance journals including the Journal of Banking and Finance, Journal of Business Finance and Accounting, Corporate Governance: An International Review and the Pacific Basin Finance Journal. Dr Yawson obtained a Bachelor of Science with honours degree from the University of Ghana, a Master of Science and a PhD in Finance from Queens University Belfast (UK). He is also a Chartered Accountant with industry experience in reputable financial institutions.

## Martin Zerfass

Mr Zerfass worked for more than five years as a Management and Business Consultant in the area of IT Outsourcing and IT Contract and Service Level Agreements. Having a legal degree, supplemented with a MBA from a top European business school, during recent years, he has worked in Strategic Sourcing and M&A divisions. He is currently working in Shanghai in Business Development/M&A for a worldwide automotive and industry supplier. He combines both in-depth knowledge of IT with a high degree of M&A know-how.

# Reviews for
# Value in Due Diligence

*This is a book all corporate decision-makers should be reading prior to their next merger or acquisition. It shows important aspects that need to be considered to ensure the success of a deal. It is also enlightening for university professors and their students.*

*Many of the chapters highlight the reasons for past M&A blunders and all chapters cover remedial and contemporary strategies for Due Diligence. The international team of contributing authors truly offers a global perspective on this crucial issue for corporate growth.*

Martin Scholich, Board Member,
PricewaterhouseCoopers AG

*This comprehensive book targets all managers, and their team members, responsible for corporate Due Diligence. It is also a must read for consultants, controllers, accountants, lawyers and both professors and students.*

*The contributing authors, selected for their global expertise on a wide cross-section of M&A issues, offer both a theoretically sound treatise but also a handy and expedient 'how-to' guideline to better ensure your M&A strategies will succeed.*

Dr Axel Steiger-Bagel, Board Member,
Bayer MaterialScience AG

# I

# Strategy Development and Target Identification

# 1 Due Diligence on Strategic Fit and Integration Issues: A Focal Point of M&A Success

MICHAEL N. A. COBBLAH
*Ecobank Development Corporation, Accra, Ghana*

DR MICHAEL A. GRAHAM
*School of Economics, Finance, RMIT University, Melbourne, Australia*

DR ALFRED YAWSON
*Business School, The University of Adelaide, Adelaide, Australia*

## Introduction

Mergers and acquisitions (M&A) are a major part of the corporate restructuring process and one of the fastest strategic management tools to grow a business. Many M&A deals run into hundreds of millions, or even billions, of dollars. It is no wonder then that they arouse strong feelings and grab the headlines when deals are announced. According to the SDC Platinum database, M&A transactions involving acquirers in G7 countries in the 2007–2008 period alone totalled 29,131 with a transaction value of USD 3,128,954 million as presented in Table 1.1.[1] Out of the total number of transactions, 79 per cent and 21 per cent were domestic and cross-border deals, respectively. The transaction value of the domestic deals was USD 2,253,472 million.

Synergy is proposed as the main motivation behind these M&A activities. However, the literature suggests that most M&As have a less than stellar record in meeting the financial and synergistic expectations of stakeholders (for example, Rau and Vermaelen (1998); Moeller, Schlingemann and Stultz (2005); Fuller, Netter and Stegemoller (2002)). Both the academic and industry literature suggest that over 50 per cent of all acquisitions have failed (for example, Pautler (2003); Homburg and Bucerius (2006); Chatterjee (2009)). Given the data presented in Table 1.1, this implicitly translates into a loss of USD 1,564,477 million to shareholders in the G7 countries during this 2007–08 period. The many recorded abysmal performances, and indeed outright failures, in M&As are worrying and demand thorough investigation into the factors underlying this phenomenon.

---

1 Takeovers are defined as deals where the acquiring firm holds less than 50 per cent of the target's stock pre-takeover and successfully achieves more than 50 per cent at the takeover completion date.

**Table 1.1    Acquisitions by Firms in G7 Countries during 2007–08[2]**

| Country | No. of deals | % of domestic deals | % of cross-border deals | Value ($M) | Domestic deals (% of value) | Cross-border deals (% of value) |
|---|---|---|---|---|---|---|
| Canada | 2,717 | 69.64 | 30.36 | 236,134.59 | 61.80 | 38.20 |
| France | 1,956 | 64.47 | 35.53 | 217,477.24 | 37.34 | 62.66 |
| Germany | 912 | 62.61 | 37.39 | 143,311.25 | 37.26 | 62.74 |
| Italy | 817 | 72.34 | 27.66 | 165,194.35 | 58.71 | 41.29 |
| Japan | 2,771 | 93.04 | 6.96 | 126,381.05 | 80.49 | 19.51 |
| UK | 4,559 | 70.74 | 29.26 | 523,989.73 | 61.99 | 38.01 |
| US | 15,399 | 83.75 | 16.25 | 1,716,465.31 | 84.43 | 15.57 |
| Total | 29,131 | 79.00 | 21.00 | 3,128,953.53 | 72.02 | 27.98 |

In the finance literature, the inability of M&A activities to engender good returns is often explained by the simple fact that the acquirer overpaid for the target. This literature has mainly examined M&As from the perspective of returns accruing to bidding and target firms' shareholders, with a focus on the relationship between the market for corporate control (for example, mode of payment, type of transaction, and number of bidders) and shareholder gains (Jensen and Ruback (1983); Loughran and Vijh (1997)). The contribution of this body of research has, undoubtedly, been momentous. However, these studies only provide a partial insight into the factors that influence M&A outcomes, as many documented failures are left unexplained. Nonetheless, both industry participants and the strategic management literature (see for example, Shelton (1988); Seth (1990); Birkenshaw, Bresman and Hakanson (2000); Waldman and Javidan (2009)) have regularly cited 'people' problems and cultural issues as the top factors in failed mergers.

Typically, the M&A process starts with the identification of an opportunity to create value. Once a decision has been made to progress the acquisition, advisors are appointed to lead the effort in structuring the transaction. These advisors undertake preliminary background work to assist in determining an optimal bidding price subject to due diligence and other regulatory approvals. The due diligence process mainly involves financial, technical, and legal issues which collectively, lead to a business valuation of the target. The valuation takes into account all transactions impacting issues that may directly or indirectly affect the initial bid. Once this process has been successfully completed, negotiations begin. What most due diligence processes fail to unearth is what we consider to be the 'soft' issues within the organization. These include people issues and operational due diligence which are intangibles and, hence, difficult to quantify and adjust within the context of the actual valuation of the target.

The objective of this chapter is to highlight the importance of strategic fit, organizational and cultural issues at this early stage of the merger process. Balmer and Dinnie (1999) note firms pay significant attention to the legal and financial considerations when

---

2    The table reports the volumes and values of mergers by the G7 countries. The acquisition data is compiled from the SDC Platinum database of domestic and international acquisitions.

conducting due diligence but neglect the implications for corporate identity. Knowing how to manage the strategic and people challenges that are bound to arise can enhance the chances of a successful merger. As such, in this chapter, we also draw upon both the academic literature and industry commentary to make a case for paying attention to intangible factors that are predictors of merger success at the due diligence stage. Isolating deal making from integration challenges creates problems for the merger. The imbalance between closing the deal and post-acquisition integration results in the loss of an important source of leverage to produce a value-added asset combination. As such, we propose that due diligence should begin in the acquiring firm before a decision to approach a potential target is finalized. Subsequently, the due diligence process must go beyond legal and financial matters to include organizational and human consequences. Further, the advisors involved in the transaction should approach strategic, organizational and cultural due diligence with a dynamic attitude since the business environment is also dynamic. The rest of the chapter is structured as follows. In Section 2, we discuss the content of strategic fit. Section 3 focuses on organizational and cultural fit issues. Following that, we relate strategic fit and integration issues to due diligence in Section 4. Section 5 concludes.

# Strategic Fit

The concept of strategic fit has its theoretical underpinning in contingency perspectives found in both the strategy and organization theory literature (Ginsberg and Venkatraman (1985)). In business studies, the general notion of fit is rooted in the concept of 'matching' or 'aligning' organizational resources with environmental opportunities and threats (Andrews (1971); Chandler (1962)). According to Miles and Snow (1994), the process of achieving fit begins by aligning the company to its marketplace and this practice defines the company's strategy. Zajac, Kraatz and Bresser (2000), in a model of dynamic strategic fit, identify environmental and organizational contingencies that influence changes in the firm's strategy. Generally, strategic fit is viewed as having desirable corporate performance implications. These implications include cost reduction due to economies of scale and the transfer of knowledge and skills. Strategic fit is, thus, an important factor to consider when firms make investment decisions that result in the combination of assets as with M&As.

## STRATEGIC FIT IN MERGERS AND ACQUISITIONS

The merger contingency framework espoused by Lubatkin (1983) posits that the benefits accruing to a merged firm are contingent upon the degree to which the two firms achieve a strategic fit. This, in turn, can contribute to the competitive advantage of the merged firm. Different types of firm combinations are capable of achieving different degrees of strategic fit. Generally the stronger the fit, the greater the performance gain to the merged firm. Accordingly, related mergers should provide superior value creation compared with unrelated mergers (Salter and Weinhold (1979); Lubatkin (1983)). Such synergistic benefits arise out of economies of scale and scope. Furthermore, there is the possibility of transferring core skills, across the firms involved, in such amalgamations. Selecting a related merger partner would imply the bidding firm is striving to achieve a strategic fit between the merged entities. Surprisingly, Seth (1990) finds no significant difference in the overall value creation (combined for the bidding and target firms) between related and unrelated acquisitions. However, Lubatkin (1987), Singh and Montgomery (1988) and Shelton (1988) provide some empirical support for the relatedness hypothesis. Broadly, these studies conclude that mergers with more similar characteristics are more likely to create value for shareholders.

Additionally, common business sense suggests that, finding a better-fitting partner will lead to less complicated mergers. The business consulting and academic literature are in agreement that anticipated synergy gains from M&A may not be realized if firms do not choose their partners well.

## MEASURING STRATEGIC FIT

The consensus viewpoint in the literature is that there must be good strategic fit between the acquiring firm and the target to achieve success in M&A. Therefore, an explicit measurement of strategic fit is required to make decisions about whether or not there is in fact a fit. Socorro (2004) proposes the cost of technological transfer, which affects the diffusion of technology across firms, as a measure of strategic fit. He argues that if manufacturing firms merge and they decide to operate the production lines of both firms, the most efficient firm transfers its technology to the less efficient one. Given that there are considerable costs involved in transferring technological knowledge, the amount of resources deployed to accomplish a successful transfer can be used as a measure of the transfer cost. The transfer cost could be high when the technology is complex and the recipient firm does not have the capacity to absorb it, indicating difficulties in achieving strategic fit (Teece 1977).

Shelton (1988) presents an alternative model for measuring strategic fit by focusing on how well the assets of the merging firms can be combined to facilitate production. The model depicts how assets combinations change the product market opportunities of the bidding firm. The model further shows that whilst a merger, as a whole, can create value, certain combinations of assets may destroy value. As a result, a system of classifying M&As that measures the various types of strategic fit between target and bidder assets will provide an indication of the amount of value mergers can create. This will provide the bidder with a much clearer idea of which types of asset combinations they should be aiming for.

The system of classifying acquisitions by Shelton (1988) is based on the related-complementary and related-supplementary concepts developed by Salter and Weinhold (1979). A related-complementary fit, and a related-supplementary fit, are denoted by vertical and horizontal integration, respectively. In a related-complementary fit, the target assets provide the acquiring firm with new products and skills for product markets currently served by the bidding firm. This strategy provides the merged firm with the opportunity to strengthen its market position by serving current customers with new products and improved technology. A related-supplementary target asset, on the other hand, provides the acquirer with access to new customers and markets with the same product.

Even though related-supplementary and related-complementary fits both provide opportunities for reducing marketing and production costs, the former provides greater opportunities to harness excess capacity in managerial talents. Related-supplementary fit involves expansion into new markets with new customers. This is achieved by utilizing managerial creativity in order to use combined assets effectively in exploiting the new markets made available by acquiring the target. According to Shelton (1988), strategic business fits can be ranked in descending order of synergy creation potential as follows:

a)  Identical: where the merger results in similar products being offered to similar customers.
b)  Related-supplementary: where similar products are offered to new customers.
c)  Related-complementary: where new products are offered to similar customers.
d)  Unrelated: where new products are offered to new customers.

Different categories of fits create different values for the merged firm. There is evidence that unrelated fits provide the least amount of value creation in mergers (for example, Lubatkin (1983); Shelton (1988)).

## LINKING STRATEGIC FIT TO ORGANIZATIONAL AND CULTURAL FACTORS

There is considerable diversity in the findings relating to the relevance of strategic fit. Many published research articles have concluded that strategic fit is relevant (Lubatkin (1987); Chatterjee (1986); Elgers and Clark (1982)), while, in contrast, there are other studies that do not provide evidence supporting the theory (Singh and Montgomery (1988); Shelton (1988)). While these studies provide no clear ruling about the value of strategic fit in mergers, they do provide important insights for further research. Strategic fit, though important, is not a sufficient condition, by itself, for superior acquisition performance (Jemison and Sitkin (1986)). While relatedness indicates that potential synergistic benefits may be present, the expected superior post-acquisition performance would only be realized if the implementation process gets underway smoothly.

There is wide recognition that human elements can, and do, make or break mergers. These human elements, grouped under the umbrella term of 'organizational and cultural differences', such as, company identity, processes, leadership, ego clashes, commitment to change and cultural integration (Bastien (1987); Buono and Bowditch (1989); Cartwright and Cooper (1993)). By this, an M&A deal that is financially sound could, eventually, fail to deliver the promised gains, if the implementation process is insensitive to the workforce and their cultural differences. Surprisingly, despite widespread interest in this topic, many deal makers have neglected this side of the M&A process.

# The Effect of Organizational and Cultural Differences on M&As

The empirical literature documents an inverse relation between cultural differences and shareholder gains over time (see for example, Chatterjee *et al.* (1992); Very *et al.* (1997)). Hence, organizational and cultural impediments associated with integration can clearly result in ineffective post-takeover operations. Incompatibilities may exist in areas such as organizational structure (for example, management style, operating procedures and reward and evaluation systems) and/or organizational cultures (for example, values, beliefs and assumptions). Organizational and cultural integration is, obviously, more complicated in international M&As as these involve the blending of national cultures and unique cross-border firm structures.[3]

## ORGANIZATIONAL FACTORS

There is recognition that it is the people within the organization who must implement the consolidation, however, integrating two companies can be difficult even under the best of circumstances (Haspeslagh and Jemison (1991); Larsson and Finkelstein (1999); Pablo (1994)). This difficult challenge could be exacerbated by the size of the deal. For example, Exxon combined 80,000 employees of their own with Mobil's 43,000 in their merger in 1999. In another merger, Compaq combined 33,000 employees with DEC's 54,000 (in 1998). Daimler-Benz and Chrysler's merger, also in 1999, involved a combination of 421,000 employees. The complexity involved in combining these firms, given the size of their respective personnel, is mind-boggling.

Organizational fit also influences the ease with which the bidder and the target can assimilate after a merger. Tetenbaum (1999) finds that many differences in organizational structure between the target and the acquirer may be evident early on, for example, one party to the deal may be highly centralized in its operations while the other is highly decentralized. Further, one firm may be highly bureaucratic, while the other is less bureaucratic. Such organizational differences become pertinent when certain decisions, such as those pertaining to the unification of organizational systems, (for example, purchasing, information systems and payroll) become more relevant during the implementation stage.

Organizational alignment could follow two possible paths – integration and absorption. Organizational integration could be seen as 'the unification of relevant organizational elements (for example, assets, structures, employees, operating procedures and reward systems) between merging firms through the use of collaborative processes' (Waldman and Javidan (2009), p. 133). Collaborative processes are those that are transparent and entail criteria for change that are explicit and clear. Absorption occurs when one firm attempts to assimilate the practices of the other (Marks and Mirvis (2001)). An example of absorption is an acquiring firm bringing in new management or forcing the target firm to adhere to the acquirer's organizational policies and structures. While this may be desirable to the acquiring firm, it could entail negative ramifications, such as resistance, especially when one structure is inappropriately forced onto another (Waldman and Javidan (2009)). Effective organizational integration would clearly delineate the chain of command and enable the new organization to exercise full control over its functions and activities.

## CULTURAL FACTORS

Cultural differences may also be an obstacle in M&A implementation. Sathe (1985) defines culture as 'the set of important assumptions (often unstated) that members of a community share in common' (p. 10). Generally, culture affects how members of a group interact with each other. Every group, corporate or otherwise, has a unique culture that is shaped by its members' shared history and experiences. Culture is invisible to the naked

---

3    See Table 1.1 for the importance of international acquisitions in M&As.

eye but critical in shaping the moral fiber of the workplace (Schein 1985). Although invisible, cultural differences may be evidenced in many spheres of corporate life. At the top management level, culture influences organizational practices such as rules of conduct, leadership styles, administrative procedures and perceptions of the environment (Donaldson and Lorsch (1983); Bhagat and McQuaid (1982)). In terms of risk propensity, value of individual freedom and initiative may be pervasive in liberal firms, while the more conservative firms may tend to place higher value on compliance and stability. Indeed, Pablo and Javidan (2002) largely attribute the difficulties in the Daimler-Chrysler merger to risk propensity differences. Furthermore, fundamental societal and cultural dissimilarities could also come into play in the case of cross national mergers (Tetenbaum (1999). Culture differences may also be manifest in executive compensation practices, as often reported in the popular press.

The full force of organizational culture, evidenced during a merger, creates a series of cultural collisions that ripple through the organization (Buono, Bowditch and Lewis (1985)). Albert and Whetten (1985) and Fiol (1991) point out the distinctive organizational attributes that often remain hidden to employees until the organization's collective identity is challenged. A merger, invariably, threatens this collective identity. When a culture clash does emerge, the acquiring firm may discover itself facing hidden costs with soaring monetary price tags. This may add substantial costs to the integration process and, indeed, likely hinder the ability of the organization to achieve the desired value creation (Blake and Mouton (1985); Haunschild, Moreland and Murrell (1994); Weber (1996); Bligh (2006)). Kotter and Heskett (1992) document some financial costs of ignoring cultural elements in M&As. They find that merged companies that managed their cultures well, as opposed to those that did not, respectively showed revenue increases of 682 versus 166 per cent, stock price increases of 901 per cent versus 74 per cent, and net income increases of 756 per cent versus 1 per cent. Tetenbaum (1999) also reports findings by Mercer Management Consulting that companies with strong cultural integration plans created above average value in their industries. It is, therefore, beneficial to examine organizations from a cultural viewpoint in M&A because it helps to draw attention to aspects of organizational life that, historically, have been ignored.

Similar to organizational alignment, various options for reconciling cultural differences in an M&A are available, including complete integration of the two cultures of the merging parties, or alternatively, an assimilation of one culture by another. There is also the added possibility of 'deculturation' which will result in an eventual loss of both cultures and the creation of a new one. The optimal strategy adopted depends on the degree of cultural difference that exists between the organizations and the extent to which each party values its own culture and identity. Whereas organizational integration revolves around formal systems reconciling culture involves informal systems. The informal systems will have damaging impacts on the melding of the two organizations involved if not handled properly.

## Due Diligence

The various stakeholders involved in the merger process must pay attention to strategic, organizational and cultural issues. The recorded failures in M&As indicate that somewhere between the initial M&A concept development and its execution, the anticipated synergy gains evaporate. We identify the over-weighted emphasis placed on financial and legal aspects of M&As and the neglect of organizational and cultural issues as a major factor behind these disappearing synergy gains. The neglect of such intangible issues, in the end, is a significant factor that can spell the doom of many M&As.

Sinickas (2004) defines M&A due diligence as '... where each party tries to learn all it can about the other party to eliminate misunderstanding and ensure the price is appropriate' (p. 12), the purpose of due diligence is to carefully analyze the available data from the target firm to determine whether the financial information disclosed is complete and free from material misstatements. At this point, the firms involved should determine that all major issues have been identified and the key assumptions used in the analysis are supported. Comprehensive due diligence is critical in the M&A process and industry commentators argue that it would be irresponsible to complete an acquisition without embarking on a thorough due diligence. According to Nigh and Boschetti (2006), more recent acquisitions have been more successful than their counterparts in the late 1990s and they attribute this success to better pricing as the average premium paid has dropped to a range of 20 to 35 per cent from 50 per cent or more. The implied risk has also increased from the 10 to 12 per cent to a level of 15 per cent or more. They attribute the recent drop in acquisition premium paid, and a resulting higher likelihood of success, to a greater emphasis placed on due diligence.

Given the significance of intangible factors in the M&A process, this chapter proposes an even more comprehensive approach to uncover all the relevant issues that are embedded in the potential target along the lines of the 360-Degree Due Diligence (360 3D) put forward by Nigh and Boschetti (2006). This proposal implies paying attention to all aspects of organizational life, not just an analysis of the cash flow and financial stability as has traditionally been the case. Organizational due diligence can help ensure the best strategic and cultural fit between the bidder and the target. Further this proposal is supported by Right Management, a manpower development company, which put forward that 'neglecting organizational due diligence is as irresponsible as neglecting financial due diligence, and can have consequences no less disastrous.'

To maximize the likelihood of merger success, this chapter further proposes that the due diligence process begins in the acquiring firm. An internal or in-house appraisal must clearly indicate that the acquirer is truly ready and equipped to accept and integrate the assets, processes and personnel of the target firm into their own system. This internal due diligence should indicate whether the takeover idea is consistent with the acquisition program of the firm. Chatterjee (2009) argues that acquisitions that are part of an acquisition program developed around sound business logic are the ones that have the best chance of success. Without proper internal appraisal, it is difficult to identify targets that can fit into the bidder's acquisition program. For example, Oracle, which is in business enterprise applications, made 20 acquisitions between 2005 and 2007 as part of a well designed acquisition program. Oracle had one solid acquisition program with a clear objective of becoming a one-stop-shop driven by a fusion strategy based upon integrating all applications under one platform. Having an acquisition program in place enables any bidder to identify targets and serves as a guide in the due diligence process. Answering the following questions, at the early stage of the M&A process, can help organizations to improve the quality of their due diligence process:

Does the bidding firm have a clear acquisition and post-merger integration program in place?

Is the strategic fit between the bidder and the target ambiguous or vague?

Is there a willingness on the part of the target to embrace the vision and strategy of the merged firm?

How would key strategic personnel, who are the business drivers of the target entity, be retained to guarantee continuity?

What is the culture of the target and how compatible is it with the culture of the acquiring firm?

What barriers exist to the emerging culture that might inhibit successful implementation of strategies?

What communication plans could be adopted to eliminate, or reduce, the likely incidence of anxiety?

What plans have been instituted to smooth the integration process?

Has the bidder taken into account the impact of the changing business environment on the activities of the merged firm?

Unambiguous answers to these questions would give rise to a plan that is understood by both parties to the deal. This can best happen when groups comprising people from both companies work as a team to resolve issues. Clear and open lines of communication can also facilitate finding solutions to many of the above issues. It spells out the goals for what the merged company can become and allows the whole organization to understand the immediate priorities in integrating systems, people and processes. In all of this, it is important to designate a merger integration leader, at an early stage, to coordinate the efforts directed at value creation. This manager must be cognizant of organizational and cultural differences and avoid conflicts through communication with all stakeholders. This manager must also work with the human resources managers of the merger partners and have a genuine involvement in whether the merger proceeds or not. This helps to ensure that the integration is focused on achieving the desired effect, while at the same time, assists to better assure that the core strengths and competences of the two companies are not damaged by the transition.

While due diligence may indicate a strategic, cultural and organizational fit at a point prior to the acquisition, there are potential problems that may not manifest themselves until long after the deal has been done. Managers involved in the acquisition must therefore embrace the issue of continual change throughout the due diligence process because business environments are dynamic. Approaching strategic and cultural due diligence with this dynamic attitude is consistent with Venkatraman (1989) who, after reviewing research on strategic fit, concluded that existing studies have focused on static, cross-sectional approaches for specifying and testing fit within strategy research. It will be appropriate for the acquiring firm to specify and test fit issues in a dynamic framework. This can avoid uncomfortable surprises of organizational misfit that is bound to occur as changes in the business environment emerge.

Another important factor in fit-related due diligence is that firms must pay attention to the multi-dimensionality of strategic and cultural fit. Given that organizations face multiple environmental and organizational contingencies that can affect strategic and cultural fit, it is important that due diligence is extended to cover the multi-faceted dimensions of the firm. Extending due diligence to cover dynamic strategic and cultural fit issues is challenging if one begins to conceptualize these issues in multi-dimensional terms, given that the desirability of changing strategy in response to changing environments becomes much more uncertain when it moves an organization away from its traditional or distinctive values (Prahalad and Hamel (1990); Ghemawat (1991); Selznick (1957)).

Delving into dynamic strategic and cultural frameworks involves making predictions on when the direction of, and how, the current conditions will continue to be relevant in the future. The due diligence team, and its advisors, must be knowledgeable in forecasting tools to be able to make relevant predictions which can ensure merger success on a long-term basis. This is obviously challenging given the difficulty in identifying and specifying precisely which environmental and organizational contingencies the merger partners should consider in formulating the merger strategy.

## Conclusion

In this chapter, we have examined the strategic fit, organizational and cultural issues as a pre-condition catalyst for successful acquisitions. Our analysis suggests that whilst strategic fit is essential, the many failures in M&A could, primarily, be attributed to the 'human factor' – incompatible organizations and cultural clashes. This situation is, thankfully, however, remediable. While each of the stages in the merger process (target identification, deal negotiation and post-acquisition integration) is clearly important, ultimately, it is people who create the value and are the driving force behind achieving the desired synergies. The recognition and realization of this fact should lead firms to attach equal importance to initial deal-making and subsequent integration.

Moreover, the analysis in the chapter indicates that the due diligence process should extend far beyond the traditional financial and legal investigations to incorporate organizational and cultural issues. Anecdotal evidence indicates that firms have been complacent in this regard and many failed takeovers could be attributed to such neglect. Further, acquirers should approach organizational and cultural due diligence with a dynamic attitude, being cognizant of the multi-dimensionality of the problem, to position the merged firm for an inevitable change that will occur in the business environment. Although we cannot predict with certainty the outcome of an M&A, done properly, strategic fit, organizational and cultural due diligence could, and should, be an effective insurance policy against failures that too often accompany M&As.

# References

Albert, S. and Whetten, D. A. 1985. Organizational identity. *Research in Organizational Behavior* Greenwich. CT: JAI Press. 263–95.

Andrews, K. R. 1971. *The Concept of Corporate Strategy*. Homewood. IL: Dow Jones Irwin.

Balmer, J. M. and Dinnie, K. 1999. Corporate identity and corporate communications: The antidote to merger madness. *Corporate Communications* 4, 182–97.

Bastien, D. T. 1987. Common patterns of behavior and communication in corporate mergers and acquisitions. *Human Resources Management* 26, 17–31.

Bhagat, R. S. and McQuaid, S. J. 1982. Role of subjective culture in organizations: A review and directions for future research. *Journal of Applied Psychology* 67, 653–85.

Birkenshaw, J., Bresman, H. and Hakanson, L. 2000. Managing post-acquisition integration process: How the human integration and task integration processes interact to foster value creation. *Journal of Management Studies* 37, 395–425.

Blake, R. R. and Mouton, J. S. 1985. How to achieve integration on the human side of the merger. *Organizational Dynamics* 13, 41–56.

Bligh, M. C. 2006. Surviving post-merger culture clash: Can cultural leadership lessen the casualties. *Leadership* 2, 395–426.

Buono, A. F. and Bowditch, J. L. 1989. *The Human Side of Mergers and Acquisitions*. San Francisco: Jossey-Bass.

Buono, A. F., Bowditch, J. L. and Lewis, J. W. 1985. When cultures collide: The anatomy of a merger. *Human Relations* 38, 477–500.

Cartwright, S. and Cooper, C. L. 1993. The role of culture compatibility in successful organizational marriage. *Academy of Management Review* 7, 57–70.

Chandler, A. D. 1962. *Strategy and Structure: Chapters in the History of American Industrial Enterprise*. Cambridge, MA: MIT Press.

Chatterjee, S. 2009. The keys to successful acquisition programmes. *Long Range Planning* 42, 137–63.

Chatterjee, S. 1986. Types of synergy and economic values: The impact of acquisitions on merging and rival firms. *Strategic Management Journal* 78, 119–40.

Chatterjee, S., Lubatkin, M., Schweiger and D., Weber, Y. 1992. Cultural differences and shareholder value in related mergers: Linking equity and human capital. *Strategic Management Journal* 13, 319–34.

Donaldson, G. and Lorsch, J. W. 1983. *Decision Making at the Top*, New York: Basic Books.

Elgers, P. T. and Clark, J. J. 1982. Merger types and stockholder returns: Additional evidence. *Financial Management* 9, 66–72.

Fiol, C. M. 1991. Managing culture as a competitive resource: An identity-based view of sustainable competitive advantage. *Journal of Management* 17, 191–211.

Fuller, K., Netter, J. M. and Stegemoller, M. 2002. What do returns to acquiring firms tell us? Evidence from firms that make many acquisitions. *Journal of Finance* 57, 1763–93.

Ghemawat, P. 1991. *Commitment: The Dynamic of Strategy*. New York: Free Press.

Ginsberg, A. and Venkatraman, N. 1985. Contingency perspectives of organizational strategy: A critical review of the empirical research. *The Academy of Management Review* 10, 421–34.

Haspeslagh, P. C. and Jemison, D. B. 1991. *Managing Acquisitions: Creating Value Through Corporate Renewal*. New York: Free Press.

Haunschild, P. R., Moreland, R. L. and Murrell, A. J. 1994. Sources of resistance to mergers between groups. *Journal of Applied Social Psychology* 24, 1150–78.

Homburg, C. and Bucerius, M. 2006. Is speed of integration really a success factor of mergers and acquisitions? An analysis of the role of internal and external relatedness. *Strategic Management Journal* 27, 347–67.

Jemison, D. B. and Sitkin, S. B. 1986. Corporate acquisitions: A process perspective. *Academy of Management Review* 11, 145–63.

Jensen, M. C. and Ruback, R. S. 1983. The Market for Corporate Control. *Journal of Financial Economics* 11, 5–50.

Kotter, J. and Heskett, J. 1992. *Corporate Culture and Performance*. New York: The Free Press.

Larsson, R. and Finkelstein, S. 1999. Integrating strategic, organizational, and human resource perspectives on mergers and acquisitions: A case survey of synergy realization. *Organization Science* 10, 1–26.

Loughran, T. and Vijh, A. M. 1997. Do Long term shareholders benefit from corporate acquisition? *The Journal of Finance* 52, 1765–90.

Lubatkin, M. 1983. Mergers and the performance of the acquiring firm. *The Academy of Management Review* 8, 218–25.

Lubatkin, M. 1987. Merger strategies and stockholder value. *Strategic Management Journal* 8, 39–53.

Marks, M. L. and Mirvis, P. H. 2001. Making mergers and acquisitions work: Strategic and psychological preparation. *Academy of Management Executive* 15, 80–92.

Martin, J. 2002. *Organisational Culture: Mapping the Terrain*, Thousand Oaks, CA: Sage.

Miles, R. E. and Snow, C. C. 1994. *Fit, Failure and the Hall of Fame*. New York: Macmillan.

Moeller, S. B., Schlingemann, F. P. and Stultz, R. 2005. Wealth destruction on a massive scale? A study of acquiring firm returns in the recent merger wave. *Journal of Finance* 60, 757–82.

Nigh, J. O., and Boschetti, M. 2006. M&A due diligence: The 360-degree view. *Emphasis* 1, 6–9.

Pablo, A. L. 1994. Determinants of acquisition integration level: A decision-making perspective. *Academy of Management Journal* 37, 803–36.

Pablo, A. L. and Javidan, M. 2002. Thinking of a merger: Do you know their risk propensity profile? *Organizational Dynamics* 30, 206–22.

Pautler, P. A. 2003. Evidence on mergers and acquisitions. *Antitrust Bulletin* 48, 119–221.

Prahalad, C. and Hamel, G. 1990. The core competence of the corporation. *Harvard Business Review* 68, 79–91.

Rau, P. R. and Vermaelen, T. 1998. Glamour, value and the post acquisition performance of acquiring firms. *Journal of Financial Economics* 49, 223–53.

Salter, M. S. and Weinhold, W. A. 1979. *Diversification through acquisitions: Strategies for creating economic value*. New York: Free Press.

Sathe, V. 1985. *Culture and Related Corporate Realities*. Homewood, IL: Irwin.

Schein, E. H. 1985. *Organizational Culture and Leadership: A Dynamic View*. San Francisco, CA: Jossey-Bass.

Selznick, P. 1957. *Leadership in Adminstration*, New York: Harper and Row.

Seth, A. 1990. Value creation in aquisitions: a reexamination of performance issues. *Strategic Management Journal* 11, 90–115.

Shelton, L. M. 1988. Strategic business fits and corporate acquisition: Empirical evidence. *Strategic Management Journal* 9, 279–87.

Singh, H. and Montgomery, C. A. 1988. Corporate acquisitions and economic performance. *Strategic Management Journal* 8, 377–86.

Sinickas, A. 2004. How to do due diligence research. *Strategic Communication and Management* 8, 12.

Socorro, M. P. 2004. Mergers and importance of fitting well. *Economic Letters* 82, 269–74.

Teece, D. 1977. Technology transfer by multinational firms: The resource cost of transferring technological know-how. *The Economic Journal* 87, 242–61.

Tetenbaum, T. 1999. Beating the odds of merger and acquisition failure: Seven key practices that improve the chance for expected integration and synergies. *Organizational Dynamics* 28, 22–36.

Venkatraman, N. 1989. The concept of fit in strategy research: Toward verbal and statistical correspondence. *Academy of Management Review* 14, 423–44.

Very, P., Lubatkin, M., Calori, R. and Veiga, J. 1997. Relative standing and the performance of recently acquired European firms. *Strategic Management Journal* 18, 593–614.

Waldman, D. A. and Javidan, M. 2009. Alternative forms of charismatic leadership in the integration of mergers and acquisitions. *The Leadership Quarterly* 20, 130–42.

Weber, Y. 1996. Corporate cultural fit and performance in mergers and acquisitions. *Human Relations* 49, 1181–203.

Zajac, E. J., Kraatz, M. S. and Bresser, R. K. F. 2000. Modeling the dynamics of strategic fit: A normative approach to strategic change. *Strategic Management Journal* 21, 429–53.

# 2 *Maximizing the Impact of M&A Controlling: Due Diligence's Link to Corporate Values. Practical Experience from the Consumer Goods Industry*

DR ANDREAS BROKEMPER AND THOMAS HERRMANN

*Henkell & Co. Sektkellerei, Wiesbaden, Germany*

## Chapter Highlights

- The instruments of M&A controlling support a successful transaction process and minimize overall M&A investment risks.
- In-house acquisition and investment controlling, accompanies the acquisition process starting from the analysis and searching phase and ending with the target integration.
- While strategic M&A controlling evaluates the conformity of acquisition goals, within the overall corporate strategy, operational M&A controlling focuses on an effective due diligence audit, a sustainable business plan and a profound business valuation.
- Only a fluid link between the due diligence and cquisition strategy paves the way to success.
- Different types of due diligence and their critical areas are discussed with a focus on financial due diligence, including practical examples.
- If corporate values are intangible – the due diligence process should make these assets visible. For example, the brand is the most important asset for the consumer goods industry. Therefore, the specific features of a 'Brand Due Diligence' and brand valuation are illustrated.

## Introduction

The success or failure of mergers and acquisitions (M&A) correlates strongly with the ability of organizations to manage effective M&A controlling. Due to the speedy and tight timelines of most M&A processes, and the limited availability of information and secrecy restrictions, the challenge to accomplish effective M&A controlling is comparatively more difficult than traditional controlling functions.

Due diligence plays a key role in M&A controlling. The principle role is a reduction of information asymmetry between the seller and buyer and the avoidance of negative surprises in the post-acquisition and integration phase. For mergers and acquisitions in foreign countries, the complexity clearly increases as a result of different legal, tax and accounting systems and, finally, the socio-cultural differences which are often underestimated when integrating companies. However, considering the due diligence process as just another audit, such as, the annual audit does not suffice. Due diligence should always be a focused operation on the most critical points of a transaction scope, encompassing a variety of investigation objects, including everything from commercial, human resource, tax, and legal to financial issues.

The inherent challenges of a due diligence process are often less self-evident than those of evaluating financial performance or assessing tax risks. These after all seek to answer a direct question, 'In what condition is the target company?' The real value of due diligence lies in its ability to answer the question 'Why, or why not, is the company an attractive target?'

The content of this chapter is based on the authors' respective experience as a CFO and Acquisition Controller at Henkell & Co. Sektkellerei, a 100 per cent subsidiary of the Oetker Group. Henkell & Co. Group is one of the leading international sparkling wine and spirits producers with affiliates in more than ten countries. In the last decades, the company has successfully acquired a series of companies and brands in order to internationalize its business, build a leading market position in different European countries and consolidate the domestic market in Germany.

## M&A Controlling in the Transaction Process

The measurement, controlling, examination and evaluation of an acquisition can be summarized under the term M&A controlling (Strauch 2004). M&A controlling accompanies the acquisition process and supervises this purposeful process (Littkemann, Hotrup and Schrader 2005). This includes the search for information and the evaluation of all accessible data to minimize any takeover risks. The acquisition process can be subdivided into three phases (Figure 2.1):

- the strategic analysis and searching phase;
- the transaction and audit phase;
- the integration phase.

The first phase encompasses market and target analyses, the preparation and updating of watch lists with all the relevant data of the takeover candidate, the permanent and systematic market and competitor screening process, as well as, integration calculations with a focus on synergies. This process enables the company to define and proactively select acquisition targets instead of passively waiting for opportunities. It is helpful to implement a company-wide standard, in order to standardize sensible functions across all divisions or departments, raise their awareness and prepare them for the screening and searching phase. For instance, the sales force and market research departments can make valuable contributions based on their expertise in finding the right target.

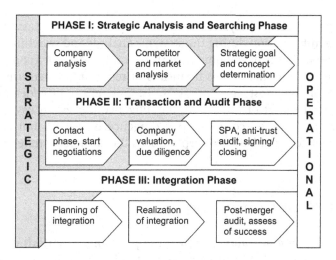

**Figure 2.1    Typical Phases of M&A**

*Source*: Jansen 2000

In the audit and due diligence phase, described in more detail overleaf, interdisciplinary teams are formed which closely analyze the target. The most important areas of analyses are – besides the areas of finance, taxation and legal – the market environment and production facilities. The integration phase includes the planning and implementation of the integration project. However, apart from this stepwise phase concept, post-merger-integration considerations always play an important role and are crucial issues during all phases of an acquisition process. Due diligence provides valuable insights into the target that save time and effort during this integration phase across all the different corporate functions. With respect to the controlling function in the integration phase, a smooth, fluent transition from M&A controlling to corporate controlling will be essential. Hence, it is highly-recommended to integrate it functionally.

## Strategic M&A Controlling

The starting point for strategic M&A controlling is a formulated acquisition strategy, which is updated continuously within the scope of the overall corporate strategy. The objective is to track only those takeover targets that are consistent with the corporate strategy (Littkemann, Hotrup and Schrader 2005). Ideally, the acquisition strategy leads to a list of potential acquisition candidates, including a clear ranking showing their importance, as well as, the takeover probability of these potential targets.

This acquisition list, with both national and international acquisition candidates, forms the basis of a systematic and on-going screening of takeover opportunities. The subsequent screening and analyses of the target includes, for example, country, market and company analyses and a detailed integration calculation between the operations of the acquirer and the target. This integration calculation allows for a preliminary appraisal of the synergy potentials and their ultimate effect on the financial and earnings position after takeover.

The realization of market analyses, as well as, company and brand assessments requires suitable sources of information during the strategic analysis and searching phase. In order to complete this analysis the development, and constant update, of a competitor database and the screening of potential targets by means of relevant key performance indicators (KPIs), are some of the most appropriate tools. This effort provides an information advantage prior to the start of the actual due diligence process. A key factor to always keep in mind for a successful corporate due diligence is that it's not an isolated task. Effective due diligence should always keep in focus the corporate strategy as its principle guideline.

## Operational M&A Controlling

Operational acquisition controlling involves the planning, monitoring and conducting of the transaction. Significant aspects are impacted by due diligence and valuation of the target company. When starting the due diligence process it is advisable to form interdisciplinary teams of in-house experts and also external consultants.

The scope of due diligence, in the context of a share deal, covers all corporate fields, especially market analyses, production, human resources, finance, legal and tax matters. It is perhaps obvious that the demand for external consulting rises, if the takeover target is active in new, or unfamiliar, market segments or countries. The insights and results from these different aspects of due diligence are then summarized and evaluated. All key findings are evaluated especially against the background of the 'future cash relevance' and are condensed into a discounted cash flow valuation. This cash focused analysis applies to possible future payment obligations, as well as, the necessary investment in fixed assets, working capital or the assessment of positive cost synergies. All financial aspects of due diligence should result in an integrated forecast, where balance sheet, profit and loss, cash-flow statements and discounted cash flow (DCF) valuation are consistently linked. Because every acquisition is basically a cash investment, the valuation should answer the question of an expected payback period. The single aspects of the due diligence are handled more thoroughly in the following sections below.

In the negotiations phase of the transaction, the results of the due diligence have a corresponding influence on the purchase price, as well as, the sales and purchase agreement (SPA) and, in particular, on the SPA guarantees. In this phase, controlling can support the negotiation leader via an effective presentation of the due diligence (DD) results, by an alternative valuations proposal, as well as, the preparation of an appropriate purchase price mechanism to reflect these DD findings in the sales and purchase agreement.

While the closing of a significant transaction is always an important milestone in corporate development, the 'real' work often begins after the purchase and this can take years to complete. In the integration phase, coaching teams from different functional divisions – similar to the due diligence team – should help to integrate human resources, cultural and business processes. This operational controlling is, among other aspects, responsible for the integration of internal reporting and the ongoing review of the success of the acquisition. Companies operating internationally require an integration of internal and external financial reporting with a view to follow group accounting procedures and guidelines, as well as, standardized budgeting and planning guidelines and assumptions. However, possibly incompatible organizational and company cultures, as well as linguistic barriers, should not be underestimated within the context of controlling international takeovers.

# Due Diligence

M&A has proven to be clearly one of the most risky and complicated corporate decisions. Moreover, stepping beyond one's national borders raises the risk of possible acquisition failure even higher. A significant number of M&A transactions do not result in the expected increase in value for the buyer. Moreover, follow-up review of the acquisition progress is not always straightforward to investigate, because defined valuation parameters may have become obsolete in the business plan due to constantly varying and unpredictable market changes. Reasons for M&A failure can be an ineffective integration, an overestimation of the synergy potentials or a lack of 'strategic fit'. A systematic, goal-oriented due diligence can serve to reduce the prevalent high failure rates of many M&As.

The term due diligence is often defined as an investigation with due care to evaluate a target company, in the scope of a business transaction, with the intention to reduce the information asymmetric between the seller and buyer (Berens 1999). The due diligence audit contains, in particular, a systematic strengths and weaknesses assessment of the target, analyses of the risks linked to the purchase, as well as, a sound valuation of the assets (Peemoeller 2005). An audit with due care and a transaction-oriented focus, limits unexpected risks and gives advice for the measures to be taken in the integration phase. However, it should be mentioned, that even though a thorough due diligence can significantly reduce acquisition uncertainty it never completely eliminates the entrepreneurial risk of embarking on a M&A.

## SUBFIELDS OF DUE DILIGENCE

Within the scope of a commercial due diligence, market analyses are of special importance as they contain an evaluation of market share and brand awareness, changes in the company's products, as well as, an assessment of customer and distribution channels. When undertaking a due diligence analysis, the assessment of a company's assets is often focused on hard facts with easily accessible information. The effort of an additional systematic collection of information on so-called 'soft' facts, or soft critical success factors, will lead to equally valuable insights, especially considering the fact that in the majority of share deals, a significant part of the purchase price is paid for goodwill. Goodwill, defined as the excess of a company's acquisitions price above the sum of net assets, consists mainly of intangible assets not separately capitalized on the balance sheet.

The assessment focus on market and customers includes all market-related intangibles that give a company its competitive advantage. A strong brand leads to higher identification with a company's products and services. High customer loyalty leads to repeat buying and a steady cash flow. Therefore, criteria like market share, customer strength and brand loyalty, customer satisfaction, the durability of customer loyalty and price sensitivity and elasticity can all explain why, or why not, a premium price should be paid for the target. The valuation of the brand is of pronounced significance within the consumer goods industry – and discussed in greater detail in the following – when acquiring brands in an asset deal transaction.

The due diligence investigation can be further expanded by analyzing the target's internal organization. Within the scope of a production and technology audit, among other aspects, the technology level, the production facilities, the capacity utilization or the necessary investment expenditures are all determined. The required capital expenditure volume is an important item in the business plan as it evaluates the company's free cash flow. Depending on the production type and production history, procedures may require an additional environmental due diligence and especially in countries with low environmental standards, one needs to consider that going forward these lower national standards will likely need to be aligned to satisfy higher international regulations.

Legal due diligence contains the legal classification of the target, the review of the legal corporate structures and an assessment of all contractual and other legal risks of the transaction. The results of this legal due diligence can expose off-the-balance sheet risks, which are – if applicable – considered in the valuation model and, finally, in the SPA. Within the scope of the tax due diligence, respective risks are examined and valuable knowledge is gained for the subsequent tax structuring of the transaction. Here, possible topics could be the ability to depreciate trade mark rights, within the scope of an asset deal, or to transfer or carry forward a tax loss.

The historical and projected financial and profit situation of the acquisition target is analyzed by financial due diligence, including, in part, the analyses of financial statements, management reports, business plans and by thorough personal inquiries with management. Depending on the target, an audit of human resources can also be advisable as the high failure rate of many M&As is often caused by human resource problems stemming from different corporate cultures. Thus, especially in cross-border acquisitions, special attention should be paid to the sensitive areas of staff and company culture to avoid or mitigate unpleasant surprises in the integration phase.

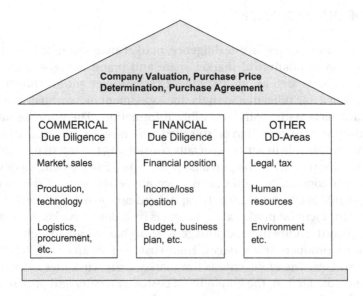

**Figure 2.2    Essential Audit Fields of Due Diligence**

*Source*: Own illustration

## PLANNING AND REALIZATION OF DUE DILIGENCE

The planning and realization of due diligence encompasses, in particular, defining the fields of the analyses, as well as, classifying the review areas. Standardized due diligence checklists can be particularly helpful to ensure that all fields of the audit are covered. These check lists need an individual adaptation to the acquisition target considering the special features and conditions of each transaction. Subsequently, the single fields of analysis are assigned to team members, taking into consideration a split of the audit field of internal experts from all departments, as well as, external consultants such as chartered accountants or tax consultants (Peemoeller 2005). To ensure a high quality audit, the choice of suitable consultants and legal experts should be handled with extreme care, especially in foreign markets where the acquirer may depend on previously unknown external experts. In this respect, the coordination task between internal and external experts should not be neglected, so that an optimum information exchange is guaranteed and the whole team can efficiently follow the overall superior acquisition goals.

The audit volume naturally depends on the size of the acquisition target, the transaction phase or the acquisition concept. An audit within the scope of a share deal is clearly extensive and is afflicted with significantly higher risks than the purchase of single assets within the scope of an asset deal. With an asset deal, often single trade mark rights and/or selling rights are acquired. The best conditions of a brand purchase are offered to organizations that are most capable of, and experienced in, integrating brands without larger investments, using existing marketing, distribution and production resources. The realization of a unique brand due diligence is explained further in this chapter.

# Financial Due Diligence

The financial due diligence is often seen as the core of the due diligence process and comprises the analysis of the target's financial statements and management reports, as well as, its business plan (Pack 2002). With cross-border transactions, it likely requires a transformation of the financial statements, prepared under national accounting rules, to the group guidelines of the acquirer. Only by a reconciliation from national generally accepted accounting principles (GAAP) to the acquirer's group accounting rules, can the real financial effects on the acquiring company be made visible.

The financial due diligence is based on the annual reports and accounts, as well as, the internal accounts and budgets (Pack 2002). Additionally, the financial due diligence should also allow insights into the quality of the internal and external accounting system. This appraisal could lead to the discovery that an integration of the reporting systems may not be as straightforward as previously envisioned and could, therefore, result in higher investments in staff and/or IT infrastructure.

As mentioned, the analysis of the financial situation contains an audit of the annual accounts, usually of the last three years, with a critical analysis of the valuation guidelines. Audit examples are:

- Fixed assets: a basic appraisal of the extent of hidden reserves, in particular, non-operating assets; a review of depreciation in terms of depreciation policy and depreciation versus additions to fixed assets; and an impairment test on intangibles.

- Accounts receivable: a determination of doubtful debts and insufficient write-offs.
- Inventory: a review of valuation and aging structure, inventory turnover, and a determination value of write-offs.
- Working capital analysis with a determination of a normalized average working capital demand to avoid surprises of unexpected additional cash demand after the transaction closing.
- Pension reserves: an assessment of both the guidelines and the inherited pension liabilities.
- Off-balance sheet risks: contingent liabilities; loan commitments; guarantees and comfort letters.

The audit of the financial situation also contains an analysis of the cash-flow statements and this serves as a basis for the acquirer's pay-back or cash-flow projections. These analyses give valuable insights into the target's future cash flows with consequences for the financing of the transaction or operating business. While the investigation of the assets and liabilities determine the takeover risks, the audit of the profit and loss status serves to calculate the future income perspectives. The review of the profit situation is based on an analysis of the profit-and-loss statement, usually over the last three years, with a detailed analysis of the turnover segments and other revenue drivers and cost types. Business specific ratio and benchmark analyses, with comparative companies, will deliver the primary results. One objective here is the determination of a 'normalized', sustainable annual result by the elimination of past exceptionally unusual or infrequently occurring circumstances, such as, extraordinary expenditures or income (reorganization expenses, subsidies), considering throughout that there is no authoritative standard with respect to what items to include or exclude. The final quality of the profitability should be assessed and verified by more face-to-face enquiries with the managers of the target organization.

The assessment of the medium-/long-term financial planning data should contain a plausibility analysis of the business plan for at least the next three to five years. The evaluation of past budgeting accuracy often provides a first impression of the quality and 'philosophy' of the target's planning. Due care is advised with unrealized cost reduction programs, the recurring or non-recurring impact of programs realized and exaggerated, projection sales increases from any new products/markets without sufficient budget or so-called 'hockey-stick' estimates. These are budgets with a carefully planned immediate future, followed by a steep increase which significantly affects the terminal value of a valuation and, hence, the entity value itself. In new unknown markets or countries, turnover planning can be checked by comparing them with externally available marketing research and comparative benchmark studies to provide a plausibility of the cost structures.

The analysis of the vendor's business plan is the basis for a revised business plan that includes the company valuation. All findings from due diligence should flow into the revised planning to determine the ultimate synergies. This requires an interdisciplinary approach to market inquiry and an assessment of cost synergies from all of the different fields of due diligence. A synergy-oriented audit approach examines all possible purchasing, production, marketing, as well as, administration and distribution synergies and attempts to find a realistic assessment of the synergy potential.

Additionally, possible 'dis-synergies' – for example, loss of sales quantity when integrating the sales portfolio with a common customer base – are also issues that need to be considered. The revised business plan forms a sound basis for the following company valuation model. The company valuation should provide a standalone value of the target, as well as, a valuation after synergies. The findings of due diligence, and the synergy assessment, should together avoid an overly -inflated purchase price premium.

## Due Diligence for Brand Purchasing

Especially with the consumer goods industry, brands are a company's most important asset. Hence, it is obvious to concentrate on the company's real value and to seek to acquire these assets directly from within the scope of an asset deal. While a share deal involves the sale of a stock of shares, that is, partially or entirely, an asset deal is merely the purchase of fixed or intangible assets (Berens 1999). The risks of a share deal are usually significantly higher due to the fact that all liabilities and contingencies pass to the acquirer in relationship to the share value. Therefore, an asset deal is an attractive alternative when buying brands due to the avoidance of risks and future contingencies and also for an easier integration into the acquirer's organization. An additional advantage is that acquired assets can usually be more effectively written-off for tax purposes, making an asset deal more attractive for the buyer. The obvious precondition is the fact that the seller is willing to sell – often within the scope of a strategic reorganization – assets or specific brands out of its portfolio.

The definition of a specific brand strategy and the positioning of the brand within its own brand portfolio, as well as within, the competitive environment, take place prior to the start of due diligence in the strategic analysis and searching phase. This could imply, for instance, a realistic assessment of the potential for the internationalization of the brand, focused on the relevant research from national markets. If this judgment precipitates positively, synergies from the use of a common distribution platform and greater international corporation may be gained. With the purchase of international brands, special care is necessary in the legal audit of trade mark rights in the foreign markets which includes the choice of approved international, as well as local, trade mark rights experts. If due care is omitted at this point, the 'immaterial nature' of the acquired assets can quickly appear through possibly losing the legal brand and distribution rights. Infringement of copyright has often appeared in past M&As and these legal attacks against registered brands provide important evidence to take heed of these issues while performing the risk assessment. Nevertheless, with all brand acquisitions in countries with less stable legal systems, a residual risk always remains regardless of how well the audit may have been conducted.

Within the scope of brands due diligence, the sustainable profitability of the brand has to be assessed, as well as, the total brand value. Thereby, the attractiveness of a brand is often based on considerable investments in marketing activities which are not to be neglected when assessing the future profit strength factors. Subject, type and scope of the 'marketing analysis' makes up the composition of the marketing budget, the assessment of the market share figures and the analyses of available marketing research studies. The brand due diligence also focuses on the audit of sales development and sales trends, as well as, on an investigation of the profit contribution for the brand. For a consumer goods manufacturer, the assessment of the 'net sales' per unit is absolutely essential. This key figure implies a detailed inquiry of the net sales after all deductions, including rebates and discounts, listing fees based on the customers' contracts and any other possible side arrangements. Key figures and the seller's statements should be defined in the sales and purchase agreement and secured with a purchase price mechanism. Any variations in the defined contributions margin per unit from the real figures, detected after acquisition, should lead to a purchase price reduction based on a multiple of the total profit margin per year. A purchase price holdback facilitates this kind of procedure.

To determine the future expected profit contribution margin, the premises for production planning and related variable costs, after integration of the brand, are defined. The cash flow, derived from the profit contribution resulting after budgeted marketing expenses shown in the business plan, forms the basis for the brand assessment. After a brand acquisition, additional investments in manufacturing plants could become necessary, which is a factor to consider in the brand assessment model. These findings, as well as, possible cash-effective effects from the change in working capital after brand acquisition, should flow in the valuation. The determination of the brand value can be summarized in the following simplified schedule in Table 2.1.

**Table 2.1    Example of a Simplified Brand Valuation**

| Brand valuation | | | | |
|---|---|---|---|---|
| € Mio | t1 | t2 | t3 | tn |
| Brand profit | 10.0 | 10.0 | 10.0 | 10.0 |
| Brand profit after depreciation* | 2.0 | 2.0 | 2.0 | 2.0 |
| Tax on brand profit (40%) | −0.8 | −0.8 | −0.8 | −4.0 |
| Additional working captial | −8.0 | −2.0 | 0.0 | 0.0 |
| = Brand free cash flow | 1.2 | 7.2 | 9.2 | 6.0 |
| Discounted factor (7.2%) | 0.933 | 0.870 | 0.812 | 9.811 |
| Discounted present value | 1.1 | 6.3 | 7.5 | 58.9 |
| **Brand Value after Tax**    ⇨ | **87** | | | |

* Simplified assumption for illustration purposes: Brand purchase price of €40 Mio; depreciation period of five years.

## Summary

Acquisitions are often the only opportunity for growth in saturated markets. Thus, M&A controlling throughout the acquisition process should become a company's core competence. The M&A controlling function has the responsibility to support top management's need to access reliable information by processing and presenting the relevant information, as well as, coordinating the whole transaction process. A well prepared due diligence team, with experienced internal and external experts, is thus of central importance.

As discussed, with international transactions, special care is required in the analysis of local markets, as well as, in the consideration of national features and peculiarities in the financial, tax and legal systems. The knowledge gained in due diligence forms a valuable basis not only for the purchase decision but also for the subsequent integration phase. To reduce transaction risks, the purchase of brands, instead of shares, is often advantageous. The audit approach may need to be tailored depending on transaction and business specific requirements. A 'brands due diligence' focuses on the determination of a sustainable brand profit margin, taking into account the specific circumstances of the integrated organization, in the assessment of the brand value.

Finally, a fluid link between due diligence and the corporate acquisition strategy should more likely lead to a successful M&A. Considering this, due diligence, in the end, does not only answer the question of 'What is acquired?', but also provides the ability to answer the critical strategic question 'Why a company is, or isn't, an attractive target?'

# References

Berens, W. and Brauner, H.U. 1999. *Due Diligence bei Unternehmensakquisitionen.* 2nd Edition. Stuttgart: Schaeffer-Poeschel, 5–30.

Jansen, S.A. 2001. *Mergers & Acquisitions, Unternehmensakquisitionen und -kooperationen.* 3rd Edition. Wiesbaden: Gabler Verlag, 150–222.

Littkemann, J., Hotrup, M. and Schrader, C. 2005. Besonderheiten der Bewertung hochinnovativer Unternehmen im Rahmen des Akquisitionscontrollings. *Zeitschrift für Controlling & Management,* Sonderheft 3, 40–6.

Strauch, J. 2004. *Unternehmensbewertung und Grundsätze ordnungsmäßiger Due Diligence.* Dissertation. Muenster: Westfälische Wilhelms-Universität.

Peemoeller, V.H. 2005. *Praxishandbuch Unternehmensbewertung.* 2nd Edition. Berlin: Verlag Neue Wirtschafts-Briefe, 160–7.

Pack, H. 2002. Due Diligence in: *Handbook of International Mergers and Acquisitions: Planning, Execution and Integration,* edited by G. Picot. New York: Palgrave Macmillan, 162–4.

# 3 Accounting for Real Options in the Due Diligence Process

MATHIAS GERNER AND PROFESSOR ULRICH HOMMEL
*Strategic Finance Institute (SFI), EBS Business School,
Wiesbaden, Germany*

## Introduction

It is a well established insight, from applied finance literature, that companies tend to prefer external growth via merger and acquisition (M&A) over internal growth. The academic finance literature has further shown that M&A transactions are generally value creating for the sell-side while, in contrast, the buy-side suffers from value destruction in the majority of cases.[1] It is striking then that companies appear to systematically engage in practices which are often to the detriment of their shareholders. Negative transaction returns could be the result of a poorly managed post-merger integration process or perhaps be the consequence of poor target selection and deficient deal structuring. This chapter uses the latter hypothesis as a starting point and examines to what extent other problems in the due diligence phase may contribute to negative M&A performance.

The objective herein is to outline the benefits of real options thinking (rather than formal real option valuation[2]) in the due diligence phase from the buyer's, as well as, the seller's perspective. We argue that applying a real option framework can help to protect the acquirer against deal-specific downside risks. Doing so can also act as an enabler for the buyer to select targets with more promising long-term business prospects, as well as, an adequate strategic fit that can help the seller to realize higher transaction prices.[3]

All companies strive toward stabilizing and strengthening their competitive positioning by improving existing products and services, inventing new ones, entering new markets or by developing long-term and mutually beneficial relationships with key stakeholders, such as, customers and suppliers.[4] Doing so provides a continuous challenge to senior management to reinvent their company's value chain in order to meet the challenges from market rivals and to cope with market dynamics in general (such as the evolution of customer preferences). This stands in stark contrast with the value metric tools, commonly used nowadays in management, which are perfectly suited to administer a real investment portfolio 'as is' but which offer little direction for the

---

1   See Copeland, Weston and Shastri (2005), pp. 760–772 for an overview of the relevant literature.

2   See for instance Müller (2000) and Koch (1999) for the valuation aspect in the context of M&A.

3   See Baecker and Hommel (2004) for an extensive review of the real options literature.

4   See for instance Bollen (1999) for the real option valuation in the context of product life cycles.

shaping of a company's strategic development. The real option method offers unique and novel ways to create, identify and realize growth opportunities.[5] It explicitly recognizes that corporate risk-taking does not only entail downside potential but is also an essential prerequisite for creating shareholder value on a consistent basis. This chapter does not want to contest the fact that the formal valuation of real options is generally a difficult and technically challenging task, not the least because of the difficulty in quantifying the value levers of a real option, as well as, to select and to properly apply mathematically challenging option pricing techniques. Working with the real options framework in a qualitative sense, however, helps to structure the problem conceptually and also provides a terminology which allows finance, strategy and operational specialists to equally participate in the discussion on the future direction of the company.

Due diligence is a key phase of the M&A process which allows the seller to provide the potential buyer with extensive business planning information which should enable them to analyze the financial and economic implications of following through with the acquisition. While the seller is providing argumentative support for a higher minimum willingness to accept, potential buyers are put in a position to come up with a proper estimate of their maximum willingness to pay. Environmental factors may, however, heavily influence the quality of the data supplied by the seller, as well as, the care invested in reviewing the documents by the buyer. Intense bidder competition may, for instance, lead to premature trigger happiness on the buy-side and more restricted information provision on the sell-side. Both were widely observed phenomenon during the New Economy bubble.

This chapter analyzes the relevance of real options thinking for the design and management of the due diligence process. Real options represent – on the one hand – opportunities for future growth by expanding existing activities or by leveraging the target's investment portfolio for the entry into new markets. They may – on the other hand – help to curtail the downside risk of an acquisition by enabling the acquirer to engage in defensive actions in response to negative events. Real options may already reside in the target's investment portfolio or may emerge as part of the takeover transaction. They are mostly 'owned' by the acquirer after deal completion (long position[6]) and therefore represent a source for future value growth. In contrast, explicit or implicit contractual obligations embedded in the target's investment portfolio are equivalent to short option positions which should be carefully analyzed by the buyer during the due diligence process in order to negotiate insurance-type provisions into the acquisition contract. This chapter also provides a detailed discussion of the relevance of all of these different aspects for the due diligence process, as well as, general guidelines for realizing real option value in the M&A process from the buyer's, as well as, the seller's perspective.

The remainder of this chapter is structured as follows: The next section will provide a general motivation for adopting a real options perspective in the due diligence phase of a M&A transaction and also include a rough-and-dirty introduction to real options. Section 3 explains how real options associated with the transaction can be identified and managed by the potential buyer in an effort to manage growth, as well as, to curtail

---

5       See for instance Bowman and Moskowitz (2002) in the context of real options and strategic decision-making.

6       The holder of an option (owner) has acquired the option by paying the option premium and can exercise the option by paying the exercise (strike) price. The option grantor (writer) represents the counterparty and therefore holds the 'short' position. She receives the option premium upfront and is required to exchange the underlying asset against the exercise price at the discretion of the option holder.

downside risks. Additionally, the necessary steps from the seller's perspective to realize some, or all, of the real option value embedded in the company or the assets available for sale are outlined. Section 4 discusses how transaction risks can be mapped into the acquisition agreement in the form of protective contract clauses. Section 5 concludes the chapter with a brief summary of the key arguments.

## General Relevance of Real Options Analysis for the Due Diligence Process

Three different valuation approaches are commonly applied in a M&A setting:

1. discounted cash flow (DCF) analysis (which determines the investment's net present value or NPV)
2. trading multiples
3. comparable transaction analysis.[7]

In addition, an accretion/dilution analysis is commonly carried out to determine how the acquisition impacts the buyer's price/earnings (P/E) ratio. While (2) and (3) typically play a key role in determining the ultimate purchase price, (1) is used to evaluate the target's future business prospects and to quantify deal-related synergies.[8] DCF analysis, however, suffers from the deficiency that it treats the firm as being operated on 'auto pilot', that is, it does not explicitly account for the ability of management to respond to the resolution of business uncertainty by adjusting real investment strategies.[9] In a valuation context, management flexibility is equivalent to a portfolio of real options and represents a collection of rights (but not obligations) to undertake certain actions in response to the arrival of new information relevant for the company's real investments. As management typically 'owns' any such options (also called the 'long' position), accounting for real options leads to the discovery of additional value. In other words, DCF analysis leads to a systematic undervaluation of investments and, hence, adopting a real options perspective during the due diligence phase can help to improve the precision of the valuation estimate from the buyer's perspective.[10] The seller also obviously has every interest in incorporating real options into the bargaining process, as it could support a higher purchase price.

Investments have to display three characteristics in order for management flexibility to qualify as an option right in a financial sense.[11]

---

7    See for instance Damodaran (2002) for a methodological overview. Kruschwitz and Loeffler (2006) have assembled the most extensive treatment of the DCF methodology available so far.

8    The main difference between the valuation based on trading multiples and comparable transactions that the latter captures.

9    In other words, the DCF method does not lend itself directly to the evaluation of the target firm's future business development potential. See for instance Dunis and Klein (2005).

10   See Hommel, Scholich and Becker (2003).

11   See Hommel and Pritsch (1999), pp. 9–12 and Trigeorgis (1993).

a) *Uncertainty*: Cash flows associated with the real investment are uncertain, that is, the market has not fully revealed the economic prospects of the respective business activity.[12]

b) *Flexibility*: Management has the ability to adjust investment strategies in response to the arrival of new information.

c) *Irreversibility*: The usage of management flexibility is a resource-using activity, that is, there are sunk costs associated with the adjustment of the investment strategy.

It is important not to confuse real options with simple action alternatives such as, for instance, the selection of a least-cost dealing strategy with several purchasing alternatives available to the buyer.

If all three characteristics are present, then the investment project's payoff profile displays the typical 'hockey stick' format of a financial option (see Figure 3.1). As a consequence, its economic value can be determined with standard contingent claims analysis.[13] Specifically, formal option pricing determines the total value of the investment (also called *expanded NPV*) while the value of the option feature of the investment can be calculated by deducting the investment's DCF value (also called *passive NPV*).[14]

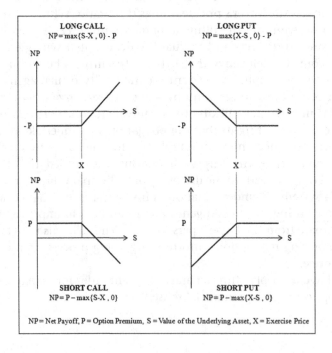

**Figure 3.1    Payoff Functions of Financial Call and Put Options**[15]

---

12    Economic uncertainty (market risk) is relevant in this context. See Pritsch (2000), pp. 206–213 for a differentiated treatment of differentiated risk types in the context of valuing pharmaceutical R&D projects.

13    See Dixit and Pindyck (1994) for a formal treatment of contingent claims analysis in a real options setting. Baecker, Hommel and Lehmann (2003) provide a review of different (analytical and numerical) option valuation techniques.

14    See Trigeorgis (1995), p. 2 for a more detailed exposition of this aspect.

15    Accounting for the option premium leads to a downward shift of the payoff functions for long positions (owner pays the option premium) and an equivalent upward shift for short positions (option grantor receives the option

# Expanded NPV = Passive NPV + Option Value

The analogy between real and financial options[16] can be highlighted with the following example. Management rarely encounters 'now or never' type investment opportunities and can typically delay an investment decision for some time, for instance, with the objective to learn more about the project's profitability. It represents an *Option to Wait/Defer* which is equivalent to a financial call option. The project value can be determined with standard option pricing techniques and by identifying the equivalent value levers. Management has the right to carry out an investment over a certain time period (equivalent to the *time to maturity*[17]) by committing the costs associated with the investment (equivalent to the *exercise price*). The implementation of an investment enables the firm to realize the project's gross cash flows which are defined as the net cash flows plus the investment costs (corresponding to the *value of the underlying*). Delaying the investment implies that the firm is foregoing the cash flows associated with the project (equivalent to *dividend payments* on the underlying asset). The project value will further be impacted by the liquidity premium (represented by the *risk-free rate of interest*) and the overall variability of gross cash flows (expressed by the *volatility* of the underlying). Other standard real options include:[18]

- *Option to Expand*: Option to scale up an investment, for example, by adding more capacity (equivalent to a financial call option on the gross cash flows associated with new capacity).
- *Option to Contract*: Option to scale down an investment, for example, by retiring existing capacity (equivalent to a financial put option on the gross cash flows of retired capacity).
- *Option to Shut Down and Restart*: Option to temporarily mothball capacity (equivalent to a financial call option on the cash flows of mothballed capacity with variable costs as the exercise price).
- *Option to Abandon*: Option to terminate a project altogether by leaving the respective market (equivalent to a financial put option on the gross cash flows of the project).
- *Option to Switch*: Option to exchange one asset for another (equivalent to a financial exchange option which is equivalent to a call on one asset and a put on another with both options to be exercised simultaneously).[19]
- *Option to Grow*: Option to generate new investment opportunities by carrying out a particular investment (equivalent to a financial compound option – a financial call option on another financial call option).

---

premium).

16    See Black and Scholes (1973) for financial option valuation.

17    'European' options can only be exercised at maturity, that is, at the time of expiration. In contrast, 'American' options also allow for early exercise, that is, exercise prior to maturity. While exchange-traded financial options are mostly of the European type, real options are typically of the American type. An American option will always be at least as valuable as a European option and strictly more valuable if the probability of early exercise is positive.

18    See Trigeorgis (1996), pp. 2–4 and Trigeorgis (1995), pp. 3–4. A managerial exposition can be found in Brach (2003), pp. 67–103.

19    Exchange options are actually the most general representation of an option right. In fact, any option can be represented and valued as an exchange option. See for instance Hommel and Müller (2000) for a formal treatment of this claim.

- *Time to Build Option*: Option to stage an investment and to abandon an investment after each stage if milestones have not been met (equivalent to a financial compound option – a financial call option to enter the next investment stage which itself represents a financial call option on subsequent stages).

The value prospects associated with a project can be represented by a probability distribution with the expected value being equivalent to the risk-neutral NPV.[20] Real options may impact such a distribution in two different ways (see Figure 3.2).[21] Call options tend to generate more upside potential (extend the right tail of the distribution)[22] while put options generally limit the potential downside of project (push in the left tail of the distribution). While accounting for (long positions in) real options always increases the expanded NPV, the impact on the risk-neutral NPV depends on the costs of acquiring and exercising the real option. The main difficulties in formally valuing real options are the quantification of the corresponding value levers (in particular the value of the underlying and its volatility) as they may not be directly observable, as well as, determining the value impact of early exercise features.[23] A particular investment project may also include several real option rights so that interdependence must be explicitly accounted for.[24]

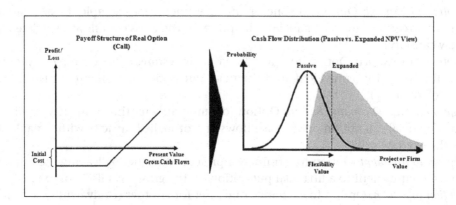

**Figure 3.2    Expanded versus Passive NPV Distribution**[25]

---

20    As explained by Pritsch (2000), modeling economic uncertainty as a value distribution requires discounting with the risk-free rate rather than with the cost of capital in order to avoid the double-counting of risk.

21    The different option types can actually be categorized into (1) generalized 'growth options (expand, grow) (2) 'learning options' (wait, time to build) and (3) 'insurance options' (contract, abandon, shut down and restart). See Hommel and Pritsch (1999), pp. 13–15 and Pritsch (2000), pp. 204–206.

22    See in particular Amram (2002) for a discussion of this aspect.

23    See for instance Copeland and Antikarov (2001) and Pritsch (2000) for an extensive discussion of implementation practices and barriers.

24    The complexity of the valuation problem can, however, be reduced by recognizing that there are diminishing returns to accounting for additional real option features. Hence, while a typical project may easily include 20 or more real options, it may be fully sufficient to focus on a subset of the most important ones. See Pritsch (2000), pp. 173–182 and Hommel and Pritsch (1999), pp. 15–19 for an extensive treatment of common difficulties in applying the real options method in corporate practice.

25    See Hommel and Pritsch (1999), p. 10. An extensive managerial description of the impact of real options on firm value can also be found in Amram and Kulatilaka (1999).

The due diligence process plays a key role in aligning the value perceptions of the buy- and sell-side in a M&A transaction. Effective due diligence leads to a reduction of information asymmetries between buyer and seller and, therefore, raises the efficiency of the takeover market. It provides potential buyers with internal planning data of the target firm which can be used to update and fine-tune valuation estimates. Due diligence should also help to uncover transaction-related risks which can subsequently be managed with contractual provisions or by adjusting the purchase price. There are various benefits associated with applying a real options perspective during the due diligence phase, specifically the following abilities:

- To differentiate between the value-reducing impact of economic risk on projected cash flows and the value-enhancing effect of volatility on embedded option values.[26]
- To identify the value of growth opportunities to be captured with the acquisition. They may be embedded in the target's investment portfolio already or may be part of the deal-specific synergy.
- To identify downside risks associated with the acquisition which can then be hedged with contractual guarantees from the seller (insurance-type option clauses to be included in the acquisition contract) or by upfront payments (reduction of the purchase price).
- To evaluate the potential benefits of a partial acquisition combined with a performance-linked option to purchase the remaining stake from the seller at a later point in time.
- To value the equity of the target firm within an option framework by recognizing that equity is equivalent to a down-and-out barrier option.[27]

Next to due diligence, the focus of this chapter argues that applying real options thinking can improve the buyer's:[28]

- *acquisition strategy* by generating a more reliable evaluation valuation of 'strategic' degrees of freedom for management
- *target screening* by prioritizing targets on the basis of the value drivers of real options
- *communication with capital markets* by providing sound economic justification for takeover premiums[29]
- *post-merger integration* by controlling for real options and ensuring optimal exercise decisions.

The subsequent sections of this chapter will outline how buyers and sellers can incorporate the real options perspective into the M&A process and what the likely impact is on M&A outcomes, in particular deal structuring, as well as, on the design of the due diligence phase from the buyers' and sellers' perspective.

---

26    See also Boer (2002) for the impact of different types of risk on option values.

27    Equity represents a call option on the company's assets with the market value of debt as the exercise price. See Hommel and Pritsch (1999) for a general description and Grass (2009) for the down-and-out feature (which captures the insolvency case.

28    See Leithner and Liebler (2001) for an extensive discussion of all these aspects.

29    See Farag (2003) for an extensive discussion of option-based value reporting for growth companies.

## Accounting for Deal-Related Real Options in the Due Diligence Phase

The due diligence phase represents the part of the M&A process where the buyer has the opportunity to evaluate all of the potential upside and downside risks present in the target firm. A company needs to determine the passive NPV, as well as, the value of any embedded options. The total willingness to pay must exceed the seller's total valuation (which is equivalent to the minimum willingness to accept), otherwise, the bargaining space between the two parties will be empty and no mutually beneficial deal can be successfully negotiated. The difference between the buyer's maximum willingness to pay, and the seller's minimum willingness to accept, represents the maximum value impact to be generated by the deal from the buyer's perspective (defining the value range for fixing the purchase price). The buyer can generate value above and beyond the seller's minimum willingness to accept by capturing synergies and by generating gains from the restructuring of the stand-alone target. The value enhancement may show up in the passive NPV or in the option value of the target's real investment portfolio.

While Figure 3.3 summarizes the argument for a stand-alone acquisition of the target firm, one has to recognize that bidding competition may influence the bargaining space significantly. Specifically, the buyer's relative valuation must be based on post-acquisition values which are impacted by the fact that either the buyer, or some direct competitor, may end up acquiring the target firm.[30]

Buyers must utilize the due diligence process to identify their maximum willingness to pay, and in addition, the specific sources of value. Key questions in this context are whether the value is actually 'real' and whether the buyer is in fact capable of realizing the economic potential embedded in the target firm. The task of valuing the firm's investment is straightforward for 'cash cow' type projects but becomes progressively more difficult

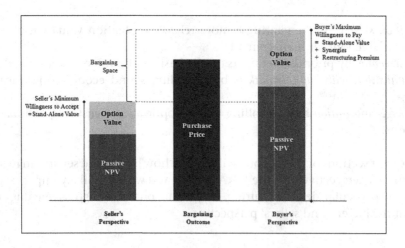

**Figure 3.3    Price Determination in Mergers and Acquisitions**

---

30    M&A performance studies are ignoring this fact as well and, hence, the evidence on negative transaction performance may simply be the consequence of using the wrong benchmark (and therefore the result of ignoring the M&A dynamics of the respective industry).

as the distance to cash returns increases. In M&A practice, the estimation of deal-specific synergies is often based on 'wishful thinking'. Real options tend to be even more abstract and cash-flow remote. Leaving them aside altogether – which is frequently done by M&A advisors – is, however, definitely not sensible as it implies a systematic undervaluation of the target firm.

The real options method is particularly suited to capture two aspects of M&A transactions which ultimately shape the deal's performance. First, M&A transactions are frequently motivated by the strategic growth potential associated with the target firm. The buyer acquires the ability to use the target's investment portfolio as a foundation for new investments, such as, entering new markets, scaling up ongoing activities or expanding the target's product lines. The potential to grow can best be characterized as a set of real investment opportunities which are to be valued as options in order to capture the ability of management to respond to the resolution of economic uncertainty (also called growth options). Second, an acquisition typically involves an array of downside risks which need to accounted for in the due diligence process. They may represent outright short option positions in the form of contractual commitments and guarantees via third parties. In the case of simple risk exposures, management may have certain degrees of freedom to react to negative developments which again represent real options (and fall into the category of learning options). Finally, the acquirer may actively hedge downside risks by requiring contractual guarantees from the seller (which are equivalent to insurance options). Real options may, therefore, already be part of the target's investment portfolio or may be created in the context of the acquisition.

Applying the real option approach in the context of a transaction-related due diligence requires three distinct steps (see Figure 3.4). The acquirer must initially verify its general applicability by identifying existing real options and their ultimate economic relevance as well as the potential to create more options as part of deal structuring. Once confirmed, the acquirer must derive data room requirements which yield the ability to quantify the input parameters for option pricing. The option identification stage is followed by the valuation of the target on the basis of the real option method. It poses the particular challenge of quantifying the relatedness of the real options embedded in the acquirer's and the target's investment portfolio. Finally, the real options need to be managed in the context of negotiating and structuring the M&A deal.

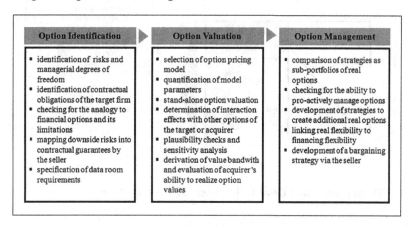

**Figure 3.4   Option-Based Organization of the Due Diligence Process**

The real option method should always be applied with great care as it may be a useful tool to identify deal-related value but can also serve as a justification of value-destroying transactions. Real options are generally cash-remote and their value levers are typically difficult to quantify. Methodological short-cuts can further contribute to a systematic over-valuation of the target firm. Potential buyers may, therefore, become more susceptible to the 'winner's curse' problem by over-bidding for the target firm, especially if faced with pressures from financial markets to use excess cash reserves for the funding of external growth.

The general usefulness of the real option method in M&A is summarized in Figure 3.5. Based on Luehrman's (1998) famous tomato garden example (see Figure 3.5a), real options can be grouped into six subcategories ranging from options with close to zero time value (exercise immediately) to options with basically no intrinsic value (exercise never).[31] In the context of an acquisition, the tomato garden must be mapped onto Figure 3.5b. Some features of the target firm can be characterized as option rich and the seller may be able to credibly defend the relevance of these options in the bargaining phase. In this case, the application of the real option method is unavoidable (Quadrant C). If the seller lacks such credibility, then the buyer may, in the end, get away with not paying for these option features (Quadrant D). Quadrants A and B represent a similar differentiation with respect to the seller's credibility but refer to parts of the target's investment portfolio with little optionality.

Figure 3.6 highlights the linkage between the different facets of due diligence and the subsequent determination of the purchase price. Within the strategic due diligence, real options thinking is most relevant in the context of financial, operational, marketing, legal, tax and environmental due diligence. 'Long' call option structures can mostly be found along the financial, operational and marketing dimensions while 'short' positions tend to be more prevalent in the other areas. External due diligence will yield insights on exogenous risk exposures relevant for acquisition performance which can potentially be hedged away by the buyer via contract design.

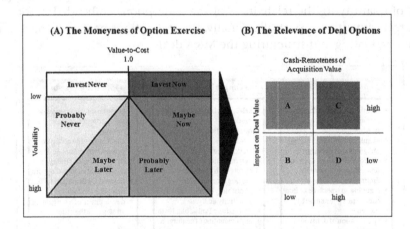

**Figure 3.5    Moneyness and Deal Relevance of Real Options**

---

31    The total value of an option is the sum of its intrinsic value (payoff from immediate exercise) and its time value (value associated with keeping the option alive).

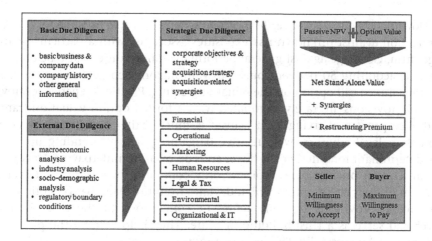

**Figure 3.6   The Path from Due Diligence to Purchase Price**

In order to capitalize real options into the ultimate purchase price, the buyer must accept the seller's claim that the option value is 'real' and 'realizable'. Particularly problematic in this context are real options written on a non-existing underlying (that is, the underlying is to be created with option exercise). The underlying then needs to be valued by determining the present discounted value of, at this point, still fictitious gross cash flows and volatility must be derived using a Monte Carlo simulation.[32] Buyers will typically try to reject the relevance of these types of options on the basis of excessive cash remoteness while sellers must attempt to provide credible data underpinning their formal pricing.

From the seller's perspective, one needs to distinguish between option values which can also be justified with alternative valuation methods such as comparable transactions or simple multiples analysis and those which can only be explained with real option analysis. As a general rule, formal real option valuation should be used as the method of last resort and, if feasible, option values should be rationalized, as much as possible, with reference to observed market prices (paid for comparable firms or implicit in the stock prices of traded firms). 'Pure' option values are typically difficult to directly capitalize into the purchase price which may force the seller to take the route via earn-out provisions guaranteeing post-transaction compensation at the time when the buyer actually exercises the option. These and other contract provisions are discussed in the next section.

## Creating Acquisition Value by Mapping Transaction Risks into the Acquisition Contract

Buyers can protect themselves against deal-related downside risks by adding clauses and provisions to the M&A contract. These are especially useful in cases where the buyer is concerned about the potential losses associated with a particular risk exposure and the

---

32   See for instance Razgaitis (2003) for the practical usage of Monte Carlo simulation in the context of real option valuation. See Pritsch (2000) for an application in the context of pharmaceutical R&D projects.

seller is downplaying its relevance. To a certain extent, it is also possible for the seller to offer protection against unknown risk exposures associated with a particular activity of the target firm. Coverage against general performance shortfalls can also be obtained by, for instance, acquiring 50 per cent plus $x$ to gain majority control and by obtaining a performance-linked call option on the remaining equity. Practical experience shows that contractual provisions are rarely negotiated with a formal option valuation framework in mind. The process of fixing such clauses is much rather dominated by economic intuition than legal advisors, with relative bargaining strength, ending up to be the primary determinant for whether the buyer ends up over- or underpaying for contractual protection. Option pricing issues typically only come into play once the buyer has to decide when to exercise an option which deviates from the 'bang bang solution'.[33]

Contractual provisions typically represent concessions of the seller in favor of the buyer and serve as a trust-building measure. They help to raise the probability of completing a deal successfully. The most common examples are:[34]

- *Earn-out provisions* offer the seller the opportunity to condition the final transaction price on several parameters which influence the future performance of the acquisition target.[35] As a consequence, the acquirer will be released from the difficulties of negotiating a final acquisition price in the face of forecast uncertainties and the limited availability of planning data. The contractual purchase price is defined to be preliminary with either side potentially receiving additional compensation depending on the target's future business performance (for example, based on earnings before interest (EBIT) or earnings before interest and taxes, depreciation and amortization (EBITDA)). While earn-outs may appear to be an attractive instrument to gain buyers' trust, the seller is faced with the risk that buyers manipulate post-acquisition performance downward by shifting profits to other legal entities within their conglomerate.[36]
- *Warranties* and *guarantees* provide the buyer with the right to ask for pre-defined compensation in case particular properties of the acquisition target are not in line with the specifications laid down in the acquisition contract within a certain time period. In this context, one has to distinguish between the legally guaranteed compensation defined by national M&A law and payments offered by the seller above and beyond the legal minimum. In financial terms, these provisions typically represent put options which are equivalent to insurance contracts. They may also be defined as so-called spread options if the guarantee also includes a *bagatelle clause* (defining a minimum performance delta for the provision to come alive), as well as, a *cap clause* (defining a maximum compensation).[37]

---

33    Bang bang solutions represent outcomes where the option is either exercised with certainty or not at all.

34    See Leithner and Liebler (2001) for a discussion of these provisions in a real option context. Picot (2002, 2004) provide an extensive discussion from a legal perspective.

35    Performance-linked vendor loans are sometimes used as a substitute to earn-outs. See Richter and Timmreck (2003) for a formal discussion and an exemplary valuation.

36    Ernst and Thümmel (2000) discuss this aspect in the context of applying real options thinking to M&A.

37    Formally speaking, a spread option is a combination of several plain vanilla options. In this context, the (so-called bear) spread option can be modeled as a combination of long call with exercise price $X'$ and a short call with exercise price $X''<X'$. See Hull (2006), pp. 228–229.

- A *right of withdrawal* provision grants the acquirer the right to withdraw from the sales contract altogether if certain conditions are met (sometimes also called *material adverse change clause*). It is equivalent to a put option on the company's assets. The specific terms and conditions which may lead to a potential revocation of the initial sales contract have to be clearly defined and depend on hitting certain indicator thresholds which are typically external to the firm. Rights of withdrawal are of particular relevance for joint ventures or syndicated deals granting participating companies the ability to sell out their stakes to the remaining contractual partners at a guaranteed price.
- *Rights of first refusal* put the buyer in the position to gain preferred access to other holdings or assets of the seller, either the equity stake excluded in the initial acquisition or related companies and assets. In financial terms, these provisions represent call options which, in principle, may be granted by the seller or the buyer, in the latter case as part of a conditional asset swap.

The main purpose of contractual provisions is to bridge any remaining valuation gaps between buyer and seller during the negotiation process with conditional concessions. As it turns out, valuing the array of potential provisions adds very few additional data requirements for the due diligence stage as they are typically directly linked to total firm value. The contracting parties may, nevertheless, have to cope with considerable ambiguities regarding the legal enforcement. Contractual guarantees may for instance be defined as 'hard' (based on objective facts) or 'soft' (a violation is preconditioned on the seller being aware of the facts at the time of the sale) and the burden of proof may be placed either on the buyer or the seller.[38] From a real option perspective, guarantees must be 'hard' with the burden of proof placed on the seller in order for the provision to be fully covered by the analogy of financial and real options.

## Summary

Practitioners typically reject the real option approach as being too technical and overly abstract. Indeed, the non-observability of key input parameters and the faulty application of the option pricing methodology can easily generate results which overstate the true economic value of an acquisition target. Sticking to more traditional valuation methods is, however, also not satisfactory as it either leads to a systematic under-valuation of the target firm (DCF) or quantifies the strategic potential of an acquisition on the basis of market sentiment (multiples and comparable deal analysis)[39] which may be equally fictitious.

In this chapter, we have argued that, if applied with care, the real option approach can significantly enhance the efficiency of the M&A process. Buyers can more easily protect themselves against downside risks and sellers are better able to capitalize on the target firm's upside potential. The strategic prospects of an acquisition are valued in line with their true economic characteristics, as non-linear payoff structures analogous to financial options. This chapter has outlined how practitioners can cope with the downsides of the

---

38    See Picot (2008), pp. 238–240 for a legal treatment of contractual guarantees.

39    This aspect is for instance discussed in Schwetzler (2003).

real options method during the due diligence phase of a M&A transaction. In particular, data availability requirements must be expanded to yield a more informative picture of the target's risk profile. Overall, the recommendations herein reflect a more general need to put acquisition planning on a more scientific footing.

# References

Amram, M. 2002. *Value Sweep: Mapping Corporate Growth Opportunities*. Boston: Harvard Business School Press.

Amram, M. and Kulatilaka, N. 1999. *Real Options – Managing Strategic Investment in an Uncertain World*. Boston: Harvard Business School Press.

Baecker, P. and Hommel, U. 2004. 25 Years Real Options Approach to Investment Valuation: Review and Assessment. *Zeitschrift für Betriebswirtschaft*, Supplementary Issue No. 3, 1–53.

Baecker, P., Hommel, U. and Lehmann, H. 2003. Marktorientierte Investitionsrechnung bei Unsicherheit, Flexibilität und Irreversibilität: Eine Systematik der Bewertungsverfahren, in *Reale Optionen: Konzepte, Praxis und Perspektiven strategischer Unternehmensfinanzierung*, edited by Hommel, U., Scholich, M. and Baecker, P. Berlin: Springer Verlag, 15–35.

Black, F. and Scholes M. 1973. The Pricing of Options and Corporate Liabilities. *Journal of Political Economy*, Vol. 81, 637–54.

Boer, F. P. 2002. *The Real Option Solution: Finding Total Value in a High-Risk World*. Hoboken, NJ: Wiley.

Bollen, N. 1999. Real Options and Product Life Cycles. *Journal of Management Science*, Vol. 45, Issue 5, 670–684.

Bowman, E. and Moskowitz, G. 2002. Real Options Analysis and Strategic Decision-Making. *Organization Science*, Vol. 12, No. 6, 772–77.

Brach, M. 2003. *Real Options in Practice*. Hoboken, NJ: Wiley.

Copeland, T. and Antikarov, V. 2001. *Real Options – a Practioner's Guide*. London: Texere.

Copeland, T., Weston, J. F. and Shastri, K. 2005. *Financial Theory and Corporate Policy*. Boston: Pearson.

Damodaran, A. 2002. *Investment Valuation: Tools and Techniques for Determining the Value of Any Asset*. New York: Wiley Finance.

Dixit, A. and Pindyck, R. 1994. *Investment under Uncertainty*, Princeton: Princeton University Press.

Dunis and Klein 2005. Analysing Mergers and Acquisitions in European Financial Services: An Application of Real Options. *The European Journal of Finance*, Vol. 11, No. 4, 339–55.

Ernst, D. and Thümmel, R. 2000. Realoptionen zur Strukturierung von M&A Transaktionen. *Finanz Betrieb*, 11, 665–73.

Farag, H. 2003. Möglichkeiten des realoptionsbasierten Value Reporting für Wachstumsunternehmen, in *Reale Optionen: Konzepte, Praxis und Perspektiven strategischer Unternehmensfinanzierung*, edited by Hommel, U., Scholich, M. and Baecker, P. Berlin: Springer Verlag, 547–91.

Grass, G. (2009). *The Impact of Corporate Diversification on the Option Value of Equity*, unpublished working paper.

Hommel, U. and Müller, J. 2000. Tauschoptionen: Kernbausteine realoptionsbasierter Investitionsrechnung. *Finanz Betrieb*, Vol. 2, No. 1, 72–7.

Hommel, U. and Pritsch, G. 1999. Investitionsbewertung und Unternehmensführung mit dem Realoptionen Ansatz, in *Handbuch Corporate Finance*, edited by Achleitner, A.-K. and Thoma, G.F., Köln: Deutscher Wirtschaftsdienst, 1–67.

Hommel, U., Scholich and M., Becker, P. 2003. *Reale Optionen: Konzepte, Praxis und Perspektiven strategischer Unternehmensfinanzierung*. Berlin: Springer.

Hull, J. C. 2006. *Options, Futures, and Other Derivatives*. 6th edition. Upper Saddle River, NJ: Prentice Hall.

Leithner, S. and Liebler, H. 2001. Die Bedeutung von Realoptionen im M&A-Geschäft, in *Realoptionen in der Unternehmenspraxis*, edited by Hommel U., Scholich M. and Vollrath R., Berlin: Springer Verlag, 131–53.

Luehrman, T. 1998. Strategy as a Portfolio of Real Options. *Harvard Business Review*, September–October, 89–99.

Koch, C. 1999. *Optionsbasierte Unternehmensbewertung: Realoptionen im Rahmen von Akquisitionen*. Wiesbaden: Deutscher Universitäts-Verlag Gabler.

Kruschwitz, L. and Loeffler, A. 2006. *Discounted Cash Flow: A Theory of the Valuation of Firms*. Chichester: Wiley Finance.

Müller, J. 2000. *Real Option Valuation in Service Industries*. Wiesbaden: Deutscher Universitäts-Verlag Gabler.

Picot, G. 2002. The Implementation of Mergers and Acquisitions under Business Law Aspects: The Formation of the Transaction Agreement, in *Handbook of International Mergers and Acquisitions*, edited by Picot, G., New York: Palgrave Macmillan, 61–152.

Picot, G. 2004. Vertragsrecht, in *Unternehmenskauf und Restrukturierung*, 3rd edition, edited by Picot, G., München: C.H. Beck, 1–246.

Picot, G. 2008. Vertragliche Gestaltung des Unternehmenskaufs, in *Handbuch Mergers & Acquisitions*, 4th edition, edited by Picot, G., Stuttgart: Schäffer-Poeschel, 206–69.

Pritsch, G. 2000. *Realoptionen als Controlling-Instrument: Das Beispiel pharmazeutische Forschung und Entwicklung*. Wiesbaden: Deutscher Universitäts-Verlag Gabler.

Razgaitis, R. 2003. *Deal-Making Using Real Options and Monte Carlo Analysis*. Hoboken, NJ: Wiley.

Richter, F. and Timmreck, C. 2003. M&A Optionen sind Real(e) Optionen, in *Reale Optionen: Konzepte, Praxis und Perspektiven strategischer Unternehmensfinanzierung*, edited by Hommel, U., Scholich, M. and Baecker, P. Berlin: Springer Verlag, 243–55.

Schwetzler, B. 2003. Die Bewertung von Wachstumsunternehmen mit Multiples, in *Reale Optionen: Konzepte, Praxis und Perspektiven strategischer Unternehmensfinanzierung*, edited by Hommel, U., Scholich, M. and Baecker, P. Berlin: Springer Verlag, 399–429.

Trigeorgis L. 1993. Real Options and Interactions with Financial Flexibility. *Financial Management*, Vol. 22, No. 3, 202–25.

Trigeorgis, L. 1995. *Real Options in Capital Investment: Models, Strategies, and Applications: Models, Strategies and Applications*. Westport, CT: Praeger Publisher.

Trigeorgis, L. 1996. *Real Options: Managerial Flexibility and Strategy in Resource Allocation*, Cambridge, MA: MIT Press.

Trigeorgis, L. 2005. Making Use of Real Options Simple: An Overview and Applications in Flexible / Modular Decision-Making. *The Engineering Economist*, Vol. 50, 25–53.

# *Due Diligence and Results Evaluation*

# 4 *Marketing Due Diligence*

EMERITUS PROFESSOR MALCOM MCDONALD
*Cranfield School of Management, Cranfield, United Kingdom*

DR BRIAN SMITH
*Pragmedic, Hertfordshire, United Kingdom*

PROFESSOR KEITH WARD
*Cranfield School of Management, Cranfield, United Kingdom*

## Introduction

Despite what many non-marketers think, marketing is much more than just promotion. It is much more, even, than designing and delivering the 'marketing mix' of promotion, product, pricing, place (distribution), process, people and physical evidence. Methods for measuring the effectiveness of these more obvious marketing activities have been in place for years. While these tactical measures have their place, they tell us little about the effectiveness of the marketing strategy, that part of the marketing process that concerns itself with understanding the market and deciding what parts of it to focus upon and with what value propositions. It is with this aspect of marketing that the marketing due diligence (MDD) process concerns itself.

Marketing, in this broad strategic sense, is closely correlated to shareholder value. It is the choice of which customer segments to focus upon and what to offer them that lies at the root of sustainable competitive advantage. Good choices create customer preference which, in turn, creates better return on investment. Looked at through the lens of business risk, as investors would, strong strategy reduces the risk associated with a promised return. To investors, it is the risk-adjusted rate of return that matters and managing risk is as important as managing returns, sometimes more so. The MDD process involves both diagnostic and therapeutic stages. The first evaluates business risk and assesses whether the plan creates or destroys shareholder value. The second, building on the outcomes of the first, adapts the business plan to improve its risk profile and enhance shareholder value creation. Marketing due diligence begins with explicating the strategy, which is often implicit and unclear even to those who need to implement it. This explication results in a clear definition of which customers are to be served and what products, services and overall value propositions are to be offered to them. This explicit strategy is then assessed for market risk, share risk and profit risk.

Market risk arises from the possibility that the market may not be as large as hoped for in the business plan. It is, to a large degree, a function of the novelty of the business plan. Strategies involving new customers and/or new products are more likely to have a higher market risk than those involving existing products and customers.

Share risk arises from the possibility that the plan may not deliver the hoped for market share. It is the corollary of the competitive strength of the strategy. Share risk is reduced when homogeneous segments are targeted with specifically tailored value propositions which leverage strengths, negate weaknesses, avoid direct competition and anticipate future trends.

Profit risk arises from the possibility that the plan may not deliver the intended profits. It is a function of the competitor reaction engendered by the plan and of the aggressiveness of cost assumptions. Significant levels of market, share or profit risk, or some combination of the three, suggest that the returns delivered by the plan are likely to be less than promised.

The final stage of shareholder value creation is therefore to calculate whether this risk moderated return represents the creation or destruction of shareholder value. This involves calculating the full value of the assets put at risk, including intangibles. Only if the likely return is greater than the cost of this capital is shareholder value created. In addition to shareholder value creation, or destruction, a third possible outcome of this diagnostic phase is that the plan is insufficiently thought out to enable a judgement to be made about its value-creating potential. The MDD therapeutic process uses the tools of strategic marketing management to manage and reduce the risk associated with the strategy. Using the results of the diagnostic stage to direct efforts, it suggests improvements to the marketing strategy. Hence, the implications of using MDD are to improve the marketing strategy in terms of its ability to create shareholder value. The book which this chapter is based on is *Marketing Due Diligence*, Butterworth-Heinemann, Oxford, 2005 which was voted Britain's best marketing book by the Chartered Institute of Marketing in 2006.

## What is the Connection between Marketing and Shareholder Value?

Both boards and investors need a better method of assessing the probability of business plans creating shareholder value. The financial due diligence process, for all its rigour and detail, only really considers the tangible aspects of a company's valuation. Current, fashionable methods of valuing intangibles, such as brand valuation techniques, are fundamentally flawed. They assess the value of the intangibles in terms of what it might cost to replace, or against a hypothetical parallel company without that asset. However, these approaches do not allow for a fundamental truth in asset valuation: value flows from how the asset is utilized, not simply what it costs to make or replace. As a result, these current methods of valuing intangibles are necessary but not sufficient.

What is really needed, to complement financial due diligence and to give boards and investors what they need, is a way of assessing the effectiveness with which assets and resources are applied to the market. Such a process could be accurately described as a process of MDD. Executed correctly, with rigour and using well founded methods, such a process will predict accurately the likelihood of a business plan delivering the shareholder value it promises. For some, giving a process for evaluating business plans and shareholder value creation the name marketing due diligence might seem incongruous. To many, the term 'marketing' is synonymous with its highly visible aspects of advertising, sales promotion and other activities that are more accurately termed marketing operations. If one holds this limited view of what marketing is, one can be forgiven for thinking that 'marketing due diligence assesses the probability of creating shareholder value' is exaggerating the importance of marketing.

However, the wider and more accurate definition of marketing is that marketing has both strategic activities (understanding the markets, defining the target segments and the value propositions) and operational activities (delivering and monitoring value). These activities form a continuous process of marketing which draws on, and contributes to, the company's asset base. This continuous cycle of activity is the management process known correctly as marketing. It is the assessment of this process and its connection with shareholder value that is properly and accurately called marketing due diligence.

At the risk of being simplistic, the connection between marketing (in the broad strategic and not just marketing operations sense) and shareholder value is quite simple. Despite this, the number of companies that fail to understand the link is such that it bears a simple illustration here. In most commercial organizations, shareholders or other providers of funds (banks, venture capitalists, and so on) provide money with which to create assets. These assets, whether plants and/or buildings, patents, brands or something else, are then utilized in the market to create goods and services for a group of potential customers. The sale of these goods and services creates revenues which, once costs are subtracted, become profits or returns on the shareholders' original investment. The shareholders hope that this return is greater than that which might have been obtained by investing the same money in another investment of similar risk. If investors suspect that the return will not be superior to the alternatives of similar risk, they are, within some practical constraints, at liberty to invest elsewhere. The aggregate decision of many investors determines the price of the company's shares. In this simplified world of capital economics, therefore, shareholder value, the combination of share price and dividends, is directly linked to the risk-adjusted rate of return achieved by the company.

In the simple, and hypothetical, case of there being one company in each market and one type of customer in each market, shareholder value is simply a function of the operational efficiency with which the company uses its shareholders' funds. In the real world, however, there are competitors and not all customers are the same. In real markets, being efficient is not enough. As Michael Porter famously said, 'operational efficiency is usually a necessary but insufficient condition for creating shareholder value' and so strategic effectiveness becomes important.

The importance of marketing strategy arises from the fact that, in anything but the most embryonic or regulated of markets, there are competitors and different types of customers. Together, the activity of competitors and the heterogeneity of the market means that companies have to make decisions about how to focus their (that is, their shareholders') resources. Even the biggest and richest company does not have the resources to meet the needs of all customer types perfectly and profitably. If they attempt to do so, competitors who have focused on one part of the market have a local superiority of resources that allows them to create a stronger, more compelling and more attractive value offer to the customer. In a free market, customers choose whichever supplier provides the best value to them. For some customers, 'best value' might mean superior technical performance, for others high service levels, for others low cost.

Whatever the customers' definition of value, it takes resources to create superior value to that being offered by the competition. So, the critical implication of competitor activity and market heterogeneity is that companies must choose which customers to focus on. Think, for example, of the way in which business-type hotels, motel chains and small country hotels offer not just different value propositions, but also target different types of customers.

Nor is marketing strategy simply a case of picking the most attractive market segment. Different companies have different distinctive capabilities, which may determine the best choice of segment. Consider, for instance, the different capabilities of Mercedes, Toyota and Ferrari, and what that implies for their choice of target customers and what value proposition to provide. In most cases, the choice of which segments to target and what to offer them is a difficult one, requiring an understanding of the market opportunities and threats, as well as, the company's strengths and weaknesses. A poor choice leads to an inferior or merely adequate proposition to the customer and the concomitant lack of customer preference.

Alternatively, making and implementing the right choice of target segments and value propositions results in customer preference and sustainable competitive advantage. Higher returns (from higher share, higher margin or both) follow from this customer preference and lead to superior shareholder value. As companies like Tesco, Dell and BMW have found out, it is marketing strategy which drives shareholder value, even as operational efficiency and technical ability underpin it. This is the logic summarized in Figure 4.1.

This strong and direct connection between marketing strategy decisions and shareholder value lies at the root of MDD. Half a century of research reveals a remarkably clear correlation between certain characteristics of a marketing strategy and the shareholder value that flows from it.

## What is the Marketing Due Diligence Diagnostic Process?

Before we consider what MDD is, it is worthwhile considering at what level in the organization it is applied. Strategy (that is, resource allocation) decisions are made at all

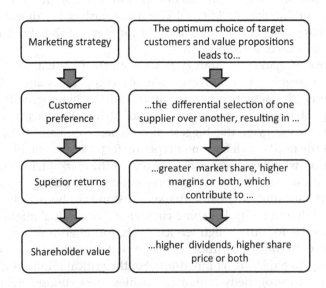

**Figure 4.1    From Marketing Strategy to Shareholder Value**

levels. At corporate levels, these decisions involve which businesses to be in. At lower levels, smaller scale decisions are made about, for instance, single products in a certain country. Between these two extremes lies the Strategic Business Unit (SBU), a unit of the firm that is usually defined as having three distinct characteristics:

1.  It is fairly independent in its activities, which do not interact much with those of the rest of the firm.
2.  It deals with a relatively self-contained market.
3.  It is able to address the market on its own, without much direct support from the rest of the company.

Typical examples of a SBU include the therapy area of a pharmaceutical company, the PC division of an IT hardware company or the B2B (business-to-business) division of a telecom company. SBUs should not be confused with the functional divisions of a firm, such as manufacturing or R&D, which could not meet the three criteria listed above. It is at this SBU level that MDD is applied. At organizational levels higher than the SBU (for instance, with the board of a multiple SBU business) MDD can assess shareholder value creation by aggregating the results of each SBU. Below the SBU level, the strategy decisions at product, channel or country level aggregate to determine the MDD of the SBU. For the rest of this chapter, the descriptions of MDD therefore refer to processes and analysis carried out at the SBU level, rather than at corporate or functional levels.

MDD is a sophisticated process. It is not easily reduced to simple mnemonics and acronyms, a fact that reflects the complexity of the strategy/shareholder value linkage. However, the process can be understood by considering each layer of this complexity one step at a time. The first of these layers is to consider MDD as consisting of a three-stage process, as shown in Figure 4.2. Stage one makes the marketing strategy explicit and so provides the input into stage two. In this second stage, the risks associated with the marketing strategy are thoroughly examined. In stage three, the risk evaluation is used to calculate whether or not the marketing strategy will create shareholder value.

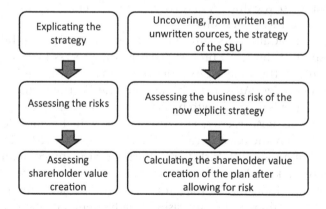

**Figure 4.2   The Outline Process of Marketing Due Diligence**

## Explicating the Strategy

The first step of MDD may seem superfluous. It is a reasonable, if ultimately false, assumption that the strategy of a SBU is laid out in its business plan. Certainly, the length and complexity of the typical annual planning cycle, together with the size of the resultant document, suggests that all that is needed here is to read the plan. In practice, this is not the case. Although all business plans contain the basic outline of the strategy, use of MDD reveals that, in practice, most plans do not provide a full picture of the strategy.

The important detail of the strategy, which reveals its inherent risk, is more often held in a labyrinth of unwritten or informal forms. Sometimes these are easily accessible, such as supporting marketing research reports or product design documents. Often, however, they are held in the heads of the executives as implicit and unspoken strategy decisions that have important ramifications for the probability of the plan working. Obviously, to avoid a superficial and incorrect assessment, it is necessary to surface all of the strategy before assessing the risk. In doing so, however, we also realize one of the very important benefits of the MDD process, which is additional to assessing shareholder value creation. In the act of explicating the strategy, the management team identifies the gaps, inconsistencies and errors that can result from even the most rigorous strategic planning process. This is a very valuable outcome of the process that occurs even before the risk assessment is begun.

Uncovering the unwritten, often implicit, elements of the strategy requires that a structured set of questions are answered. In simple terms, these are:

- What is the business of this SBU?
- Where will its growth come from?
- How will it achieve that growth?

Usually, only a partial answer to these questions will emerge from a careful consideration of the written plan. To uncover the implicit strategy, a detailed set of questions, derived from the three basic questions, are needed. These are summarized in Figure 4.3, although an effective explication of the strategy may require some detailed and intelligent variations and extensions around these questions.

These questions, in addition to being a useful tool for explicating the strategy, reveal a fundamental aspect of the MDD process. That is, the process looks especially hard at the growth elements of the strategy. Experienced managers will see in the basis of the questions in the work of Igor Ansoff and his famous matrix. The focus on growth reflects the essential truth that it is in the growth parts of the strategy – for example, new products or new markets – where most risk lies. This discovery was the foremost lesson of Ansoff's work and is appropriately included in the MDD process. The fact that, in business plans, 'new' is almost synonymous with 'risky', also means that many companies are habitual and unconscious risk takers. The constant expectations of shareholders to outgrow the market and the competition means that, for many companies, submitting a low/zero growth plan is not an option, and taking risks is inadvertently demanded by investors.

Let this not be considered as a criticism of growth-oriented plans, or a recommendation in favour of low-growth, non-innovative, strategies. However, the correlation between growth and risk and between risk and shareholder value does mean that shareholders are making an implicit but insistent demand on companies and their boards: we want you to

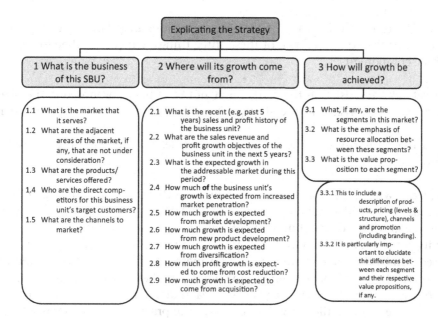

**Figure 4.3   Questions to Explicate the Strategy**

grow, but at the lowest risk possible. Such a demand requires that managers do all they can to ensure that their strategies minimize risk. Before that can be done, however, the risks inherent in the current strategy must be uncovered and understood.

## Assessing the Risks

Having explicated the strategy and made clear what the SBU is about, where it is looking for growth and how it intends to realize it, we have to assess objectively the business risk inherent in the strategy. Only then can we make a rigorous assessment of the shareholder value created by the plan. At first sight, assessing the risks associated with any SBU's business plan seems an impossible task. If we think for a moment what could go wrong, then an endless list of frightening possibilities opens up. There are innumerable things that could go wrong and all of them look unquantifiable and, therefore, practically useless.

However, a more detached look at why some plans work, and others fail, enables a more practicable understanding of business risk, based on the fundamental assertions made in all business plans. In essence, and at the highest level of detail, all business plans say the same thing. They make three basic assertions, which can be summed up as:

1.   The market is this big.
2.   We're going to take this share of the market.
3.   That share will make this much profit.

Each of these assertions carries a level of risk that it may be wrong. The market may not be as big as asserted, the plan may not deliver the share anticipated and the share may not deliver the profit. Each of the three assertions may fall short of its promise. Business risk is the combined risk of these three things, which can therefore be said to have three components:

1. Market risk – the risk that the market may not be as big as promised in the plan.
2. Share risk – the risk that the strategy may not deliver the share promised in the plan.
3. Profit risk – the risk that the strategy may not deliver the margins promised in the plan.

It is worthwhile here to reflect for a moment on this three-part structure of business risk, because it is fundamental to the concept of MDD. As simplistic as it appears, this structure captures all of the hundreds of possible reasons a business plan can fail to deliver its promises. Fickle customers, aggressive competition and flawed forecasts are all addressed within the three components of business risk. Thinking of risk assessment in these terms shifts the problem from one of complexity (have we counted all of the risks?) to one of rigour (have we accurately assessed each of the three risks?). This problem of rigour is all the more challenging due to one of the practical requirements for MDD. It is not enough to simply assess with rigour; it must be done using information that is practically accessible to the organization rather than requiring lots of new and difficult-to-access data. It is this challenge that is addressed in turn, in the following paragraphs, for each of the components of business risk.

## Assessing Market Risk

If market risk is the probability that the market will not be as large as the business plan promises it to be, assessment of it depends on asking questions that inform an objective judgement of that probability. The research that underpins this paper revealed that market risk was accurately quantified if five sub-components were assessed and combined into an aggregate value for market risk. These five sub-component risks are described in Table 4.1 with their respective contributing factors to market risk. It is sufficient to understand what each of the sub-component risks represents and why they are an effective diagnostic for market risk. Each of the subcomponents represents a set of assumptions that are built, implicitly or explicitly, into any strategy or business plan. Assumptions, to the extent that they are not completely tested, are sources of risk because they may prove ill-founded and erroneous. Together, the five sub-components represent all of the significant assumptions made and risks taken regarding market size. There will be, in some cases, overlap between the categories. This means not only that the five sub-components cannot simply be added, but also that no important assumptions or risks will be missed. Equally, the risk impact of each sub-assumption is not equally weighted and varies from case to case. These complicating factors mean, on one hand, that some qualitative judgment is needed but, on the other hand, that the assessment is comprehensive.

**Table 4.1   Sub-components of Market Risk**

| Sub-component | Explanation of market risk |
| --- | --- |
| Product-category risk | This is the risk that the entire product category may be smaller than planned. The risk is higher if the product category is novel and lower if the product category is well-established. |
| Market existence risk | This is the risk that the target segment may be smaller than planned. The risk is higher if it is a new segment and lower if the segment is well-established. |
| Sales volumes risk | This is the risk that sales volumes will be lower than planned. The risk is higher if sales volumes are 'guessed' with little supporting evidence and lower if the sales volumes are well supported by evidence such as market research. |
| Forecast risk | This is the risk that the market will grow less quickly than planned. The risk is higher if forecast market growth exceeds historical trends and lower if it is in line with or below historical trends. |
| Pricing risk | This is the risk that the price levels in the market will be lower than planned. The risk is higher if pricing assumptions are optimistic and lower if they are conservative. |

Assessing market risk accurately, therefore, requires careful questioning of the written and unwritten business plan, using the five-sub-component framework in Table 4.1 with rigorous graduated scales. However, as a general rule of thumb, we can observe that new products and new markets, poorly researched and aggressively forecast on price and volume, constitute high market risk. Existing products and mature markets, with extensive market research and conservative forecasts, have inherently less market risk. As discussed later in this chapter, our market risk assessment can be used to moderate the market size assertions in the business plan. The next task is to consider how great a share of that moderated market the strategy might win.

## Assessing Share Risk

While market risk is a function of both market choice and strategy design, share risk flows solely from the strategic decisions on which the plan is based. In short, share risk is the corollary of strategy strength. A strong strategy has a high probability of delivering the planned share, whilst a weak strategy has a high probability of failing to meet its promises.

The challenge, therefore, is to understand what constitutes a strong strategy compared to a weak one. More particularly, a useful process must be able to make an objective judgement of strategy strength (and therefore share risk) independent of the SBU's market context. As with market risk, this appears initially to be an impossible task. How can one judge the strength of a strategy without a mountain of market-specific detail and without making lots of error-prone value judgements?

As with market risk, the research foundations of this chapter considered the issue of strategy strength and share risk. Again, a pattern of consistent factors emerged which clearly differentiated strong strategies from weak, risky strategies. This pattern revealed that the choice of target markets and value propositions can be objectively assessed against five criteria, again representing five sub-components of share risk. These are summarized in Table 4.2.

It is important at this stage to grasp what these different risks represent. Instead of assumptions leading to risk, as with market risk, these five factors represent error or wastage in allocation of resources so that the plan has an increased chance of failure. In short, a plan which targets a tightly defined segment, all of whom want the same thing, is more effective than one in which the target is a broader and necessarily heterogeneous group (for example, ABC1 males or 'blue-chip companies'). Similarly, plans work when the customer is offered a tailored value proposition and fail with a 'one size fits all' approach. The rare exception to this rule is a situation in which one supplier has a quasi-monopolistic position, in which customers have little choice.

In the situations we more commonly face, then, the best plans understand and use internal strengths and weaknesses, and align them to market opportunities and threats. The worst plans ignore or neglect such 'SWOT alignment'. Low-risk strategies sidestep the competition and anticipate market changes. High-risk strategies go head-on and plan for yesterday's market. Although, as described later, there are other minor factors contributing to share risk, these five factors are a functionally complete tool by which to assess whether or not the strategy will deliver the promised share.

**Table 4.2   Sub-components of Share Risk**

| Sub-component | Explanation of share risk |
|---|---|
| Target market risk | This is the risk that the strategy will work only in a part, not all, of its target market. The risk is higher if the target market is defined in terms of heterogeneous customer classifications and is lower if it is defined in terms of homogeneous needs-based segments. |
| Proposition risk | This is the risk that the offer to the market will fail to appeal to some or all of the target market. The risk is higher if all the market is offered the same thing and lower if the proposition delivered to each segment is segment specific. |
| SWOT risk | This is the risk that the strategy will fail because it does not leverage the company's strengths to market opportunities or guard its weaknesses against market threats. The risk is higher if the strategy ignores the firm's strengths and weaknesses and lower if the strengths and weaknesses of the organization are correctly assessed and leveraged by the strategy. |
| Uniqueness risk | This is the risk that the strategy will fail because it goes 'head-on' with the competition. The risk is higher if the choice of target market and value proposition are very similar to the competition and lower if they are very different. |
| Future risk | This is the risk that the strategy will fail because the market's needs have changed or will change in the time from strategy conception to execution. The risk is higher if the strategy ignores market trends and lower if it assesses and allows for them. |

As with assessing market risk, the sub-components of share risk overlap to some degree and vary in relative weighting between cases. Hence, some judgement is still necessary in the assessment. However, the graduated scales for each sub-component and cancelling out effects of multiple errors mean that share risk can be judged accurately and comprehensively. An objectively moderated view of the probable share can then be combined with the expected market size to calculate the likely future revenue of the SBU. The next task is to see if that revenue will deliver the planned profit.

## Assessing Profit Risk

Market risk flows from the strategic decision to allocate resources to a market and assumptions about that market. Share risk flows from strategic decisions about which customers within that market to target and what to offer them. Profit risk, however, arises from assumptions about the implementation of the strategy in the chosen market. In particular, profit risk arises from assumptions about competitor response and from planned versus actual costs and prices. Again, it initially presents as an insuperable task. How can we possibly predict, with any accuracy, what will happen during implementation, how the market will move and what the competition will do? Again however, this seemingly impossible task is simplified and made practical by considering the implementation failures and successes of good and bad plans. By looking at the detail of why some strategies deliver their promised margins and others do not, we can discern five sub-components of profit risk. These can form the basis of a comprehensive and rigorous assessment of profit risk and are summarized in Table 4.3.

As with market risk, the sub-components of profit risk represent the risks that flow from the various assumptions built into the plan. Profit is threatened when assumptions about costs prove too optimistic, ignoring experience with other similar products, or those about prices prove naïve, assuming benign and passive competitors. As before, the five sub-components do overlap to some extent and their relative contribution to overall profit risk is different in different cases. However, the deconstruction of profit risk into the five sources allows a much better judgement of risk than if profit risk were assessed as a single entity. As a rule of thumb, implementation risk is lower when the profit pool in the market is large and growing quickly, when the strategy has little impact on competitors and when assumptions about costs are realistic and supported by other similar activity. The risk of not delivering the promised margins is high when the total profit available in the market is small and shrinking, the strategy impacts heavily on a single powerful competitor and assumptions about costs are overly optimistic.

The assessment of business risk inherent in the strategy, as described above, is a complex and sophisticated part of the overall MDD process. This is entirely appropriate and any simple approach to a subject as complex as the business risk of a SBU will inevitably be naïve and misleading. In the MDD risk assessment stage, a single, monolithic judgement about the chances of the plan succeeding is broken down into three separate judgements which are much more amenable to objective evaluation. These three are then further broken down into five sub-component risks, each of which can be measured on a graduated scale using objective and accessible data. Once market, share and profit risk assessments are completed, the result is a quantitative assessment, albeit based on careful, semi-qualitative judgements of each risk. It is these quantified judgements which form a well-founded basis for the third and final stage of the MDD process, that of assessing shareholder value creation.

**Table 4.3    Sub-components of Profit Risk**

| Sub-component | Explanation of profit risk |
|---|---|
| Profit pool risk | This is the risk that profit will be less than planned because of competitors' reactions to the strategy caused by a combination of the strategy and the market conditions. The risk is higher if the profit pool is static or shrinking and lower if the targeted profit pool is high and growing. |
| Profit sources risk | This is the risk that profit will be less than planned because of competitors' reactions to the strategy. The risk is higher if the profit growth comes at the expense of competitors, and lower, if the profit growth comes only from growth in the profit pool. |
| Competitor impact risk | This is the risk that profit will be less than planned because of a single competitor reacting to the strategy. The risk is higher if the profit impact on competitors is concentrated on one powerful competitor and that impact threatens the competitor's survival. It is lower if the profit impact is relatively small, distributed across a number of competitors and has a non-survival threatening impact on each. |
| Internal gross margin risk | This is the risk that the internal gross margins will be lower than planned because the core costs of manufacturing the product or providing the service are higher than anticipated. The risk is higher if the internal gross margin assumptions are optimistic relative to current similar products and lower if they are relatively conservative. |
| Other costs risk | This is the risk that net margins will be lower than planned because other costs are higher than anticipated. The risk is higher if assumptions regarding other costs, including marketing support, are less than current costs and lower if those assumptions are more than current costs. |

# Assessing Shareholder Value Creation

The notional SBU we have addressed so far has, in the course of its business plan, promised a certain turnover and a certain return on sales. Those returns imply a certain level of shareholder value created, dependent on the capital employed to create those sales. In the traditional capital market model, investors discount this value according to the probability of the promises being delivered. The investors' judgement is based on a number of factors, such as the macroeconomic environment, the health of the sector and historical performance. Each of these factors suffers from being both a lag indicator (that is, it indicates past, not necessarily future, performance) and a general indicator (that is, not being specific to the strategy of the SBU in question). The over or undervaluation of many, if not most, companies is an indicator of the imperfect nature of this traditional approach to risk assessment. Such an imperfect, judgemental and weakly based method of valuing companies is unsatisfactory for both sides of the capital market. Boards complain that investors fail to appreciate the strategy and consequently undervalue the company. Investors accuse boards of over-promising and imperfect disclosure of key indicators and therefore discount share price valuations to protect themselves.

The MDD process addresses both the lag indicator and generalization criticisms of traditional methods. It is fundamentally different from the traditional model, in that it considers the specifics of the company's strategy (not sector or macro-economic effects) and the implications of that strategy for the creation of shareholder value in the future, rather than extrapolating the past. The assessment of shareholder value creation in MDD begins by allowing for sensitivity of the plan to business risk.

Some strategies are more sensitive to risk than others and sensitivity to the three different components of business risk varies according to the internal and external context. Strategies are sensitive to market risk (that is, they are vulnerable to poor assumptions about market size) if they involve fast growth and high market share. When the SBU's objectives have a large growth component (that is, a lot of the planned for return is from new business) and they already have a large market share, a smaller than predicted market will have a large impact on returns. Conversely, a business plan with a low growth component and which involves going from a very small share to only a slightly larger one is less sensitive to misjudgement about the size of the market. Simply put, a company trying to move from $2 million to $2.2 million in a multibillion dollar market is little affected by even a significant error in its estimate of market size. A company trying to move from $40 million to $50 million in an $80 million market is much more sensitive to market risk.

Strategies are sensitive to share risk (that is, they are vulnerable to weaknesses in their strategy) if they involve fast growth in the face of strong competition. Similar to market risk sensitivity, when the SBU's objectives have a large growth component in the face of large and effective competitors, a weak strategy will have a large impact on returns. Conversely, a business plan with a low growth component and which involves competing with small or weak competitors is less sensitive to a weak strategy. Simply put, a company trying to take a little share from much smaller and weaker competitors is less sensitive to weaknesses in its strategy. By contrast, a small, new entrant trying to make significant inroads into a market dominated by a strong incumbent is highly vulnerable to share risk.

Strategies are sensitive to profit risk (that is, they are vulnerable to poor assumptions about price and cost) if they involve fast growth and operate on low margins. When the SBU's objectives have a large growth component and planned margins are low, a lower than planned margin will have a large impact on returns. Conversely, a business plan with a low growth component and which involves very high margins is less sensitive to a weak strategy. Simply put, a SBU trying to grow slowly and with 80 per cent margins is less sensitive to a small fluctuation in its costs or prices. By contrast, an SBU planning to grow quickly with margins of less than 10 per cent is very susceptible to even small fluctuations in costs, prices or both.

Using these differing sensitivities to the various components of business risk, the MDD process then considers the market size, market share and profit assertions in the plan and moderates them in the light of the assessed risk and sensitivity.

Hence, market size is adjusted or confirmed depending on the level of market risk, share for share risk and profit for profit risk. This adjustment is not a simplistic, linear, change in line with the value of the risk assessment and the sensitivity. Typically, small levels of risk result in little or no adjustment. At the other extreme, very large levels of risk mean that the strategy is so unsound that, frankly, the probability of achieving the growth component of the plan is unknowable, rather than simply low. More usually, moderate levels of risk imply significant changes in the growth assertions. In any case, the non-growth, historical trend of the business is largely unaffected by the risk.

Obviously, the adjustments are cumulative. An adjusted profit assertion is built on an adjusted share, which is built on an adjusted market size. Taken together, the end result is a revised profit figure for the returns reasonably expected from the plan. This figure represents the original assertion reduced, confirmed or, rarely, increased after allowing for the risk associated with the plan.

The next step in assessing whether or not the SBU's strategy delivers shareholder value is to compare the revised or confirmed profit figure with that which would represent the cost of capital. MDD does not attempt to suggest an appropriate cost of capital. This is usually dictated to the SBU by either its headquarters or its financiers. The critical issue is whether the profit figure represents a return on the capital employed greater than the cost of capital. In assessing this, it is necessary to be realistic about the capital employed to realize the profits. In particular, it is important to count both tangible and intangible assets employed. It is easy, for instance, to make a high return on capital employed if valuable intangibles such as brands or intellectual property are ignored and only tangible assets are counted. This is typically the case when a SBU uses an umbrella branding approach. In doing so, it 'uses' the asset of the brand which has been created by many years of investment. If the strategy fails, that brand value, or part of it, is at risk. Accurate assessment of return on investment should count all assets employed, tangible or otherwise, as they are all 'at risk' in the investment.

So the final stage of this diagnostic phase of MDD is a relatively simple calculation. The profit figure, adjusted or confirmed in the light of risk levels and sensitivity, is compared to what is necessary to create shareholder value. That comparison figure uses the SBU's cost of capital and counts all the assets used, or put at risk, tangible and otherwise. This simple comparison results in one of two conclusions:

1.  The profit generated by the SBU's business plan, when assessed for and adjusted for all three areas of business risk, exceeds the cost of capital. The strategy is likely to create shareholder value.
2.  The profit generated by the SBU's business plan, when assessed for and adjusted for all three areas of business risk, falls short of the cost of capital. The strategy is unlikely to create shareholder value.

Whichever of these statements is appropriate is the output of the diagnostic phase of the MDD process.

There is a third outcome of the process that is actually more common than either the positive or negative results. This is the result when one or more of the 15 tests applied during MDD cannot be answered. It is not uncommon for SBUs not to know (that is, not to have considered) issues such as the existence of segments, SWOT alignment or the impact on competitors. In those circumstances, the only possible statement is that, on the basis of what is known from the written and unwritten strategy, the shareholder value creation of the SBU cannot be verified. To a large degree, this common result is worse than a negative result, in that it demands not just improvements in the strategy but a more thorough understanding of the SBU's strategic position.

## Implications of the Marketing Due Diligence Process

At a fundamental level, MDD is very simple. While it will never be possible to eliminate business risk entirely, it is possible to reduce it to a practical minimum. In doing so, what risk remains is identified, located and, most importantly, understood. To achieve this, the process does not take a naive, simplistic approach. Instead, it uses the results of many years of research in which business successes and failures are examined. Just like looking at the black box from many crashed aircraft, this allows us first to group the reasons for failure, then to suggest ways to avoid them. In that sense, MDD can be considered as analogous to pre-flight checks, with the same implications for the reliability and success of the business plan. When, in time, MDD becomes a routine process for assessing the strategic decisions of company directors, the flaws it detects and the challenges it throws up may be fewer and more routine. In the meantime, however, application of MDD will have many important implications for the board.

# 5 Marketing: Its Valuable Role in the Due Diligence Process

PROFESSOR MARY LAMBKIN
*Smurfit Graduate Business School, University College Dublin, Ireland*

DR LAURENT MUZELLEC
*Dublin City University, Dublin, Ireland*

## Introduction

At a macro level it appears that mergers and acquisitions (M&A) occur in waves, spurred by external factors such as low interest rates, a strong stock market, technological shocks and changes in regulation (Andrade *et al.* 2001; Martynova and Renneboog 2008). At a micro level, however, each individual transaction is driven by specific motivations to expand a business or to improve profitability. The evidence shows that the majority of M&A transactions are horizontal, meaning that they involve the purchase of another company in the same industry, either at home or abroad (Capron 1999; Andrade *et al.* 2001). Such horizontal acquisitions imply a motivation to expand the company's footprint or to increase market share, which is why they attract so much attention from the anti-trust agencies (Mueller 1985; Ghosh 2004). Additionally, most M&A transactions are based on a perceived opportunity to exploit synergies between the merged entities. Nowadays, such synergies are as often in marketing and distribution as in operations (Chatterjee 1986, 2007).

These motivations suggest an interest and involvement from marketing people, both academics and practitioners. Decisions about entering new markets, accessing distribution and/or increasing market share are the fundamental strategic issues that senior marketers deal with and, therefore, one would expect them to be centrally involved in the due diligence process preceding M&A decisions, as well as in the execution of such transactions. Whether or not marketing people are actually involved in such decisions, or whether they are dominated by financiers, is an empirical question that seems to call for further examination, although circumstantial evidence strongly suggests that they are not. For instance, the well documented fact that marketing personnel are so poorly represented in the boardroom of major companies suggests that they may be excluded from top level strategic decision-making such as M&A decisions (Nath and Mahajan 2008; Verhoef and Leeflang 2008).

In addition to the strategic motivations for M&A, evaluation of the post-merger synergies expected to result from mergers should also require a marketing involvement.

First of all, there is the fact that every single merger or acquisition involves a branding or, more typically, a *re*branding decision, which can possibly affect the synergies achieved and the value created by the combination of firms or businesses (Basu 2006; Ettenson and Knowles 2006; Muzellec and Lambkin 2006) Secondly, the integration of a firm's post-acquisition is a complex and challenging task that is often poorly executed with the result that hoped for synergies are not often realised (Chatterjee 1987, 2007). This stage usually involves transfers of people and resources and often results in downsizing to try to extract scale efficiencies and to remove costly duplication with repercussions for morale and co-operation. Sales and marketing resources are usually at the forefront of this process, and the success or failure of integration in this area can strongly influence whether the acquisition is a success or failure (Capron and Hulland 1999). How this is actually experienced in practice is a question requiring research but thus far it has received almost no attention.

The final test of success for M&As is in the performance they achieve over time, measured by the usual marketing and financial metrics. There is a large body of evidence in the economic and financial literature to indicate that M&As have a poor record of success, with the main beneficiaries being the sellers of businesses who reap a one-off gain from the premium paid to acquire their firm (Agrawal *et al.* 1992; King *et al.* 2004). Financial research tends to have a bias in terms of focusing on cost efficiencies rather than on revenue generation. A marketing perspective on this topic would help to redress this balance by putting greater emphasis on revenue growth either through market expansion or through value enhancement.

The foregoing points combine to suggest that marketers ought to have a central role in every aspect of M&A, both in the planning and execution of such transactions and in researching best practice. This chapter sets out to review the topic of marketing's role in due diligence, to identify the key marketing variables that should play a part in M&A due diligence, to review the theory and research on the topic from a variety of sources and to suggest areas for future conceptual development and research. It starts by examining the evidence concerning motivations for M&A transactions with a particular emphasis on building market share. It then provides an organising framework for considering marketing issues as a necessary foundation for a systematic analysis of the potential gains from combining two companies. It goes on to consider the analysis that should take place under each of the main asset headings and explains the value of this analysis. The chapter concludes with some consideration of issues involved in estimating synergies and in deciding on a price to bid.

## Motivations for Mergers and Acquisitions

Economic theory has suggested many reasons for why mergers might occur: efficiency-related reasons that involve economies of scale in production, distribution, marketing or other 'synergies'; attempts to create market power by building market share and thereby increasing industry concentration; a desire to improve market discipline, as in the case of the removal of excess capacity or incompetent target management; self-serving attempts by acquirer management to 'over-expand'; and, to take advantage of opportunities for diversification, such as, exploiting internal capital markets and managing risk for undiversified companies (Andrade *et al.* 2001; Kaplan 2006; Martynova and Renneboog 2008).

This evidence is particularly interesting from a marketing point of view because it suggests market share growth as a prime motive for M&A transactions. This rationale was borne out in five successive bi-annual surveys of large global M&A deals by KPMG (KPMG Transactions Services Surveys). The results of these surveys indicate that managers and boards of directors consider gaining market share as the single most important reason for undertaking mergers and acquisitions. For example, in their 2008 survey (KPMG 2009), growing market share was the single most important objective mentioned by 25 per cent of respondents, followed by geographic growth (18 per cent), expanding into a growing sector (10 per cent), entering a new market (10 per cent) and acquiring a brand or additional services (8 per cent). All of these objectives are concerned with growing revenue and all might be considered to have a marketing dimension. In contrast, achieving cost synergies was mentioned as a motivation by only 7 per cent and acquiring new technology or intellectual property was mentioned by only 5 per cent.

Other studies have also borne out the fact that marketing objectives are of paramount importance. For example, a study of more than 2,000 US acquisitions completed during the 1980s and 1990s, by Ghosh (2004), also found evidence in support of the hypothesis that increasing market share is an important consideration in acquisitions. In summary, this study found that a key motivation for acquiring firms, even those with a high pre-acquisition market share, is to further increase market share.

Further corroboration of this tendency may be found in the well documented fact that M&A are most likely to occur between firms within the same industry. In other words, horizontal mergers and acquisitions, in which firms acquire others in the same industry to thereby increase their market share, are the most numerous. This trend has continued from the 1970s right up to the present day with about half of all M&A deals being within the same industry in recent decades (Andrade *et al.* 2001)

In earlier waves of M&A activity, the focus of market share expansion was mostly domestic, but since the 1990s, there has been a substantial increase in the number of cross-border transactions suggesting that growing international market share has become the objective in recent decades (Martynova and Renneboog 2008). This observation ties in with the KPMG research which lists geographic expansion, after market share, as the second most important objective for M&A deals.

In summary, the evidence indicates that growing market share is a primary objective in a large proportion of M&A transactions and, therefore, this variable should be high on the list of topics to be examined in the due diligence process. This suggests a number of points. One is that the M&A project team should have a marketing professional among its members, a point that will be examined in the next section. A second point concerns how market share is to be measured and assessed. This is not a trivial matter as will be shown in later sections.

## The Mergers and Acquisitions Project Team

Since marketing objectives are frequently the raison d'être for M&A, careful assessment of prospective acquisition targets' marketing operations would appear to be strongly advisable. In practice, however, this type of analysis appears to be lacking for several reasons. First, the marketing strengths of a firm are not often perceived to be an asset in the same way as buildings, land, equipment and inventory (Capron and Hulland 1999; Ettenson and Knowles 2006). Second, individuals with a financial, rather than a marketing orientation, are often assigned responsibility for determining the value of a M&A target. For example, a survey by KPMG Transaction Services (KPMG 2006) indicated that typical M&A teams include legal people (75 per cent), finance people (56 per cent), business unit people (56 per cent), people from human resources (35 per cent), technology support (33 per cent), investor relations (21 per cent) and health, safety and the environment (20 per cent). Marketing is not even mentioned on the list unless it is assumed to reside within the representatives from the business unit.

A review of other companies which work as advisors on M&A deals suggests a similar pattern. For example, Deloitte has a model for managing the M&A process which shows the typical M&A team comprised of specialists in strategy, industry, accounting/tax, IT, HR and integration. Marketing is not mentioned at all unless it is, once again, assumed that industry and strategy specialists may carry this responsibility.

Ironically, other research evidence, from KPMG again, suggests that the most successful M&A teams are those which take an outward-focused, marketing type approach in their due diligence process (KPMG 2007). First, KPMG found that the most successful M&A teams spend from 30 to 50 per cent of their time analysing 'non-accounting' business issues such as the achievability of 'sales-force related' revenue synergies, savings to the cost structure and up-front integration costs. Second, the best teams conduct almost twice as many interviews with external experts than other companies (approximately 50 per transaction), with customers, suppliers, end users, business partners and industry analysts. Third, they are much more effective at using business unit representatives during due diligence; 90 per cent required a business unit manager to have a meaningful role in developing the synergy model and, in almost 40 per cent of these cases, the business manager led the model development effort. By involving operational managers, these teams obtained better insights into the achievability of their forecasts and received critical 'buy-in' from the managers who would eventually be responsible for implementation.

Given these three benefit areas, how can companies better improve the effectiveness of their due diligence?

- They can get experienced marketing experts involved. The new due diligence team should include people who are knowledgeable about marketing strategy, brand management, market research, logistics and distribution, marketing communications and customer service.
- Acquirers need to bring their marketing experts aboard early in the due diligence process so as to screen out less attractive prospects and to enable early planning of post-merger integration.
- The marketing experts should help to build realistic models of future sales, revenues and cash flows. Their calculations should incorporate major risks such as losing customers through duplication or defections.

# A Framework for Reviewing Marketing Assets

The concepts of brand equity and corporate reputation in marketing closely mirror the idea of goodwill in accounting so it seems appropriate to recognise both tangible and intangible categories when we consider marketing assets. In marketing terms, tangible assets are things that can be measured, quantified and tracked over time. Examples include the size and number of customers, level of market penetration, percentage market share, the amount of churn in the customer base, the number and size of contracts or orders in the pipeline, the number of distribution outlets and extent of market coverage, average prices and margins, and so on.

In contrast, intangible assets for marketing people are the positive values embodied in the corporate name and the names of the product brands which attract and keep customers, employees, investors and other stakeholders. Customer relationships, product knowledge and marketing skills are also examples of intangible assets that can add value to a company's performance.

Current due diligence processes during M&A negotiations are extremely adept at assessing tangible assets (such as property, plant, equipment and working capital) and certain of the more concrete forms of intangible assets (such as contract rights and patents). But the softer forms of intangibles (such as brands, employee and customer good will, and corporate reputation) are another matter (Ettenson and Knowles 2006). With intangible assets representing close to 80 per cent of the value of the Standard & Poor's 500, it is vital for the due diligence process to include a comprehensive analysis of intangibles that encompasses relational assets (such as brands), as well as, the more obvious forms of intellectual property (such as copyrights and patents). Of course, many executives realise the importance of dealing with corporate branding issues early on, but despite their best intentions, they often have difficulty doing so because of the lack of a comprehensive framework to guide their thinking.

Figure 5.1 provides a framework for identifying marketing assets which classifies them into tangible and intangible categories, consistent with accounting conventions. This framework lists tangible variables such as market penetration, market share, distribution networks, order-fulfillment systems and so on, which are relatively easy to measure and to assess the combined effect on costs and revenues of the merged entity. Intangible assets are also listed; these are far more difficult to measure but no less important to consider. The following sections provide guidelines concerning the questions to be asked under each of these headings in the interest of conducting a comprehensive due diligence process. These guidelines build upon a list suggested by Hise (1991).

Market penetration is a very basic but fundamental measure of performance, especially for companies selling consumer goods and services. It refers to the percentage of the available market who have bought and/or who regularly buy a company's products. It is particularly important for subscriber-based businesses where a large customer base is critical. The mobile phone business is a case in point; companies that have managed to capture a large customer base are highly valued and acquirers pay very high prices to acquire such companies, mainly predicated on the value of acquiring – and hopefully keeping – their customers.

Market share is a further refinement of this measure because it takes account of the competitive situation, that is, the percentage of total market sales controlled by each competitor. This sounds straightforward but is not as easy as it seems. First of all, there

| Marketing Assets | |
|---|---|
| **Tangible:** | **Intangible:** |
| Market Penetration | Brand Equity |
| Market Share | Corporate Reputation |
| Prices and Margins | Market Research/Knowledge |
| Patents and Trademarks | Marketing/Sales Skills |
| Product Portfolios | Customer Relationship Management |
| Distribution Networks | Customer Loyalty |
| Advertising/Communications | Customer Referrals |

**Figure 5.1   Marketing Due Diligence**

is a question about how broadly, or narrowly, the market is to be defined. For example, is it to be the financial services industry, the banking industry or retail banking? Or is it to be the telecommunications industry or the mobile phone market? Normally, there is a convention within each industry as to where the boundaries are set but it is not always clear and a judgment may have to be made by the analysts. Second, is it share of volume or value that ought to be considered as market share? The best plan is probably to measure both because these two measures can give a very different picture of the relative strength of competitive positions.

Whether there is an ideal position in terms of relative share is a matter of debate. The best evidence is that the most stable position (at least in consumer goods markets) is for the brand leader to have a share double that of the second brand, and triple that of the third. Brand leaders in this position tend to be very stable and profitable; a finding that has been termed the Rule of Three and Four (Buzzell 1981).

Market share and relative market share are useful statistics but a thorough analysis would also need to get *behind* these summary statistics to analyse the nature and composition of the customer base upon which they are based. Clemente and Greenspan (1996) outline a range of matters which should be assessed to determine the value and potential of the customer base. The objective is to unearth the information that will allow the formulation of sales, marketing and product development strategies that can be implemented after the deal is finalised. This calls for investigation of the number and size of customers, the distribution of revenue across customers, customer turnover and retention figures, revenue and profit per customer and payment history. In business-to-business markets, the due diligence should also examine the financial robustness and payment reputation of customers, and the extent to which the target relies on sales to sister companies or divisions.

Once this information is collected, it should be considered for both the M&A candidate and then for the combined entity. This dual assessment is essential because it enables identification of areas where the strength of one business can potentially compensate for the weakness of the other. Wherever feasible, it should go back for five years to provide a thorough understanding of the underlying trend and the robustness of the marketing infrastructure. The framework that is suggested for this is shown in Figure 5.2.

| Common Customers | Target Company Customers |
|---|---|
| Risk of losing sales through customer duplication | Additional sales through cross-selling |
| **Acquirer Company Customers** | **New Customers** |
| Additional sales through cross-selling | Additional new sales for the merged entity |

**Figure 5.2    Evaluating the Customer Bases**

*Source*: Adapted from Clemente and Greenspan (1996)

This framework suggests that we consider the composition of the existing customer base of both the acquirer and target individually, and then consolidate them together to assess the likely net gains and losses for the combined entity. Ideally, the customers of both companies would be added together to yield a much larger customer base with as little overlap as possible. The best scenario is probably in transnational acquisitions where there is little or no danger of customer cannibalisation. The acquisition of Abbey National in the UK by Banco Santander is a good example – this deal gave Banco Santander a major position in the UK retail banking business which was 100 per cent additional to its domestic customer base in Spain.

The recent, enforced acquisition of LloydsTSB by HBOS in the UK represents the opposite scenario in which there was a high degree of customer duplication. As two of the largest retail banks in the UK, both had branches on every high street in the country. The hope would be that considerable savings might be extracted by rationalising the distribution system so as to remove some of the duplication in the branch network, but the risk associated with this is whether customers of the individual banks would be lost in the process.

The possibility of cross-selling products to the enlarged customer base is another possibility to be explored as a potential source of increased revenue. The acquirer may have products that it can now distribute to the target's customers, and vice versa. However, such assumptions are speculative and should be treated cautiously in valuing an acquisition target and probably should not be taken into account at all in settling on the purchase price.

Research evidence on such matters shows that many acquirers rely too heavily on assumptions that are not consistent with overall market growth and competitive realities (Christofferson *et al.* 2004). For example, one global financial company estimated that a recent acquisition would net €1 billion ($1.18 billion) in synergies within five years and 13 per cent profit growth in the first year. But limited overall market growth meant that these goals could only be achieved if the company took a significant share from competitors through cross-selling, and then only if the competitors didn't respond successfully. The message is that acquirers need to calibrate the market share and growth assumptions in their pro forma analysis with the realities of the market.

## Product Portfolio

Two significant product dimensions to investigate are product liability and patent/trademark protection. Products that expose a company to potentially high levels of liability and those with little or no patent protection may not be very desirable. There are abundant examples of situations where companies have found their brand names and other intellectual property challenged or even usurped by competitors in various parts of the world, mainly due to their own failure to protect their intellectual property adequately by legal means.

A review of the product portfolio should also be undertaken to see how balanced it is. 'Twenty-eighty' analyses should be performed for the company's individual products. The ideal situation is to have a balanced portfolio with a relatively small number of brands, each of which is pulling its weight in revenue and profit terms. A more common occurrence, however, is to have 20 per cent of brands account for about 80 percent of sales which is an unhealthy situation. In such a situation, an acquiring company runs the danger of paying a high price for a portfolio of brands when, in fact, only one, or at most a few, are really worthy of purchase.

Bahadir *et al.* (2008) suggest a way to measure brand portfolio diversity which may be a helpful way to approach this topic. Specifically, they propose that brand portfolio diversity may be measured as brand portfolio size divided by the number of categories in which a firm operates. Brand portfolio size is measured as the number of brands that a firm owns. The number of categories is computed as the number of different categories in which the firm operates (using the North American Industry Classification System (NAICS) to identify product categories). For example, if the firm implements a pure corporate-branding strategy with one brand name covering all of its products which are in a single product category, the portfolio size is equal to 1. In contrast, if the firm operates in five different NAICS categories, the brand portfolio diversity is 0.2. As this ratio approaches zero, it suggests that the firm's brand is extended to many different categories which may be interpreted either positively or negatively.

On the positive side, a large ratio may be indicative of a deliberate house-of-brands strategy in which the individual product brands are consciously separated, both from each other and from connection with the parent company. This is the Procter & Gamble model. On the negative side, a large ratio may indicate an excessively long list of small and possibly weak brands with marketing investment being spread thinly across a wide range rather than being concentrated on a few strong brands. Such a situation could cause an acquirer to pay a high price for a collection of weak brands with perhaps only one, or a few, that are really worth having.

A clear appreciation of such issues should help to ensure that a realistic value is placed on the target business in which the price paid is weighted to reflect the relative values of the brands being purchased. It may also be that the acquisition is deliberately pursued in order to acquire the few strong brands, with a secondary plan to sell off weak or non-core brands immediately after the acquisition. The anticipated sale price for the non-core brands can be factored into the overall bid price for the acquisition.

## Brand Equity

A review of the available evidence suggests that branding issues are usually given low priority in M&A transactions and are typically decided on the basis of simple expediency after the deal is concluded, to bring some order to the untidy collections of names and entities that are inherited as a result of combining two firms and their collective products and markets. For example, a study of 207 mergers and acquisitions by Ettenson and Knowles (2006) found that branding issues were accorded only low or moderate priority during the negotiations in two thirds of cases.

In many instances, the corporate brand strategy receives serious attention only after the deal is approved and announced. In these cases, branding decisions become part of the post-acquisition clean-up. Furthermore, the choices made seem to be based more on expediency rather than any detailed analysis. This runs the risk that the new brand configuration may be 'sub-optimal, often reflecting a muddled process driven by short-term goals, ego or horse-trading in the final stages of the negotiations' (Ettenson and Knowles 2006). Ideally, however, branding should be driven by marketing considerations, to use the opportunity to signal a new strategic focus to the company's stakeholders and to extract synergies from the brand equities of the merged entities

Measuring brand equity is a complex issue that is still evolving but two main approaches may be identified: a consumer behaviour approach and a financial approach. Both acknowledge that brand equity represents the 'added value' endowed on a product as a result of its history and heritage as well as the accumulated effect of past investments in marketing. According to the consumer behaviour approach, a brand is said to have positive brand equity when customers react more favourably to a product and the way it is marketed when the brand is identified than when it is not (Keller 1993). Customer-based brand equity exists when the customer has a high level of awareness and familiarity with the brand and holds some strong, favourable and unique brand associations in memory that lead to customer loyalty.

Customer-based measures of brand equity are mainly assessed through market research so a due diligence investigation should start by gathering and reviewing whatever market research the target company has available. A review of this evidence should begin by looking at awareness levels for the target brands, both spontaneous and prompted. Comparing this to the awareness of the leading brands will give a good cross-check against the market share ranking. The next thing to examine is the image associations attached to the target brand, both positive and negative, to see how they compare to those of the competitors, and how they have altered over time. A further factor to look for is evidence of brand loyalty, both attitudinal (measured by preference or commitment), and behavioural (measured by proportion of purchases in the product category) devoted to the target brand. In sum, these measures will give a good sense of the customer-based equity of the target brand.

The ultimate measure of brand value, however, is the amount of profit it generates which must be sufficient to cover all of the costs involved in its production, distribution and marketing, and to provide a return on the capital employed in its production. This suggests a more stringent financial definition of what is meant by a strong brand which may be stated as: 'a strong brand is a name that influences buyers through the value it offers and which is backed by a profitable economic formula' (Kapferer 2004).

A survey of valuation experts involved in M&A transactions indicates that the dominant method of valuing brands in practice is the income approach (Bahadir *et al.* 2008). The income-based valuation is conducted in two steps. First, cash flow expectations from brands are formed and present values of future cash flows are computed. Second, this value is multiplied by a factor called the 'royalty rate.' This factor is selected from the following perspective: If the brand were subject to a licensing deal, what would be the royalty rate for the brand? Royalty rates reported for similar brands in the same and/or related industries are used as the benchmark for the royalty rate determination. As the valuation method shows, the measure captures the value of the brand in association with the product because the ultimate value relies inherently on the cash flow expectations from the brand and product.

The general tendency in M&A is that a strong firm acquires a weaker one and seeks to leverage its strength to enhance the value of the target, and thereby the value of the whole combined entity (Capron and Hulland 1999), as shown in Figure 5.3.

Acquisitions usually result in the elimination of the target firm's corporate brand in favour of the acquirer, that is, a single brand strategy in favour of the dominant brand (Basu 2006). In a study of 207 M&A deals in the US, Ettenson and Knowles (2006) found that the acquiring company name replaced that of the target company immediately in 40 per cent of cases. This strategy – which they called 'backing the stronger horse' – was by far the most prevalent approach. The opposite strategy, of keeping the status quo, was the second most frequent, representing 24 per cent of the cases studied. Finally, a new brand name may be chosen for the merged group, although this is a much less frequent occurrence – only 8 per cent of the Ettenson and Knowles' sample.

This strategy of larger companies with high brand equity buying up smaller ones with lower brand equity is akin to a commonly observed financial strategy in which companies with a high market-book (M/B) value buy companies with a lower M/B value. The hope and intention behind this type of strategy is that the brand equity or M/B ratio of the target would tend to rise to equal the level of the acquirer, resulting in an overall gain in value for the combined entity (Maksimovic and Phillips 2001).

## New Product Development and Innovation

It is also important to ask about R&D expenditure and new products. What has been the company's spending on R&D compared to industry norms? What has been the success rate of new products launched? What percentage of annual sales revenue is accounted for by new products? Answers to these questions will give a good measure of the innovativeness of the target business which is likely to be an important metric, particularly in the high technology industries.

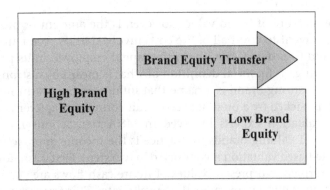

**Figure 5.3    Leveraging Brand Equity through M&A**

*Source*: Own Illustration

# Pricing

The prices charged by the target company also need to be examined. The prices need to be compared to those of direct competitors to assess the company's relative strength in the market place. A target company that is able to charge premium prices yielding good profit margins is obviously in a strong position whereas a company that is forced into a discounting position may be displaying a relative weakness in its competitive position.

Profit margins earned by the target company compared to other levels in the supply chain would also be important to consider. If suppliers or customers earn higher margins than the target company, it may suggest that the target company is in a relatively weak bargaining position which could be squeezed further in the future until it is unsustainable.

# Advertising/Communications

It is also extremely important to assess the target company's investment in advertising and other forms of communications. While the effect of much advertising investment is long-term and cannot be measured with accounting precision, there are a number of benchmarks that can be used to evaluate a company's activities. First of all, the level of expenditure can be reviewed against industry norms. Advertising expenditure as a percentage of sales is a commonly used metric and figures are published annually for all or most major industries. In 2007, for example, retail credit institutions spent 2.5 per cent of revenue on advertising while food manufacturers spent 10 per cent and cosmetic companies spent 14 per cent. A pattern of under-investment by a target company suggests a failure to support its brands and is perhaps evidence of window dressing in the financial accounts. Over-investment, in contrast, may represent a triumph of hope over expectation in a weak company which is desperately trying to increase market share.

Most companies with significant marketing communications budgets will also back this up with regular market research studies to track their awareness levels and image among their customers. This research should be carefully examined to see that the investment in advertising is actually delivering the desired results – that the brands actually do have a high level of awareness and a strong and consistent image. Any downward trends should be looked on with suspicion as possible suggestions of under-investment or increasing competition, either of which would be cause for a reduction in the price to be offered for the acquisition.

# Selling and Sales Promotion

Unlike advertising, sales promotion is typically a direct response medium with an immediate and measurable payback. The first issue to consider here is the percentage return being generated by promotions and therefore the value of this investment. A second point to consider is the overall percentage of sales being supported by promotion. The risk here is that there can be an upward migration in the rate of sales promotion until a majority of sales are being supported with a discount which becomes a standard condition of sale and amounts to an erosion in price.

If the target company has a sales force, its efficiency should be assessed by addressing the following issues:

- Selling costs as a percentage of sales revenue compared to acquirer and to industry norms.
- Sales revenue per sales employee and total costs per employee.
- Cost per sales call compared to the acquirer's sales force and industry norms.
- Average order size and repeat frequency.
- Number of customers gained and lost over a given time period.

A 20/80 analysis is also a useful way to review the sales force. It is an undesirable situation to have a small percentage of the sales force accounting for a disproportionately large proportion of sales, for two reasons: First, an unbalanced pattern may suggest a poorly performing sales force that could be a liability if taken over and, second, if some of the high performing sales people left following a merger, they might possibly take a lot of customers and sales with them.

This kind of analysis would also be useful in allowing a calculation of savings that may be made by combining the two sales forces and reducing the number of people involved and the attendant costs associated with them. Whether there are too few or too many sales people employed can be ascertained by considering the size and geographic spread of the market, the number of sales calls needed and the order size. A rationalisation following a merger/acquisition would be a good time to review the overall structure of the sales organisation and to consider fundamental questions such as whether some of the sales costs could be reduced by doing more of the work online through a call centre.

## Distribution

The supply chain and IT are two operational areas that deserve special attention because they still get relatively little attention in an M&A context (Morrison *et al.* 2008). In a recent Accenture study, respondents said a company's supply chain is often the biggest source of cost synergies, accounting for 30 to 50 per cent of the savings achieved. Rationalisation of assets such as warehouses or truck fleets, for example, is often a prerequisite to merger success. Yet nearly half (45 per cent) of supply chain managers said that during merger integration efforts, their companies focused only on generating cost savings at the expense of other metrics, such as quality, inventory turns, supply disruption and order fill rates (Accenture 2006).

The first question under this heading would be the number of distribution outlets and the extent of market coverage which the target company has. The cost of distribution as a percentage of sales revenue compared to the acquirer company and to industry norms would also have to be established. The efficiency of the distribution process would also need to be reviewed: the number of days it takes for orders to be fulfilled and to reach customers, the percentage of shipments received with damaged merchandise and the level and cost of returns received.

The nature of contractual arrangements with distributors would also need to be reviewed to ensure that continuity can be maintained, if that is the desired outcome, or that termination can occur, if that is the business decision. Qualitative issues would also need to be addressed as part of this review, such as the level of satisfaction among distributors and the likelihood of defection following a merger or acquisition. The extent to which a channel is dominated by buyers or suppliers would also need to be considered to make sure that the acquirer company could not be held up to ransom by a third party of this type.

An assessment of the physical channels of distribution and logistics system is also essential. The amount and location of warehouse space, the level of inventory maintained (measured as number of days/sales) and the cost of having this space and inventory would need to be reviewed. If the company has its own fleet of trucks and materials handling equipment, then an assessment would be needed to address such questions as the number, age, value and performance capabilities.

Distribution is an area which would usually be a prime candidate for cost savings following a merger or acquisition and the extent of the likely savings should be ascertained as part of this review process. However, Christofferson et al. (2004) found that while managers in about 60 per cent of mergers deliver the planned cost synergies, in about a quarter of all cases they are overestimated by at least 25 per cent, a miscalculation that can easily translate into a 5–10 per cent valuation error. This latter point reinforces the necessity of including a careful assessment of distribution as part of the due diligence process.

## Marketing Personnel

Evaluation of the target firm's marketing personnel may be the most significant area to be investigated by the acquiring company, for two reasons. First, much of the price premium to be paid for the firm may be a function of the calibre of the company's marketing programme. Second, evidence is strong that M&As are much more likely to be successful if the acquired firm is allowed to function as an independent unit and its management stay on to run the business (Homburg and Bucerius 2005).

The degree to which the acquired company's marketing activities will be integrated with those of the acquirer is a key question to be considered, with implications for cost savings and for implementation. If the acquired firm is to be allowed to continue as a standalone business then there is not much need for an implementation plan. If, however, marketing integration is a key element in the strategy, then considerable time and attention needs to be given as to exactly how this is to be achieved and what the new structure will be.

## Assessing Post-Merger Synergies

One of the main ways in which mergers and acquisitions can potentially deliver value is through the realisation of synergies between the merged firms, and thus estimation of the nature and magnitude of potential synergies is a key task in the due diligence process. The result of this analysis is an essential input into the valuation of a potential acquisition and in arriving at a price to bid for the target firm.

Horizontal acquisitions potentially create value by exploiting both cost-based and revenue-based synergies (Capron 1999). Economic theory has traditionally seen horizontal acquisitions as an opportunity to achieve cost savings through the exploitation of economies of scale and scope, and through divestiture of duplicated assets between the merging firms. In contrast, a marketing or resource-based view of the firm emphasises the role of revenue-enhancement synergies arising when the redeployment of the resources of the merged firms leads to revenue enhancing capabilities. Figure 5.4 summarises the main sources of potential synergy that acquirers may seek, and their possible impact on performance.

Cost-based synergies have generally received more attention than revenue-based synergies in research, as horizontal acquisitions have typically been seen as a straightforward mechanism for reducing costs through asset divestiture. Several studies show that asset divestiture, that is, the elimination of redundant activities and inefficient management practices, improves the performance of horizontal acquisitions (Capron 1999; Chatterjee 1986).

Capron (1999) carried out a detailed survey of acquiring firm managers covering 253 horizontal mergers and acquisitions that took place in American and European manufacturing industries from 1988 through 1992. Overall, these results show that both asset divestiture and resource redeployment contribute to acquisition performance; however, he found that there is a significant risk of damaging acquisition performance in the process of divesting and redeploying the target's assets and resources.

It is much more difficult to come to a definitive conclusion about the potential for revenue increase following mergers, making it highly risky to establish revenue increase as the primary justification for such mergers (Chatterjee 1986, 2007). However, there is some positive evidence that can give comfort in this regard. For example, using a sample of more than 2,000 US acquisitions completed during the 1980s and 1990s, Ghosh (2004) discovered a large increase in market share following acquisitions. The median market share of merging firms increased from 2.77 to 4.39 per cent following acquisitions, which reflected a 58 per cent increase relative to the market share in Year 1.

He also found a significant positive correlation between changes in market share and changes in long-run operating performance. Decomposing operating performance into asset efficiency and operating cost efficiency, he found that the increase in operating performance primarily resulted from greater asset efficiency. Furthermore, this study found that profitability increases with market share and the increase in profitability primarily resulted from better asset management and higher productivity. A higher market share benefits equity holders because of improvements in operating performance that results from higher asset productivity.

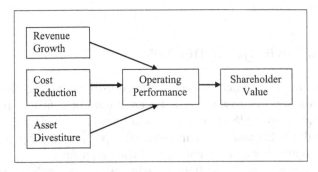

**Figure 5.4   Marketing Synergies and Performance**

*Source*: Own Illustration

The best advice, however, is that M&A teams should take great care in forecasting cost savings and revenue gains resulting from acquisitions, and to err on the conservative side in their estimates, because there is a substantial body of research evidence attesting to the fact that mergers and acquisitions have a poor record of success is delivering increased returns. Christofferson *et al.* (2004) suggest a company risks overestimating synergies if it neglects to use the available benchmarks as a sanity check. They cite the example of one European industrial company that acquired another based on predicted cost savings of €110 million from selling, general, and administrative expenses, even though precedents suggested that a range of €2.5 million to €9 million was more realistic. Still worse, it was especially risky to aim for deep cuts in sales and marketing expenditures because this approach put revenue growth at risk, and the net present value of pre-synergy revenue growth was roughly four times greater than all synergies combined.

## Price Premiums Paid for M&As

A considerable body of research evidence exists on the subject of prices paid for acquisitions and it suggests a norm of about 20–30 per cent for the typical premium paid. Andrade *et al.* (2001) reported remarkably stable target firm returns of 23–25 per cent for completed mergers spanning decades in the 1973 to 1998 period. The average acquisition premium for listed companies was 15 per cent and 22 per cent in 2004 and 2003, respectively, according to a report by Arthur D. Little.

Unfortunately, research also suggests a negative relationship between premiums paid and the returns to the acquiring firm's shareholders (Datta *et al.* 1992; Andrade *et al.* 2001; Kaplan 2006). One of the primary reasons for this negative association is that firms are unable to realize the potential synergies and their operating performance often deteriorates after the acquisition is completed. Payment of a premium to acquire a firm increases the pressure on the acquiring firm's top executives to create returns for the shareholders beyond the cost of the acquisition. If potential synergies cannot be achieved, even a small premium could be considered excessive.

Managers often justify the payment of premiums based on the potential synergies from the integration of the two firms. However, when large premiums are paid to acquired firms, creating the needed synergy becomes more challenging because of the higher returns required to cover the costs of making the acquisition. To maximize the value created, managers are motivated to reduce costs where possible and to attempt to increase the returns. Some expenses are difficult to control but human capital costs are often among the easiest to reduce, particularly in the short term. Yet, because of the value of human capital for competitive advantage, excessive workforce reductions may be detrimental to organizational performance, thereby exacerbating the original problems (Krishnan *et al.* 2007).

## Conclusion

This chapter started with an assertion that a majority of mergers and acquisitions are horizontal, involving the marriage of competitors within the same industry. This suggests that the motivation for these transactions is fundamentally market-driven – to achieve revenue growth by building market share and extending market scope. This leads to the obvious conclusion that marketing professionals – whose expertise is market analysis and brand building – ought to have a central role in every aspect of M&A, both in the planning and execution of such transactions. Available evidence does not bear this out, however, with all the indications being that marketing personnel do not get a look-in on M&A deals until after the fact, when they become involved in the tidying-up process of implementation.

This chapter has set out to correct this deficiency by arguing that marketing has a valuable role to play in every aspect of the due diligence process. It started by reviewing the evidence concerning motivations for M&A transactions to demonstrate the centrality of market share. It then provided an organising framework for considering marketing assets as a basis for a systematic analysis of the potential gains from combining two companies. Each of the asset classes identified in this model was then reviewed to suggest the types of questions that should be asked as part of a due diligence process.

The answers to these questions should then feed into estimations of the potential synergies that might be realised from the proposed merger. Such synergies might come from revenue growth, cost reductions or asset divestiture. A marketing perspective would naturally tend to emphasise revenue generation over the other possibilities, and this emphasis ought to compliment that of the other management functions which would tend to focus more on the cost reduction side. Given the widespread evidence that forecast synergies are rarely realised in M&A transactions, it seems that companies need all the help they can get to improve their record in this area.

The difficulties in extracting synergies are often exacerbated by paying too high a price for acquisitions, typically a 20–30 per cent premium over the intrinsic value. This large premium is justified on the basis of the anticipated synergies which creates an immense pressure to deliver the forecast savings. This pressure often results in taking the easy options – usually cutting personnel numbers – but this can actually have an adverse affect on the realisation of synergies by damaging morale, losing important skills and experience and damaging customer relationships. Dysfunctional effects of this type may go some way to explain the very poor record of performance that typically follows mergers and acquisitions.

It is hoped that the infusion of marketing skills and experience advocated in this chapter would help to correct some of these problems leading to a realistic assessment of synergies and a sensible bid price. It is believed that a marketing involvement could also make a contribution to post-merger implementation, assisting a smooth transition both internally and externally and leading ultimately to a superior outcome for the company and all of its stakeholders.

# References

Accenture, 2006. *Supply Chain Post-merger Study*. New York.

Agarwal, A., Joffe, J.J and Mandelker, G.N. 1992. The post-merger performance of acquiring firms: A re-examination of an anomaly. *Journal of Finance*, XLVII, Sept., 1605–21.

Andrade, G., Mitchell, M. and Stafford, E. 2001, New evidence and perspectives on mergers. *Journal of Economic Perspectives*, 15 (2), Spring, 103–20.

Bahadir, S.C., S.G. Bharadwaj, S.G. and Srivastava, R.K. 2008. Financial value of brands in mergers and acquisitions: Is value in the eye of the beholder? *Journal of Marketing*, 72 (6), 49–64.

Basu, K. 2006, Merging brands after mergers. *California Management Review*, 48 (4), 28–40.

Buzzell, R.D. 1981. Are there 'natural' market structures? *The Journal of Marketing*, 45(1), 42–51.

Capron, L. 1999. The long-term performance of horizontal acquisitions. *Strategic Management Journal*, 20, 987–1018.

Capron, L. and Hulland, J. 1999. Redeployment of brands, sales forces, and general marketing management expertise following horizontal acquisitions: A resource-based view. *Journal of Marketing*, 63, April, 41–54.

Chatterjee, S. 1986. Types of synergy and economic value: The impact of acquisitions on merging and acquired firms. *Strategic Management Journal*, 7, 119–39.

Chatterjee, S. 2007. Why is synergy so difficult in mergers of related businesses? *Strategy and Leadership*, 35 (2), 46–62.

Christofferson, S.A., McNish, R.S. and Sias, D.L. 2004. Where mergers go wrong? *McKinsey Quarterly*, (2), 92–99.

Clemente, M.N. and Greenspan, D.S. 1996. Getting the biggest marketing bang from the merger. *Mergers and Acquisitions Journal*, 31 (1), 19–25.

Datta, D.K., Pinches, G.E. and Narayanan, V.K. (1992). Factors influencing wealth creation from mergers and acquisitions: A meta-analysis. *Strategic Management Journal*, 13 (1), 67–84.

Ettenson, R. and Knowles, J. 2006. Merging the brands and branding the merger. *Sloan Management Review*, Summer, 39–49.

Ghosh, A. 2004. Increasing market share as a rationale for corporate acquisitions. *Journal of Business Finance & Accounting*, 31 (1–2), 209–47.

Hise, R.T. 1991. Evaluating marketing assets in M&A. *Journal of Business Strategy*, July/August, 46–51.

Homburg, C. and Bucerius, M. 2005. A marketing perspective on mergers and acquisitions: How marketing integration affects post-merger performance. *Journal of Marketing*, 69 (1), 95–113.

Kapferer, J-N. 2004. *The New Strategic Brand Management: Creating and Sustaining Brand Equity*. London: Kogan Page.

Kaplan, S.N. 2006. Mergers and Acquisitions: A Financial Economics Perspective. *Antitrust Modernization Commission Economist's Roundtable on Merger Enforcement*, January 19.

Keller, K.L. 1993. Conceptualising, measuring and managing customer-based brand equity. *Journal of Marketing*, 57 (1), 1–22.

King, D. R., Dalton, D.R., Daily, C.M. and Colvin, J.G. 2004. Meta-analysis of post-acquisition performance. *Strategic Management Journal*, 25 (2), 187–200.

KPMG 2006. *Benchmarking M&A Teams*, KPMG Transaction Services. Available at http://www.kpmg.com/Global/en/IssuesAndInsights/ArticlesPublications/Pages/default.aspx as accessed on 01/04/10.

KPMG 2007. *Doing Deals in Tough Times: Best Practices of Leading M&A Teams*, KPMG Transaction Services. Available at http://www.kpmg.com/Global/en/IssuesAndInsights/ArticlesPublications/Pages/default.aspx as accessed on 01/04/10.

KPMG 2009. *All to Play For: Striving for Post-Deal Success*, KPMG Transaction Services. Available at http://www.kpmg.com/Global/en/IssuesAndInsights/ArticlesPublications/Pages/default.aspx as accessed on 01/04/10.

Krishnan, H.A., Hitt, M.A. and Park, D. 2007. Acquisition premiums, subsequent workforce reductions and post-acquisition performance. *Journal of Management Studies*, 44 (5), 709–32.

Little, A.D. 2005. A user's guide to successful M&A, *Prism*, 2, 35–51. Available at http://www.adlittle. co.uk/prism_uk.html?year=2005 as accessed 01/04/10.

Martynova, M. and Renneboog, L. 2008. A century of corporate takeovers: What have we learned and where do we stand? *Journal of Banking and Finance*, 32 (10), 2148–77.

Maksimovic, V. and Phillips, G. 2001. The market for corporate assets: Who engages in mergers and asset sales and are there efficiency gains? *The Journal of Finance*, 56 (6), 2019–65.

Morrison, N.J., Kinley, G. and Ficery, K.L. 2008. Merger deal breakers: When operational due diligence exposes risk. *Journal of Business Strategy*, 29 (3), 23–8.

Mueller, D.C. 1985. Mergers and market share. *The Review of Economics and Statistics*, 67, 259–67.

Muzellec, L. and Lambkin, M. (2006). Corporate rebranding: Destroying, transferring or creating brand equity? *European Journal of Marketing*, 40(7/8), 803–24.

Nath, P. and Mahajan, V. 2008. CMO's: A study of their presence in firms' top management teams. *Journal of Marketing*, 72 (1), 65–81.

Verhoef, P and Leeflang, P.S.H. 2008. *Getting Marketing Back into the Boardroom: Understanding the Drivers of Marketing's Influence*, Marketing Science Institute, Cambridge, MA, Working Paper 08-104.

# 6 Innovation Capability Due Diligence: Investigating the Innovation Capability of Companies

JAN BUCHMANN
*Strascheg Institute for Innovation and Entrepreneurship (SIIE)*
*EBS Business School, Wiesbaden, Germany and BearingPoint*
*Management and Technology Consultants, Frankfurt, Germany*

FLORIAN KISSEL
*Rotterdam School of Management, Rotterdam, The Netherlands*

## Introduction

This chapter explores the usefulness of investigating a company's innovation capability within a commercial due diligence. Furthermore, dimensions of innovation capability that should be investigated within such a due diligence are described and followed with tips on how they can be best assessed. The final section of this chapter exposes the challenges of gathering and interpreting non-financial data, as most innovation capability dimensions are not typically related to more easily accessible financial data.

## The Relevance of Innovation and Innovation Capability

Companies achieve competitive advantage through acts of innovation (Porter 1990: 74). Without innovation, organizations simply cannot cope with continuous market change this is due to a number of reasons, such as, intensified competition or changing customer needs (Goffin and Mitchell 2005: 2–5).

Before launching into a study of innovation capability it may be prudent to examine how the term innovation is defined. Various comprehensions of the term 'innovation' can be found in literature. Generally, 'innovation' has its origin in the Latin words '*novus*' for new or '*innovatio*' for alteration, which is the basis of most definitions. However, multiple perceptions of innovation have evolved over the past decades. Vedin (1980: 22) defines innovation as 'an invention brought to its first use, its first introduction into the market'.

Afuah (2003: 13) reinforces this marketing aspect: 'invention + commercialization'. Market implementation and market success distinguish innovations from inventions (Bürgel, Haller, and Binder 1996: 14). Accordingly, an organization's innovation capability provides it with effective and efficient processes and routines to continuously generate inventions and commercialize them.

## The Relevance of Innovation Capability within a Due Diligence

A due diligence assesses a target company from a commercial, financial, and legal perspective. It is concerned with understanding more about a business, or a collection of business units being bought, by identifying the risks associated with an acquisition (Howson 2003). A central part of any commercial due diligence is to investigate whether the company is able to compete in the future and whether competitive advantage can be sustained (Howson 2006: 111–46). As will be argued in this chapter, innovation is a key component of achieving and sustaining competitive advantage. Furthermore, since the methods to calculate a company's value mostly depend on the promise of future earnings (for example, discounted cash flow analysis) (Damodaran 2006), the future orientation of innovation, and specifically innovation cability, is highly relevant for determining the value of a company. Hence, getting a meaningful picture of a company's innovation capability supports both asking and answering important questions raised during M&A processes and due diligence.

## A Comprehensive Innovation Capability Framework

Innovation capability implies that an organization is able to by itself successfully develop inventions or improvements and commercialize them within (for example, as a new process) or outside (for example, as a new product or service). The following sections of this chapter will provide an overview of innovation capability models and the determinants of innovation capability.

Like innovation itself, the term innovation capability is not universally defined. Various definitions can be found in literature leading to a large number of misunderstandings of innovation capability. The comparison and integration of three concepts of innovation capability yields a more comprehensive and appropriate approach.

Adams, Bessant, and Phelps (2006: 26–38) investigate innovation capability from an innovation management perspective. They divide innovation management into seven, mostly analytically quantifiable dimensions:

1. inputs
2. knowledge management
3. innovation strategy
4. organization and culture
5. portfolio management
6. project management
7. commercialization.

This is illustrated in Table 6.1.

**Table 6.1    Innovation Management**

| Framework Category | Measurement Areas |
| --- | --- |
| Inputs | People<br>Physical and financial resources<br>Tools |
| Knowledge management | Idea generation<br>Knowledge repository<br>Information flows |
| Innovation strategy | Strategic orientation<br>Strategic leadership |
| Organization and culture | Culture<br>Structure |
| Portfolio management | Risk/return balance<br>Optimization tool use |
| Project management | Project efficiency<br>Tools<br>Communications<br>Collaborations |
| Commercialization | Market research<br>Market testing<br>Marketing and sales |

*Source*: Adams et al. 2006

Lawson and Samson (2001: 389–95) also developed an innovation capability construct based on a dynamic capability-based view (Arthurs and Busenitz 2006: 199). Their dimensions of innovation capability (Figure 6.1) are:

1.  vision and strategy
2.  harnessing the competence base
3.  organizational intelligence
4.  creativity and idea management
5.  organizational structure and systems
6.  culture and climate
7.  management of technology.

Adams *et al.* (2006), in their research, paid more attention to resources and strategic and operational coordination processes. Even though organizational learning and culture are represented, they are treated with less importance. Moreover, their approach is extremely broad. Lawson and Samson (2001: 395), on the contrary, strongly focused on the organizational and individual levels, but paid less attention to process, products and projects. The authors state that this capability creates the potential that ultimately leads to innovation activities.

A further perspective, which incorporates the key concepts of the two previously discussed approaches, was developed by Sammerl (2006: 197–8). In accordance with the dynamic capability-based view, here the author identified five central dimensions of Innovation Capability namely, Internal and External learning (as part of Organizational Learning processes); Innovation Process Management (as an operative coordination); Innovation Portfolio (as a strategic coordination); and, Innovation Culture (considered as coordination processes). Sammerl's approach (2006; Figure 6.2) is considered by the authors to be a more balanced and comprehensive framework of innovation capability and is therefore recommended as the best model to use in order to conduct an innovation capability due diligence.

As seen in Figure 6.2, this model consists of two major areas: The first is Organizational Learning processes (Internal and External Learning), which are core components of dynamic capabilities. These processes change existing knowledge and add new knowledge (Sammerl 2006: 198). Furthermore, organizational learning consists of both individual and corporate processes. Calantone, Cavusgil, and Zhao (2002: 517–8) characterize the importance of continuous learning for innovation capability in three ways: First, learning organizations are committed to innovation, and thus, they are more likely to employ up-to-date technology. Second, they are less likely to miss opportunities arising from emerging market demand. Third, and finally, learning organizations usually have a higher innovation capability than their competitors since they better monitor their actions.

The other determinants of innovation capability proposed by Sammerl, besides organizational learning processes, are overall coordination and management processes, ensuring more effective and efficient control of activities, competencies, and resources (Sammerl 2006: 202–3). Three dimensions of processes can be deduced from this dynamic capability-based view. Innovation culture guides all actions of individuals within an organization. Moreover, the strategic level is categorized as the innovation portfolio since the innovation projects selected should reflect the organization's innovation strategy. Additionally, the management of the innovation portfolio is perceived to be the expression of and, thus, a measurement of the innovation strategy. Finally, the operational level is considered by this model by all coordinative actions regarding the innovation process.

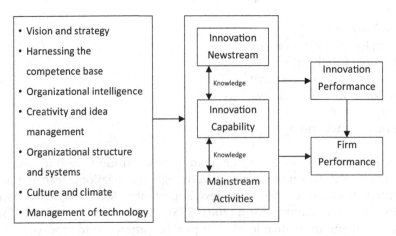

**Figure 6.1   Lawson and Samson's Innovation Capability Framework**

*Source*: Lawson and Samson (2001)

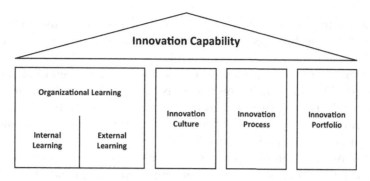

**Figure 6.2 Sammerl's Innovation Capability Model**

*Source*: Own illustration

# Innovation Due Diligence in Detail

The previously introduced innovation capability model is recommended in order to determine the dimensions that should be investigated by an innovation capability due diligence approach. This model will now be examined in greater detail.

# Organizational Learning

Organizational learning is a broadly and often inconsistently defined term and can be found with many varying definitions in literature. Kianto (2008) has identified several definitions ranging from knowledge creation, continuous improvement, and organizational agility to flexibility. The author calls the ability of learning and innovating as 'renewal capability' (2008: 71), incorporating internal and external factors. However, a consensus in literature does exist on organizational learning being an ongoing, company-wide process of learning and that organizational learning actually consists of both internal and external learning processes.

Sammerl (2006: 199–200) outlines the dimension of internal learning as the extent to which a company is able to advance internal knowledge and create new knowledge. It comprehends all processes within the organization which deal with these two options of generating and enhancing knowledge for innovation. It is, therefore, derived from the dynamic capability-based view and the knowledge-based view (Gassmann and Keupp 2007: 353).

The main source of internal learning, especially for generating new knowledge, is internal research and development. As Bürgel *et al.* (1996: 9–12) argue, internal research and development (R&D) can be sub-classified into four categories. Research can be divided into fundamental and applied research. Development can be divided into experimental and constructive development. While fundamental research is all about generating new scientific cognition without the major aim of applying this cognition, to solve a practical problem, applied research explicitly includes the goal to solve practical problems. Experimental development involves the use of existing scientific cognition in order to get new or considerably better materials, products, services, systems, or processes. Constructive development, on the other hand, is concerned with the realization of technical manufactures with a new combination of previously used phenomena, a broader application of technology and a combination derived from known construction principles.

Another source of internal learning is incremental learning often implemented in an internal suggestion system, or other mechanisms, aiming to foster incremental changes (cf. innovation culture). Schroeder, Bates, and Junttila (2002: 107–8) view internal learning with respect to the overall staff. They recommend qualifying and fostering multi-functional employees and to consider all employees' suggestions in process and product development. Employees' knowledge, they argue, is an irreplaceable source for suggestions, particularly for recurring processes, and organizational culture is an important determinant for motivating employees to contribute to innovativeness.

However, organizational learning does not only involve internal processes. Opening the organization to participation from, and the integration of, external sources of knowledge is a crucial part of innovation success. According to Sammerl (2006: 189), external learning can emerge from either integrating information and knowledge of sources from outside the organization, or by developing knowledge together *with* external partners. The former factor even includes the internal R&D department as an external learning source. As Cohen and Levinthal (1989: 593) identified, R&D does not need to solely create new information, it can utilize externally available information by assimilating and exploiting it. Hence, learning largely depends on what this chapter refers to as absorptive capacity. This absorptive capacity is the firm's ability to gather information from external sources, to assimilate this information and use it for its own purpose (Cohen and Levinthal 1990: 128–29). The latter factor of external learning, partnerships, can be established with customers, suppliers, and even competitors and includes all co-operative efforts, joint ventures, acquisitions and conventions. Gaughan (2007: 526) assumes that R&D is a major reason for forming joint ventures and strategic alliances. Narver and Slater (1990: 34) determined that orientation on the market has a strong positive effect on a company's success. Customers themselves are particularly valuable as their knowledge is hard to imitate and their involvement provides insights into their current and future needs.

## ASSESSING ORGANIZATIONAL LEARNING

The complexity and interconnectivity of organizations cause organizational learning to be multidimensional (Jerez-Gómez, Céspedes-Lorente, and Valle-Cabrera 2005: 715) and omnipresent. This has led to a 'theoretical pluralism' (Kianto 2008: 72) of organizational learning. In order to deal with learning processes: the handling of knowledge and the existing, enabling qualifications of learning need to be identified and assessed. Hence, multiple challenges in measuring organizational learning are faced.

Developing indicators for measuring organizational learning is a challenging but crucial task. In assessing knowledge, most of the indicators applied refer to numeric data which is easily available. These give a good estimate of the current state of existing knowledge assets, but they are hardly suitable for assessing the development of new knowledge (Kianto 2008: 72). Most instruments assessing organizational learning capability are based on questionnaires distributed in surveys, comprising of several items measured on scales (Jerez-Gómez *et al.* 2005: 715).

In the process of choosing indicators, previously published measures are a valuable source of examples and some are even suitable for adoption (Kianto 2008: 76). These have to fit into the dimensions of organizational learning identified in the second step. In addition to these, creating new indicators is important in pursuing one's own concept (Jerez-Gómez *et al.* 2005: 719; Kianto 2008: 76). The following paragraphs offer a sample of dimensions of organizational learning capability as measured by the respective authors (see Table 6.2).

Jerez-Gómez *et al.* (2005) propose four dimensions: (1) Managerial commitment measures managers' commitment to learning. Managers are supposed to actively support both the generation and exchange of knowledge by driving the change process and making sure that every employee understands its significance. (2) The systems perspective assesses the identity that members of the organization share and how deeply it is accepted. It determines to which degree objectives are understood and promoted. Furthermore, (3) openness and experimentation are perceived to be crucial for the learning capability. In order to achieve double-loop learning, a learning process, where not only actions but, most importantly, the very basic values are exchanged, an open climate is essential. Lastly, (4) the knowledge transfer and integration is concerned with a simultaneous process. The absorptive capacity is a major driver of the efficacy of this dimension.

Probst, Raub, and Romhardt (2006) put more emphasis on knowledge itself offering three criteria: (1) The knowledge base of the organization describes qualitatively, as well as quantitatively, the existing knowledge within the organization. (2) Interventions are regarded as being processes that trigger a change in the knowledge base. These interventions are perceived as being the outputs of the change process, and thus, can be viewed as interim results or transfer effects. Finally, the operating profit at the end of a period can be seen an indicator of (3) success of these change processes.

Chiva, Alegre and Lapiedra (2007) take a different perspective which focuses more on the attitudes and behavior of the members of an organization, for example, attributes toward experimentation, meaning the degree to which emerging ideas and suggestions are fostered. Within literature, this is the most supported dimension. The extent of risk-

**Table 6.2   Approaches on Assessing Organizational Learning**

| Approach | Emphasis | Dimensions |
|---|---|---|
| Jerez-Gómez *et al.* (2005) | Learning capability | Managerial commitment, systems perspective, openness and experimentation, knowledge transfer and integration. |
| Probst *et al.* (2006) | Knowledge | Knowledge base, interventions, success of change processes. |
| Chiva *et al.* (2007) | Attitudes and behavior | Experimentation, risk-taking, interaction with external environment, dialogue, participative decision-making. |
| Kianto (2008) | Organizational renewal capability | Strategic competence, connectivity, exploiting time, learning orientation, goal-oriented leadership, managing knowledge. |

taking, and its tolerance in this respect, is another dimension. The authors also explicitly address the interaction with the external environment, not only as an influencing factor for the dimension, but as a dimension onto itself. Further, open dialogue sustains a collective examination of processes, assumptions, and certainties. The last dimension encompasses participative decision-making, representing each member's influence in the process.

A forth concept to assess organization learning was developed by Kianto (2008). The author categorizes six dimensions of organizational renewal capability:

1.  Strategic competence should support the purposeful development of the organization, which accounts for evolvement and flexibility.
2.  Connectivity describes all relationships inside the organization, and those with external stakeholders, by both their structure and depth.
3.  Exploiting time concerns the optimum timing of change, especially of new ideas, as well as, successful outputs.
4.  The learning orientation of the organization describes not only the members' relations towards learning but also how the structure of the organization supports these.
5.  Goal-oriented leadership requires two sets of skills, namely, managing innovation processes and, on the other hand, promoting creativity and learning.
6.  Managing knowledge includes the tools for storing and sharing knowledge and information.

In an innovation capability due diligence, these dimensions should be used to assess an organization's internal and external learning capability. Additionally, two other major areas following should be investigated to assess organizational learning capability.

R&D (also part of the innovation process perspective) is a main source of organizational learning in technology-oriented organizations. Gerybadze (2004: 58–60) developed a survey about the application of resources in, and the performance of, R&D. This survey addresses questions on funds, such as an adequate amount for R&D, their optimal allocation and application, as well as, fast and flexible mobilization for the best and most promising projects. Moreover, the survey asks for the standard of capacity, such as the technological level, equipment, and infrastructure. In addition, benchmarks measuring the share of sales of new products, development time and other such indicators, as well as, the utilization of external sources of innovation are examined.

For assessing joint ventures, Anderson (1990: 20–4) asserts that most firms treat joint ventures like subsidiaries. Hence, the performance of joint ventures is often measured compared to its owners' targets. In order to achieve best results, joint ventures should be treated as standalone entities, because the interests of the joint venture may differ from those of the parent. Since joint ventures can be assessed as standalone entities, further assessment can include measures of how a company's organizational learning capability is transferred to either partners individually (to assess their respective strength) or the work of the co-operation itself. The former may cause problems of information accessibility. Additionally, Adams *et al.* (2006: 37) have identified measures of communication with external stakeholders, focusing on whether it happens at all, its degree and the correspondents. Those measures are not only subjective evaluations, but also counts of frequency.

## SUGGESTED DATA SOURCES

To assess organizational learning, the following sources can be used: Funds spent for R&D; patent statistics; documentation about knowledge management processes; knowledge management reports; documentation about idea/suggestion management systems; idea/suggestion management reports; and, information about external corporations, joint ventures and acquisitions.

# Innovation Culture

In general, corporate culture is a mechanism of co-ordination and, hence, part of an organization's overall dynamic capabilities. Corporate culture encompasses the norms and values which guide decisions and actions and as such these norms and values decrease the need for more formal co-ordination (Sammerl 2006: 209). Steinmann and Schreyögg (2005: 728–33) have identified positive, as well as, negative effects of corporate culture. The positive effects include more efficient communication, as well as, high-motivation and team spirit. Negative effects include the fact that employees are more prone to remain in traditional success patterns and to retain a collective attitude of avoidance, which results in organizational rigidity or a lack of adapting to changes. The more distinct the corporate culture, the stronger the effects. The authors conclude that it cannot be definitely clarified whether strong, or weak, cultures are preferable for innovation.

Companies that know how to innovate don't necessarily throw money into R&D. Instead, they cultivate a new style of corporate behavior that is comfortable with new ideas, change, risk, and even failure (O'Reilly and Rao 1997: 60).

This corporate behavior does not only foster idea generation but also facilitates processes to get them all the way from their emergence, through R&D, past marketing and manufacturing and ultimately, onto the customer. In practice, projects often get shot down, even in late stages, due to a lack of openness to innovation by executives (O'Reilly and Rao 1997: 60–4).

Culture is clearly an important factor for an organization's learning capability as it can enhance it to a large extent. Slater and Narver (1995: 71–2) argue that an open organization can better access a greater number of information sources, enhance methods of information sharing and offer a variety of interpretations for certain information.

One way to foster an innovative culture is to establish tools of employee participation in the innovation processes. Fairbank and Williams (2001: 68–72) specifically recommend suggestion systems. These are useful ways to obtain and utilize creative ideas. Employees are motivated to open-up, think creatively, share their information and create innovations out of their ideas. To truly motivate employees to think creatively, and to participate in the system, more than simple rewards for suggested or implemented ideas are required. By applying expectancy theory, the authors have identified three key areas to support an innovative culture via a suggestion system: (1) the rewards need to be valued by the respective employees; (2) a close link to the success of the performance is preferred; and, (3) employees need to believe that they can actually reach the goals set by management. Such rewards do not only include bonuses and career opportunities but often those that boost self-esteem play an important role.

## ASSESSING INNOVATION CULTURE

Hofstede, Neuijen, Ohayv, and Sanders (1990) were pioneers in the field of measuring organizational culture. While they did not specifically address innovation culture, their findings lay important foundations for further research. An important research question addressed in their study was whether the characteristics of organizational cultures enforce a qualitative measurement or whether they can be assessed quantitatively. The authors applied a mix of interviews and questionnaires to gather comprehensive data including background information on employees. In their study, the authors conclude that organizational culture can indeed be measured quantitatively. Furthermore, Hofstede *et al.* reason that the core of an organization's culture is its shared values.

Research on the measurement of specifically linking innovation and creativity to culture was done by Amabile, Conti, Coon, Lazenby, and Herron (1996). Their work aims to assess those aspects of the work environment that have an impact on the generation and development of ideas. The authors claim that their study yields a 'psychometrically sound tool' for a quantitative assessment of the perceived work environment regarding creativity. It was developed for scholars, as well as, professionals and was based on questionnaires.

Amabile *et al.* (1996) identified five dimensions of work environment that refer to creativity and innovation. The first dimension, encouragement of creativity, is further subdivided into three categories: organizational encouragement; supervisory encouragement; and, work group encouragement. Organizational encouragement measures not only the readiness of individual members to assume risk but also their idea generation, which requires a fair and supportive evaluation. Further factors assessed were the kinds and degree of recognition and, accordingly, the rewards of creativity. Concluding, the overall flow of ideas throughout the organization, as well as, an open management and decision-making, are important factors to assess. Moreover, supervisory encouragement relies on clear communication, whether goals are communicated clearly, if interactions between supervisors and subordinate are open and to which degree supervisors support the research of their subordinates. Work group encouragement takes a different perspective. Here, the diversity of backgrounds within the group is assessed as is the openness of all members to new ideas, their willingness to offer constructive challenges and the commitment that all members show to the project.

The second dimension from Amabile *et al.* (1996), freedom or autonomy, is supposed to ensure that employees feel free to be able to choose how to perform their work. Several studies have shown that such a perception fosters creativity.

The third dimension, the adequate allocation of resources to potential creative outputs has a strong psychological influence on cognition. Furthermore, the members of a project have to believe in its intrinsic value to show maximum motivation and creativity.

The fourth factor is pressure. While pressure usually exerts negative effects it can contribute positively if the work is intellectually challenging. The negative side is workload pressure especially if time gets too short and onerous workloads may explode and trigger stress.

The fifth and final factor presented by Amabile *et al.* (1996) is the consideration of organizational impediments to creativity, which are also negatively correlated to creativity. These can be conservatism, inflexibility, overly-formal management structures and even internal strife. This is often perceived as examination and can result in a rise of extrinsic, but also a drop of the crucial intrinsic, motivation.

Tellis, Prabhu, and Chandy (2009) in their approach to organizational culture measured the impact of corporate culture on radical innovation output in three dimensions: (1) the willingness to cannibalize existing products and markets by introducing substitutes; (2) future market focus; and (3) risk tolerance. In their empirical study, they received significant correlations for all of these dimensions. An overview of the depicted approaches and their emphases can be found in Table 6.3.

**Table 6.3   Approaches on Assessing Organizational Culture**

| Approach | Emphasis | Dimensions |
| --- | --- | --- |
| Hofstede *et al.* (1990) | Values | Shared values. |
| Amabile *et al.* (1996) | Creativity | Encouragement of creativity, freedom or autonomy, adequate allocation of resources, pressure, organizational impediments. |
| Tellis *et al.* (2009) | Impact on radical innovation | Willingness to cannibalize, future market focus, risk tolerance. |

## SUGGESTED DATA SOURCES

To assess the degree of innovation culture, recent employee surveys, information about incentive systems and corporate education programs (and their contents) could provide valuable hints. Performance measurements of suggestion or idea management systems might also give insights into the innovativeness of a company's culture. Yet another source could be the inclusion of cultural questions in interviews with management of the investigated target company.

# Innovation Process

Innovation process management covers the management of single innovation processes. It is the operative aspect of the co-ordination and management processes, and thus, it is concerned with efficiency. It involves the management of all activities performed in innovation projects, as well as, co-ordinating processes and tasks. Innovation processes are complex, dynamic, cross functional, and highly-interdependent (Sammerl 2006: 203–206).

Mischke (2007: 40–3) has identified four challenges for the successful management of innovation processes. First, the innovation process is always a cyclical investment process. This involves the need for costs of resources to be covered by sales revenue. The basic economic goal is that the return on investment (RoI) ought to be positive. However, this can only be determined at the end of the product life cycle (PLC) and ultimately depends on the outcomes of this process, and the remaining capital. Second, a basic proposition is that innovation and R&D success are reached step-by-step. The innovation process starts with a product or service idea, or the intention to introduce an innovation to the market. On this basis, an organization begins working on the realization of this innovation. During the process, it reaches several intermediate stepping-stone accomplishments, such as, marketability. These accomplishments have to be passed successively. Third, real feasibility and demand can only be determined at the end of the R&D period and the market period, respectively. The two milestones, technology success and market success, have to be passed one after another. Since they are not predictable, success can only be subsequently determined. Fourth, and finally, even small and early mistakes can have a great impact. The earlier a mistake occurs, the longer it can take and the more expensive it can be for the company to straighten it out. Because of resource constraints, only few innovation initiatives are pursued and share all available innovation resources. This leads to high cost effects, if only one, or even a few, of these initiatives fail.

## ASSESSING THE INNOVATION PROCESS

Spanning such an extensive range of steps, assessing the innovation process can clearly be a challenge. It covers the initial and preliminary screenings and assessments, market research at various stages, actual product development, several phases of product testing, production, a market launch and many more (Cooper and Kleinschmidt 1986: 74). Each of these can be measured and controlled, resulting in a myriad number of measures for the innovation process.

Adams *et al.* (2006: 36) view the innovation process in a similar perspective as that of a project. They determined that management efficiency is mostly measured in a comparison of budget and actual outcome. Such a comparison is largely carried out in the fields of project costs, revenue forecasting and project duration. A further approach is speed. This includes not only the speed of the project, but also meeting deadlines, as well as, the overall process duration. These measures demonstrate a positive correlation with product quality and customer satisfaction.

Of all of the measures for an innovation process, Cooper and Edgett (2008: 55) have identified the most popular. Among these are sales and profit measures, such as, revenue achieved compared to forecasted revenue. Further financial measures include profitability as net present value (NPV), or operating profits. Additionally, customer satisfaction gets a large share of attention. This can be measured via surveys, warrantee claims, and returns and complaints tracking. Lastly, the time to market, or on-time performance, is a widely-applied measure.

This holistic approach of measuring is not a completely new concept. In Anglophone literature, dealing with controlling and management accounting, the so-called concept of performance measurement, is well-known. Performance measurement involves the set-up and use of several Key Performance Indicators (KPIs), as for instance the above-mentioned measures costs and customer satisfaction. These KPIs serve as the basis for the evaluating of the effectiveness and efficiency of the performance and the performance potentials of different objects, in this case for example, the different steps of the innovation process. The definition of KPIs also helps to achieve more performance transparency, which can lead to more effective planning and control processes and, thus, improve the performance at all performance levels (Gleich, Henke, Quitt, and Sommer 2009: 107–8).

Davila, Epstein and Matusik (2004) identified two patterns of combined measurement systems. Measures applied individually lack a comprehensive understanding of the whole innovation process. Thus, the authors analyzed the various combinations of measures that managers use. They found that managers either use focused or balanced patterns. Focused patterns include measures at a certain stage of the process. Balanced patterns, on the other hand, include measures from different stages of the innovation process, utilizing 'leading-lagging relationships among measures' (Davila *et al.* 2004: 30) and yielding a broader picture of the whole process. Their findings suggest that managers tend to use the former pattern, but also embed aspects of the latter. Moreover, they determined a linkage between innovation strategy and the choice of the measurement system.

Hauschildt (2004: 537–42) suggests that an evaluation ought to be made throughout the whole process. This evaluation comprehends several measures at each stage. The measures are displayed in Table 6.4.

**Table 6.4    Measures Throughout the Innovation Process**

| Process Phase | Ideas | Research and Pre-development | Invention | Market Research | Product Development and Production | Introduction |
|---|---|---|---|---|---|---|
| Measurement | Number, alternatives | Technological progress, rise in output/ decrease of input | Weighted number of patents, publications, awards | Sales quantity, dispersion over time and region, number and potential of competitors | Information on improvement compared to existing solutions | Revenue, cost savings, margins, earnings |
| Information Sources | Experts referring to state of technology | Experts referring to technological performance | Controllers, managers | Market researchers and marketing managers | Marketing and production authorities | Controller, industry experts, bankers |

*Source*: Hauschildt (2004).

## SUGGESTED DATA SOURCES

Two dimensions of data sources should be also considered. First, data about the controlling mechanisms of the innovation process (are adequate controlling mechanisms in place?) is an important aspect of innovation capability. Second, the contents of the controlling systems, (for example the KPIs in Table 6.4), or measurements for the whole innovation process (for example, time-to-market), are highly-recommended to gain insight into the innovation performance and its innovation capability. Useful data could be derived from innovation controlling and project reports, as examples.

# Innovation Portfolio

The innovation portfolio comprises all ongoing and future innovation processes in an organization. It is the strategic aspect of the coordination and management process and, therefore, deals with issues of effectiveness (doing the right things) and involves the planning and control of the innovation portfolio. Naturally, the innovation portfolio has to be aligned with the overall business strategy and the innovation strategy. The portfolio management determines the fields, and the kind of, future investments. A focus on main strategic elements helps prioritize innovation projects and offers future relevance, as well as, sustainability (Sammerl 2006: 202–209).

Killen, Hunt, and Kleinschmidt (2008: 24–6) determined that product success rates remain at a rather low level despite an increase of resources allocated to new product development (NPD). Out of 100 projects started, 57 were technologically successful, 31 were introduced to the market, but only 12 were an economic success (Bürgel *et al.* 1996: 37). The best balance between levels of riskiness and the types of projects offers the highest value to the company. Moreover, the number of parallel projects should be watched closely to assure that resources are allocated effectively among the projects conducted (Killen, Hunt, and Kleinschmidt 2008: 24–6).

Cooper, Edgett, and Kleinschmidt (1999: 333–5) state that effective management of the innovation process and portfolio is vital to innovate successfully. Overall, a successful portfolio management requires the organization to regard four different areas, similar to other strategic decisions. First, strategic choices on investments in markets, products and technologies have to be made. Second, an effective allocation of resources guarantees that each project can be utilized to its capacity. This raises the question about how to spend scarce engineering, R&D, and marketing resources in order to achieve the highest value possible with an acceptable risk. The third area addresses project selection; since a company usually has too many opportunities to choose from, identifying the most promising, is as difficult as it is vital. Finally, a balance of the number of projects conducted, and the available resources or capabilities, needs to be kept.

As the project portfolio needs to be aligned with the strategy, its assessment is not only a measure of the strategy's implementation but also of the strategy itself.

## ASSESSING THE INNOVATION PORTFOLIO

Assessing the innovation portfolio implies analyzing the effectiveness of innovation (doing the right things or, in this context, projects). As stated above, only 12 per cent of all projects started are economically successful. This number confirms the necessity of an effective project portfolio management.

The success of a portfolio largely depends on the balance of individual projects and on the alignment of this portfolio with a company's strategy. A project portfolio can be balanced in several dimensions. One of these is the degree of newness. Examples for different degrees are radical innovation, improvements of existing technologies, or simple repositioning of existing products. Furthermore, the time of introduction differentiates between such portfolios that generate a constant stream of new products and those which alternate irregularly between waves of products and times without new introductions. Finally, the market perspective regards the allocation of resources according to the impact of certain markets and business units (Trott 2005: 299–300).

Cooper, Edgett, and Kleinschmidt (2001) have identified, and empirically tested, the application of six methods to evaluate projects in a portfolio. Basically, these are either methods to rank all projects or to decide on the inclusion or continuation of single projects in the portfolio.

The most popular methods to assess the innovation portfolio are financial methods. With these methods projects are ranked, on the one hand, either by their financial results or economic value or, on the other hand, versus a hurdle rate. Some companies even apply both methods.

Another method is a strategic approach, a resource allocation to 'buckets or envelopes' according to strategy. Within these buckets, individual projects are prioritized by, any and all, other methods available (for example, a financial method).

Methods less often applied are scoring models. Projects are ranked by weighted scores according to pre-defined dimensions. Criteria include dimensions such as strategic fit, financial reward, risk, probability of success, timing, technological capability, commercialization capability, protectability, or synergy between projects (ordered by frequency of application).

Another possibility are bubble diagrams, which are often used as a supporting tool. Their axes can confront:

- risk and reward
- newness
- ease and attractiveness
- strength and attractiveness
- cost and timing
- strategic and benefit
- cost and benefit (Figure 6.3).

The least popular methods are checklist models. They also tend to be applied as a supporting tool and are rather used for go/kill decisions instead of rankings. For evaluating and comparing portfolios, the ranking methods are the most valuable.

In terms of performance of project portfolios, Cooper *et al.* (2001) identified six key metrics, which distinguish high performers from their worst counterparts:

1. The alignment of projects with business objectives.
2. Whether very high value projects are in the portfolio.
3. Business strategy reflected in spending.
4. Projects completed in time.
5. A well-balanced project-portfolio.
6. The portfolio comprises the right number of projects.

The authors, as seen in Figure 6.3, have identified further characteristics of best performers. For instance, they apply much less financial models but rely rather on non-financials, their resource allocation is highly-aligned with their business strategy and, most importantly, they use multiple methods for their portfolio.

The findings of Cooper *et al.* (2001) are strongly supported by the empirical tests by Killen *et al.* (2008: 33). Strategic methods, as well as, portfolio mapping yield better balanced portfolios while financial measures alone do not reflect the true value of a portfolio. Additionally, the authors determined that project portfolio management processes are

| Rank | Type of Chart | Axis | | Axis | % |
|------|---------------|------|------|------|---|
| 1 | Risk vs. Reward | Reward: NPV, IRR, benefits after years of launch; market value | BY | Possibility of success (technical, commercial) | 44.4 |
| 2 | Newness | Technical newness | BY | Market Newness | 11.1 |
| 3 | Ease vs. Attractiveness | Technical feasibility | BY | Market attractiveness (growth potential, consumer appeal, general, attractiveness, life cycle) | 11.1 |
| 4 | Strength vs. Attractiveness | Competitive position (strengths) | BY | Attractiveness (market growth, technical maturity, years to implementation) | 11.1 |
| 5 | Cost vs. Timing | Cost to implement | BY | Time to impact | 9.7 |
| 6 | Strategic vs. Benefit | Strategic focus or fit | BY | Business intent, NPV, financial fit, attractiveness | 8.9 |
| 7 | Cost vs. Benefit | Cumulative reward | BY | Cumulative development costs | 5.6 |

**Figure 6.3   Bubble Diagrams for Innovation Portfolios**

*Source*: Cooper et al. 2001

similar in service product-based organizations and tangible product-based organizations. Moreover, the authors assert that the results of project portfolio performance measures positively correlate with the results of new product success measures. Consequently, the intrinsic value of a portfolio is also dependent on the measures applied.

## SUGGESTED DATA SOURCES

Comparable with innovation process data sources, used portfolio management methods, as well as, the portfolio contents should be examined to assess the innovation portfolio dimension. The use of sophisticated portfolio management methods, and the fit between the company's strategy and the portfolio contents, give valuable information to evaluate a company's innovation capability. Useful data can be derived from the company's strategy, project proposals, business cases, and project reports.

# Challenges in Accessing Non-Financial Information

As Lev and Zambon (2003: 598–9) state, current accounting and reporting systems fail to deliver sufficient information on intangible assets, not only for external stakeholders, but even for internal management. Intangible assets do not only lack transparent accounting, they also miss management awareness, consensus, as well as, procedures. With the rising importance of intangibles, the limits to traditional accounting become clearer. While current accounting systems are based on transactions and historical costs, the value of intangibles usually results from their current and future use, as well as, their combination with other tangible and intangible factors. Moreover, intangible assets always have a value derived from using them internally, in some cases additionally, or a value derived from a potential trade. However, since current accounting approaches focus on the latter (the value is determined using an estimated trade value), they tend to miss out the value of the internal utility, thus risking over or undervaluation of the intangible asset. Furthermore, new forms of organizations, like firm networks with blurred boundaries in-between individual companies, enhance these problems due to issues of assigning the intangibles to a specific individual.

Since innovation, to a large extent, deals with capabilities, knowledge and similar intangible matters, measuring innovation capability means measuring intangible assets which are often not reflected in financial information. The consideration of intangibles and non-financial data is often based on internal data, which has often not been previously assessed by management accounting. Therefore, it is hard to access for external valuators and one of their major tasks is to complement easily accessible financial data with relevant data from other sources.

In order to cope with the issues raised above, a definition and implementation of intellectual capital (IC) statements has been introduced in various companies, especially in the Nordic countries. The Danish Ministry of Science, Technology and Innovation (DMSTI 2003: 7), issuer of the IC statements guideline, defines its use in monitoring initiatives and results, as well as, the improvement of the 'development and management of its [a companies] knowledge resources'. The IC statements view capabilities and competencies as a productive factor whose value can be subjected to property rights. Besides their utility for external stakeholders, an IC statement's fundamental function is the self-analysis of a firm through which it becomes aware of the implicit assets (Lev and Zambon 2003: 599).

Amir, Lev, and Sougiannis (2003) have chosen to investigate the accessibility of information about intangibles differently than traditional accounting methods. They tried to overcome the problem that corporate financial reports did not often deliver sufficient information on intangible assets. This affects, in particular, intangibles-intensive companies such as highly-innovative companies with high R&D expenses. However, investors do have access to information beyond these reports, such as managers' direct communication with the capital markets, as well as, analysts' reports. These include firm and industry analyses and forecasts of KPIs such as earnings and sales. Accordingly, the goal of their research was to determine how, if at all, these non-accounting sources compensate for the missing information on intangibles in reports and financial statements. In a large sample of US companies, three findings were identified: First, analysts' information contribution, and thus their ability to value intangibles, is effectively higher in intangibles-intensive firms than in those with fewer intangibles. Second, the contribution increased significantly in the 1990s compared to the 1980s, showing that analysts, in the interim, had access to more and more information about intangibles. However, the final result was that the comprehension of this information was far from complete, especially in terms of R&D intensity.

Analyzing the value-relevance of reported financials, compared to non-financial information to investors, Amir and Lev (1996: 28–9) chose the fast-changing, highly innovative wireless communications industry. They found that financial accounting information by itself was mostly irrelevant while non-financial data, on the other hand, was highly value-relevant. Moreover, non-financial information incremental to financial data also provided value-relevant information. Therefore, non-financial information clearly contributed to a higher share in value to investors.

## Implications for Gathering Data in a Due Diligence

Even though information about intangibles is not thoroughly being published in financial statements, access to this data is not restricted to internal employees. A proper due diligence allows external stakeholders to review internal documents process handbooks, project reports and similar information. Reviewing this same information is also suggested in the previous sections of this article. External stakeholders are also able to retrieve information through various outside channels: managers' direct communication with capital markets, analyst reports and interviews with top management.

## Conclusion and Outlook

Innovation capability is an important determinant of a company's value and should, therefore, be a part of any due diligence undertaking. This chapter has proposed to assess innovation capability within four key dimensions based on Sammerl's Innovation Capability Model: Internal and external organizational learning; innovation culture; innovation process; and portfolio management. Because these dimensions must, in most cases, also be assessed by non-financial indicators, therefore easy and fast access to data becomes a challenge. While gathering this data can be problematic, the results of an innovation capability due diligence, by providing valuable information about the future prospects of the investigated company, make the effort worthwhile. The development of advanced accounting standards, as well as, sophisticated internal innovation controlling systems, in the future, will likely facilitate the collection of this relevant data.

## References

Adams, R., Bessant, J. and Phelps, R. 2006. Innovation management measurement: A review. *International Journal of Management Reviews*, 8, 21–47.

Afuah, A. 2003. *Innovation Management: Strategies, Implementation, and Profits*. 2nd Edition. New York: Oxford University Press.

Amabile, T.M., Conti, R., Coon, H., Lazenby, J. and Herron, M. 1996. Assessing the work environment for creativity. *Academy of Management Journal*, 39, 1154–84.

Amir, E. and Lev, B. 1996. Value-relevance of nonfinancial information: The wireless communications industry. *Journal of Accounting and Economics*, 22, 3–30.

Amir, E., Lev, B. and Sougiannis, T. 2003. Do financial analysts get intangibles? *European Accounting Review*, 12, 635–59.

Anderson, E. 1990. Two firms, one frontier: On assessing joint venture performance. *Sloan Management Review*, 31, 19–30.

Arthurs, J.D. and Busenitz, L.W. 2006. Dynamic capabilities and venture performance: The effects of venture capitalists. *Journal of Business Venturing*, 21, 195–215.

Bürgel, H.D., Haller, C. and Binder, M. 1996. *F&E Management*. München: Vahlen Verlag.

Calantone, R.J., Cavusgil, S.T. and Zhao, Y. 2002. Learning orientation, firm innovation capability, and firm performance. *Industrial Marketing Management*, 31, 515–24.

Chiva, R., Alegre, J. and Lapiedra, R. 2007. Measuring organizational learning capability among the work force. *International Journal of Manpower*, 28, 224–42.

Cohen, W.M. and Levinthal, D.A. 1989. Innovation and learning: The two faces of R&D. *The Economic Journal*, 99, 569–96.

Cohen, W.M. & Levinthal, D.A. 1990. Absorptive capacity: A new perspective on learning and innovation. *Administrative Science Quarterly*, 35, 128–52.

Cooper, R.G. and Edgett, S.J. 2008. Maximizing productivity in product innovation. *Research Technology Management*, 51, 47–58.

Cooper, R.G. and Kleinschmidt, E.J. 1986. An investigation into the new product process: Steps, deficiencies, and impact. *Journal of Product Innovation Management*, 3, 71–85.

Cooper, R.G., Edgett, S.J. and Kleinschmidt, E.J. 1999. New product portfolio management: Practices and performance. *Journal of Product Innovation Management*, 16, 333–50.

Cooper, G., Edgett, S.J. and Kleinschmidt, E.J. 2001. Portfolio management for new product development: Results of an industry practices study. *R&D Management*, 31, 361–80.

Damodaran, A. 2006. *Damodaran on valuation*. 2nd Edition. New York: John Wiley & Sons, Inc.

Danish Ministry of Science, Technology and Innovation (DMSTI). 2003. *Intellectual Capital Statements – The New Guideline* [Online]. Available at: http://en.vtu.dk/publications/2003/intellectual-capital-statements-the-new-guideline [accessed: 12 January 2009].

Davila, T., Epstein, M.J. and Matusik, S.F. 2004. Innovation strategy and the use of performance measures. *Advances in Management Accounting*, 13, 27–58.

Fairbank, J.F. and Williams, S.D. 2001. Motivating creativity and enhancing innovation through employee suggestion system technology. *Creativity & Innovation Management*, 10, 68–74.

Gassmann, O. and Keupp, M.M. 2007. The competitive advantage of early and rapidly internationalising SMEs in the biotechnology industry: A knowledge-based view. *Journal of World Business*, 42, 350–66.

Gaughan, P.A. 2007. *Mergers, Acquisitions, and Corporate Restructurings*. 4th Edition. New Jersey: John Wiley & Sons, Inc.

Gerybadze, A. 2004. *Technologie- und Innovationsmanagement*. München: Vahlen Verlag.

Gleich, R., Henke, M., Quitt, A. and Sommer, L. 2009. New approaches in performance measurement: Methods for specification and operationalisation within the context of supply management. International Journal of Business Excellence, 2, 105–23.

Goffin, K. and Mitchell, R. 2005. *Innovation Management: Strategy and Implementation Using the Pentathlon Framework*. Basingstoke: Palgrave Macmillan.

Hauschildt, J. 2004. *Innovationsmanagement*. München: Vahlen Verlag.

Hofstede, G., Neuijen, B., Ohayv, D.D. and Sanders, G. 1990. Measuring organizational cultures: A qualitative and quantitative study across twenty cases. *Administrative Science Quarterly*, 35, 286–316.

Howson, P. 2003. *Due Diligence: The Critical Stage in Mergers and Acquisitions*. Aldershot, UK: Gower Publishing, Ltd.

Howson, P. 2006. *Commercial Due Diligence. The Key to Understanding Value in an Acquisition*. Aldershot, UK: Gower Publishing, Ltd.

Jerez-Gómez, P, Céspedes-Lorente, J. and Valle-Cabrera, R. 2005. Organizational learning capability: A proposal of measurement. *Journal of Business Research*, 58, 715–26.

Kianto, A. 2008. Development and validation of a survey instrument for measuring organisational renewal capability. *International Journal of Technology Management*, 42, 69–88.

Killen, C.P., Hunt, R.A. and Kleinschmidt, E.J. 2008. Project portfolio management for product innovation. *Journal of Quality & Reliability Management*, 25, 24–38.

Lawson, B. and Samson, D. 2001. Developing innovation capability in organisations: A dynamic capabilities approach. *International Journal of Innovation Management*, 5, 377–400.

Lev, B. and Zambon, S. 2003. Intangibles and intellectual capital: An introduction to a special issue. *European Accounting Review*, 12, 597–603.

Mischke, G. 2007. The Innovation Game: Mythen und Realitäten im Management von Forschung und Entwicklung. In *Innovationsmanagement: Von der Idee zum erfolgreichen Produkt,* edited by K. Engel and M. Nippa. Heidelberg: Physica-Verlag, 35–60.

Narver, J.C. and Slater, S. F. 1990. The effect of a market orientation on business profitability. *Journal of Marketing*, 54, 20–35.

O'Reilly, B. and Rao, R.M. 1997. The secrets of America's most admired corporations: New ideas, new products. *Fortune*, 135, 60–4.

Porter, M.E. 1990. The competitive advantage of nations. *Harvard Business Review*, 68, 73–93.

Probst, G., Raub, S. and Romhardt, K. 2006. *Wissen managen: Wie Unternehmen ihre wertvollste Ressource optimal nutzen*. 5th Edition. Wiesbaden: Gabler.

Sammerl, N. 2006. *Innovationsfähigkeit und nachhaltiger Wettbewerbsvorteil: Messung, Determinanten, Wirkungen*. Wiesbaden: Deutscher Universitäts-Verlag.

Schroeder, R.G., Bates, K.A. and Junttila, M.K. 2002. A resource-based view of manufacturing strategy and the relationship to manufacturing performance. *Strategic Management Journal*, 23, 105–117.

Slater, S.F. and Narver, J.C. 1995. Market orientation and the learning organization. *Journal of Marketing*, 59, 63–74.

Steinmann, H. and Schreyögg, G. 2005. *Management: Grundlagen der Unternehmensführung; Konzepte, Funktionen, Fallstudien*. Wiesbaden: Gabler Verlag.

Tellis, G.J., Prabhu, J.C. and Chandy, R.K. 2009. Radical innovation across nations: The preeminence of corporate culture. *Journal of Marketing*, 73(1), 3–23.

Trott, P. 2005. *Innovation Management and New Product Development*. 3rd Edition. Harlow: Financial Times Prentice Hall.

Vedin, B. 1980. *Large Company Organization and Radical Product Innovation*. Lund: Studentlitteratur.

# 7 IT Due Diligence: Why Information Technology Can Make or Break a Deal

UWE BLOCH
*Avato Consulting, Alzenau, Germany*

MARTIN ZERFASS
*Schaeffler Holding (China), Shanghai, China*

## Introduction

A company acquires another company, or sells parts of its own, for any number of reasons including, for example, eliminating competition, diversifying a product range or concentrating on its core business. One of the most important, but also one of the most difficult tasks during such a transaction, is the due diligence (DD). Done under time pressure the DD in buy-side projects must determine all necessary information for a well substantiated offer. In a sell-side project, it must paint a clear, but correct picture, of the assets to be sold. In today's world, where information technology (IT) supports basically every process step, the IT-DD forms as vital a part as any other business area in a merger and acquisition (M&A) project.

In such projects, IT can be many things from a strategic consideration when buying or selling know-how or cutting-edge technology to synergy potential which helps refinance a deal. This leads to the conclusion that the IT-DD is of vital importance to the success of a deal as a whole and, as such, must be undertaken with the proper preparation and professionalism.

This chapter shall look at the challenges, but also the limitations of an IT-DD. When examining the task in this chapter, the focus will lie on a buy-side DD. But generally, the same rules and examples apply in a sell-side project albeit with a little difference in focus. A sell-side DD is more about giving the right answers in a data room, or in question-and-answer (Q&A) sessions to a potential buyer to achieve the best possible purchase price. The DD, in a buy-side project, focuses on a correct evaluation of the target and getting the right information.

Having said this, IT can actually make or break a deal even before a binding offer is considered. This chapter will look into the following aspects of an IT-DD as seen in Figure 7.1.

| Due Diligence Preparation | Due Diligence | Binding Offer / Negotiations | Signing & Closing | Post-merger Integration | Steady State IT Environment |
|---|---|---|---|---|---|
| • Strategic goal of transaction in relation to IT<br>• Project staffing<br>• Analysis internal IT<br>• Information gathering on 'foreign' IT<br>• Draft of possible integration scenarios<br>• Draft for possible synergies | • In depth analysis of 'foreign' IT<br>• Evaluation of IT environment<br>• Refinement of post merger integration scenarios<br>• Analysis on synergies<br>• IT relevant purchase contract stipulations | • Input for binding offer – especially synergies and post merger integration costs<br>• First draft 100 days plan | • Refinement of chosen post merger integration scenario<br>• 100 days plan<br>• Project plan for prioritized integration projects<br>• Staffing of projects | • Project controlling<br>• Refinement of individual project plans<br>• Execution of individual projects<br>• Analysis if synergy goals can be reached<br>• Cost controlling | • Conclusion of post-merger integration projects<br>• 'Business as usual' |
| 4–6 weeks | 2–4 weeks | 4–6 weeks | 8–12 weeks | Depending on project between 4 weeks and 18 months | 'Business as usual' |

**Figure 7.1   Merger and Acquisition Transaction Timeline**

## How to Prepare for an IT Due Diligence (IT-DD)

The first part of this chapter will describe the necessary preparation, but also the potential limits, concerning an IT-DD.

In every M&A transaction high expectations, as well as, significant efforts are associated with the DD phase. With the exception of private equity houses or venture capitalists, M&A transactions, data room phases, Q&A sessions, and so on, are not 'business as usual' for most of the operation's staff. Many companies today keep their own corporate M&A departments which will coordinate and manage such projects. For them, the project management is business as usual. However, especially during the DD phase, operational experts from different divisions (finance and controlling, IT, human resources, production, processes, and so on) are expected to look at and analyze large of amounts of information and recommend courses of action. For them, a DD phase is normally not part of everyday work and thus they need to be prepared for these special requirements during this time. In addition, most times M&A projects are not communicated very well within the organization so only a relatively small number of people will be involved in this work. This implies a heavy work load which is imposed upon these experts, in addition to, their normal work.

This also holds true for the IT organization. Documentation needs to be structured and prepared, organizational and project responsibilities need to be determined and made clear and strategic focus and directives need to be understood and communicated to all of the people involved. All of these aspects determine the workload to be prepared, as well as, the processes during the DD phase itself.

Whereas the rationale for the whole M&A transaction might be entering new markets, or diversification in the product portfolio, in many cases, a special focus for the IT department will be on potential synergies and cost savings of a joint IT department. Of course, this might not be the only focus but generally this is one of them. However, before the actual DD and data room phase, calculating synergies and potential cost savings is not easy because it is not yet known under which hard and software a joint IT department might operate, which standard applications can be used and which personnel and skills will finally be necessary to operate the joint IT.

## PREPARATION FOR THE IT-DUE DILIGENCE (IT-DD)

Like all the other areas of a DD, IT must also prepare systematically and comprehensively. Without a deep understanding of its own IT environment regarding all aspects it will not be possible to analyze joint future IT-strategies, synergy potentials or other strategic goals of the transaction. The main areas which must be understood are generally:

1. data center and network strategy
2. hard and software architecture and hard and software currently in use
3. hard and software maintenance
4. future hard and software development and strategy
5. software licensing models
6. desktop systems and desktop maintenance
7. human resources and skills necessary to run the IT
8. headcount for IT operations
9. capacity utilization and usage of hard and software / capacity limits
10. current IT projects
11. IT procurement
12. usage of outsourcing and external staff (consultants, freelancers, and so on).

Looking to the goal of an (IT)-DD, it becomes clear that not only one's own IT requirements need to be understood, but the IT requirements of the possible target as well. Considerations must must be given to how a possible joint IT could look in the future, which requirements it will have to meet and what kind of evolvement it will probably face. Initial thoughts like 'We will integrate the systems when the time comes' or 'We can always make the systems compatible by programming the relevant interfaces'[1] will only lead to misconceptions and to an underestimation of the risks, costs and time involved in realizing synergies or efficiency targets. Most of the time problems do not originate in the big differences of, for instance, hardware platforms in use, but from seemingly small discrepancies in active software versions or proprietary systems which simply cannot be easily hooked up to modern standardized software architecture. Only through an in-depth analysis can the upcoming questions be answered and the challenges to achieve the strategic goals become clear.

In the beginning, the goal normally is set that the more proficient IT organization shall prevail in a merger situation no matter if it is the buyer's or the target's IT. However, in reality, normally the IT of the buyer or the larger partner in a joint venture prevails without too much discussion (the bigger the better). This can lead to crucial challenges since large and historically grown IT systems, more often than not, are pieced together around an outdated system with company specific add-ons and modifications which are hard to transfer and, on the other side, are not able to incorporate additional functionalities. In addition, just imposing one IT over another will lead to frustration for IT personnel which can likely lead to lower efficiency or even the loss of key resources.

On paper, the integration of two systems might look relatively straight forward. However, in today's IT environment, with its often highly-integrated and interdependent

---

1    Statements made in real projects – hot data center consolidation of two banks, integration of IT of two insurance companies – by members of the executive boards.

IT systems, integration is often harder to accomplish than anticipated. In the German banking system, the trend in the year 2000, was towards specialty institutes such as private banks on the one hand, investment banks on the other and specialists institutes for the supporting functions with one of these functions being transaction services. Institutes were created which, in theory, should buy the relevant IT from its customer banks and integrate it into their system thus being able to render these transactions services for any number of banks and thereafter generate lower costs through standardization and economies of scale. The process of transaction services was, and is, mainly an IT-driven process with ideally straight through processing of transactions.

However, when setting up such a transaction institute, and only after the first banks had moved into the new transaction platform, it became clear that the transaction service needed to go deep into each associated banks system to interface with customer data, accounts data, as well as, regulatory systems. In Germany, each of the banks in question, had built-up their own proprietary core banking system and, therefore, no single IT interface could accommodate all of the necessary links and requirements. In the end, the synergies never came as intended and, due to mistakes in the due diligence which had been performed on each new customer bank, the prices for the transactions which had been expected in terms of cost savings, eventually never materialized. This institute never made it into the black.

On the other hand IT, and its synergies, can be a major factor in the success of a deal and, as such, must be examined accordingly. To evaluate the chances, and also the risks, correctly it is vital to best answer the questions on future strategy and possible synergies. To set the correct framework for the IT-DD, the following questions therefore must be answered both truthfully and as comprehensively as possible:

1. Relating to IT, what is the goal of the M&A project?
2. Are there different scenarios for a future joint IT? Which ones, and how likely, are they to be implemented?
3. What is the role of the acquirer's own IT in the M&A project regarding:
   - An open examination of possible outcomes. Is the discussion really open regarding which IT system shall survive? Are there any hidden agendas?
   - Are synergies to be calculated favourably so that IT does not become a road block for the M&A transaction?
4. Is the IT organization prepared for a DD-phase regarding:
   - documentation (hard and software landscapes, architecture, processes, etc.)
   - personnel and skill discussions
   - resources needed during the DD-phase and beyond.
5. Is documentation of the IT strategy in place, namely:
   - in the short-term
   - in the mid- and long-term
   - is the strategy compatible with potential M&A transactions?
   - which systems are running at their capacity limits and/or cannot be evolved to accommodate further needs and requirements
   - which investments are planned (short- and medium-term) and how will these investments look like in a post-merger situation.

6. Regarding the 'Foreign' IT:
   - What is known about the 'foreign' IT (press, consultants, former employees, personal knowledge, and so on)?
   - Is the hard and software landscape well-known (totally or in part) and is it mainly comprised of standard or proprietary applications?
   - Is the culture of the 'foreign' IT, and its environment, thoroughly known and how does it fit with one's own cultural environment?

When all these questions above have been answered satisfactorily the next steps in preparing for the IT-DD can be made, such as, collecting and sifting through the necessary documentation.

It is advisable to collect and structure all necessary information in a 'document register' for ease of reference and use during the IT-DD. This register will perform several functions. In the preparation phase, it will show which information is readily available and which will have to be generated. During the DD-phase, it can serve as a guideline for relevant information and as a tool for a gap analysis regarding missing or incomplete information.

A document register could look something like that shown in Figure 7.2 (contents need to be adapted for individual use).

In addition to this documentation, another major factor while preparing the IT-DD is to decide who shall participate on the DD-team. On the one hand, specialists are needed from all disciplines (hard- and software architects, programmers, management, procurement, organizational experts, and so on). However, more often than not, participants during a DD-phase are limited and, so in order to cover all the subjects necessary, a plan needs to be developed to include which functions and personnel should participate, and when, during the DD-phase. All of the relevant people need to be instructed, well in advance, in order to give them time to prepare but also to shift their individual calendars to accommodate the DD. Sometimes, perhaps a vacation ban for key resources may need to be considered.

After comprising the document register, and defining the relevant people, a checklist to determine strategic questions on how to deal with these issues can be developed. For instance, if IT consolidation is being planned, an analysis of the strategic fit of the IT environments will be necessary. To help with preparation, again, a checklist can prove to be very helpful. This checklist should comprise questions pertaining to:

1. Geographic allocation of IT (central or non-central IT, localized, or global IT etc.)?
2. Software and application development to be done in-house or outsourced?
3. Hardware, data centers and desktop management to be in-house or outsourced?
4. Support services to be in-house or outsourced?
5. Percentage of usage of standardized software vs. self-developed software?
6. Which standard/non-standard software is to be used and which versions?
7. System landscape to be host based or client-server based?
8. What is the age of current hard and software?
9. What are the existing maintenance contracts (partners, duration etc.)?
10. What is the IT project list for the next 24 months?
11. What is the optimal headcount considering a thorough identification of key resources (management, specialists, and so on).

| No. | Heading | Document | Document Link | Document Version |
|---|---|---|---|---|
| 1 | IT Strategy | Strategy goals | | |
| | | Strategy papers | | |
| 2 | IT Organization | Organizational charts | | |
| | | Personnel and processes | | |
| | | IT governance | | |
| 3 | IT Landscape | Application landscape | | |
| | | Application evolution roadmap | | |
| | | Infrastructure landscape | | |
| | | Infrastructure evolution roadmap | | |
| | | Core systems | | |
| | | Archiving | | |
| 4 | IT Projects | Project portfolio | | |
| | | Status of projects | | |
| | | Priorities of projects | | |
| | | Finishing date of projects | | |
| | | Project roadmaps | | |
| 5 | IT Contracts and procurement | Contract portfolio | | |
| | | Supplier portfolio | | |
| | | Internal contracts | | |
| | | Procurement strategy | | |
| 6 | Security Management | Security handbook | | |
| | | Security reports | | |
| 7 | IT Personnel and Human Resources | Headcount and allocation | | |
| | | Special agreements | | |
| | | Regulatory documents | | |
| 8 | IT Quality | Quality reports | | |
| | | Quality checks schedule | | |
| | | Customer satisfaction analysis | | |
| 9 | IT Costs and Budget | Summary IT Budget (current year) | | |
| | | IT Budget mid term planning | | |
| | | IT costs | | |
| | | Benchmark studies | | |

**Figure 7.2   Document Register**

To better visualize a strategic fit, Figure 7.3 can be used.

With this information in hand, as well as an understanding about the IT strategy within the M&A project, the same questions and information can now be sought about the 'foreign' IT in the DD-phase.

## LIMITS TO THE PREPARATION OF THE IT-DD

Sometimes not everything can be prepared in every detail. If not all of the required documentation can be in place at the beginning of the DD-phase, decisions will have to be made about where to place the priorities and which documentation is absolutely vital and which is not. Even if it is easier to undertake the DD with a guideline in hand, many IT specialists can overcome these missing documents and arrive at sensible conclusions

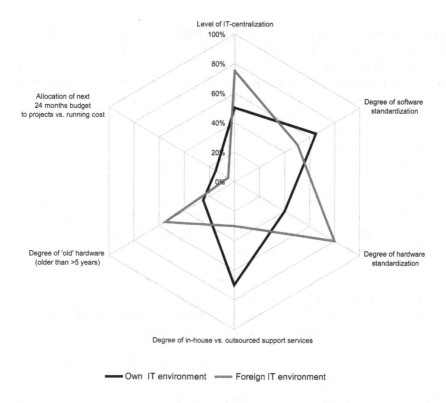

**Figure 7.3   Analysis Strategic Fit**

within a short period of time. Thus, in this circumstance, specialists will be extremely vital to the process itself for without them this stage may become an operational risk (single point of failure).

Even with in-depth preparation, the DD-phase itself will still likely remain a strenuous exercise. Additionally, possibly due to a lack of hard evidence and information during the preparatory phase, concepts and strategies during this time can only be on an aggregate level and, thus, may likely be filled with assumptions and uncertainty. Nonetheless, this DD-phase still needs to dig down deeply to get the relevant and concrete information needed to determine values, develop strategies and further ideas about a post merger scenario.

## What to Do during the Due Diligence Phase

The goal of any (IT) DD-phase is to collect and analyze all of the relevant information and evaluate the 'foreign' IT. The IT-DD, however, does not stop at a financial evaluation. In addition, the information needs to also be put into an IT concept for further use after a possible acquisition and in the resulting post-merger integration scenario. This will obviously relate to synergies, but also to the costs associated with the resulting projects. The risks of integration and the costs of different integration scenarios need to be evaluated to arrive at a comprehensive and in-depth understanding of all the issues involved and to derive the right decision regarding future IT strategy. Without this knowledge, a correct and true representation of the value (or cost) will not be possible.

The tasks during the buy side of DD are similar for all of the divisions involved, be they finance, tax, human resources, operations or IT. The goal is always to gain transparency over the target in order to determine a possible purchase price. There are several steps associated with the DD phase for IT:

1.  Identifying available information
2.  Analyzing information or documents for gaps.

(These first two steps are ideally done using the 'document register' developed during the DD-preparation. When overlapping the existing information/documents with the ones available, and performing a gap analysis, the missing information/documents can readily be identified and requested from the target).

3.  Understanding and analyzing the available documents
4.  Developing question scenarios for the Q&A sessions
5.  Developing questions for the management sessions (when applicable)
6.  Developing questions and concepts for possible workshops.

All of this information must be absorbed quickly and aligned with the prepared scenarios to determine the risks and benefits of each scenario. This can be most easily done via a SWOT Analysis (Strengths, Weaknesses, Opportunities, Threats) for each of the scenarios.

In addition, internal discussions on the strategy, and possible post-merger scenarios, need to proceed to be ready to react if any new situation or circumstance should arise, for instance, if the information found should cater to a new integration scenario or should preclude a common future IT strategy.

Cost and resource requirements (especially personnel) should not be underestimated during an IT-DD or during the following post-merger scenarios. These costs can actually determine if the whole deal will be advantageous or not. This holds true especially for smaller transactions where synergy effects are important to offset the purchase price and integration costs can be prohibitive given the value added by the acquisition. These

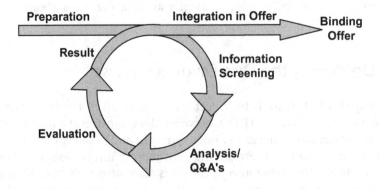

**Figure 7.4   Approach IT Due Diligence**

synergies, often looked for in IT through consolidation and reduction in personnel, need to be calculated carefully, keeping in mind timelines (no integration is completed in a few weeks), risks (some integration bring problems in IT performance, that is, system stability), investments (capacity limits might lead to the necessity to invest heavily into new hard or software), as well as, regulatory requirements and legal aspects (for instance laying off redundant staff). All of these considerations need to go into the calculation of possible synergies in order to arrive at a correct evaluation of the IT itself. These determinations can then be considered in the context of the overall binding offer.

## Q&A Sessions (Question-and-Answer Sessions) during a DD-phase

Normally, during the DD-phase, the potential acquirers are allowed to post questions regarding any unclear or incomplete information provided. In some processes, IT has to fight for its right within these sessions since finance or product-line questions are often considered to be more urgent. In most processes, the amount of questions allowed to be asked is limited either by time allocations or by a total number for the duration of the DD-phase. Thus, all the different areas of expertise compete for these limited questions. Again, IT has to position itself as an independent and essential player within this DD process in order to be able to pose its necessary questions. The questions need to be carefully prepared in order to generate the information needed.

One crucial mistake during these sessions can also be that assumptions about the information given from the acquirer's own IT experts may lead to a wrong interpretation of the information provided. If, for instance, no information is provided on the version of a central piece of application, it would not serve the DD team to assume this application is the most current version and/or the most up-to-date. Such a small miscalculation could directly lead on to higher costs for upgrades and difficulties in integrating this application later on. However, it is prudent to think about possible answers to the questions posed since this might lead to follow-up questions at an earlier stage or guidance can be given to the target and what kind of answers are expected for any particular question. The answers then should be evaluated, as fast as possible, and analyzed using the same framework as for the whole IT-DD.

All information needs to be structured in order to be fully analyzed. Again, the previously developed document register can greatly assist here. It ensures a fast way to compare and analyze the information at hand and draw the correct conclusions for the following crucial step – the binding offer.

Every piece of analyzed information and data, in one way or another, needs to be considered in the binding offer. In smaller transactions, IT integration costs can be prohibitive for the deal as a whole and synergies from IT alone are not enough to offset these costs. However, most of the time, there is not one correct solution for every given challenge. Part of the IT-DD objective, therefore, is to show and calculate alternative ways for post-merger scenarios. This might be difficult given the short time during a DD but it is unavoidably necessary and often alternative strategies for post-merger integration, not thought of beforehand, can emerge to help save a deal as a whole. Some thoughts along these lines could be:

1.  IT landscapes may not need to be consolidated right away. If running two environments or systems in parallel is not too expensive this might be an alternative to consider. Of course, this can greatly diminish potential synergies but might save money in the long run if a significant future investment can be changed to accommodate the new situation.
2.  An outsourcing strategy might be a solution to an otherwise hard to come by synergy. Due to an increase in IT via an acquisition, outsourcing might be more interesting to a relevant service provider than before. This service provider might actually have fewer problems integrating legacy systems into the environment. Of course, the consolidation topic will also arise with the service provider but it could be that through clever pricing (decreasing prices over time and with ongoing consolidation) this will, in the end, be cheaper than an in-house integration project. Other considerations will come into play with this strategy (project cost for outsourcing, fees to the service provider, and so on) and they may be worthwhile looking into. One word of caution though: an outsourcing strategy needs to be prepared with great care. Outsourcing problems, without knowing and understanding the solution or the final environment, will give rise to other problems and might jeopardize the success of outsourcing.
3.  Consolidation can be limited first on the quick wins, such as, trying to achieve easy synergies and cost savings before looking at the more complex problems. This might mean consolidation of only certain systems while the consolidation of the data centers may have to wait. Synergies will be lower but so will the risk associated with them and it may provide the opportunity to determine a potentially better long-term IT strategy options.

Clearly, the calculation of these synergies needs to be done with great care and objectivity. There are guidelines which need to be followed in order to arrive at the correct amount of savings through consolidation and improvement of efficiency. Most of these guidelines are common sense but time and time again are not always heeded:

1.  Do not overestimate synergies just because some target number has been set. Rather, calculate the synergies conservatively, including a realistic time frame in which these synergies can be achieved.
2.  Determine the capacity needs after the merger and calculate necessary investments in order to comply with these requirements.
3.  Include costs for the synergy projects within your calculation in order to be able to give a number of net savings.
4.  Detail the risks and possible challenges along the way.
5.  Think about related problem areas. If personnel reduction is one of the synergies, legal and contractual points like required notice periods might hinder the realization of synergies over a short period of time. Give these questions to other experts in the DD (legal team) and ask them to analyze the employment contracts.
6.  Develop different scenarios from full-integration, to integration of only selected systems, to the parallel running of most of the IT in order to get a feeling for the differences in potential synergies. Develop the pros and cons of each. Strategically select the one best scenario which is to be incorporated into the binding offer. Nevertheless, the other scenarios should also be calculated and discussed with the M&A team in order to maybe change the strategy as needed.

7. Evaluate risk management. This is an important factor during the DD. Many challenges cannot be solved by the acquirer alone but need the support or contractual agreement of the selling partner. For instance, guarantees for software licenses, transition periods, and so on, can be incorporated into the share purchase agreement to alleviate the financial risks associated with these specific IT issues.

8. Consider contractual agreements. For instance, to not lay off staff after acquiring a company, or to not close certain locations, can contradict synergy plans. This needs to be discussed within the M&A team and reflected accordingly within the relevant scenarios.

Of all of the potentially troublesome issues that need to be addressed, software licensing and transition period planning are key in today's transactions. For instance, current software licensing contracts normally contain some kind of 'Change of Control' (CoC) clause allowing the software vendor to terminate existing licenses of the target and negotiate new ones with the acquirer. Especially for integration periods, some licensing issues will need to be resolved. From experience, however, an early involvement of the software vendor, and a clear-cut strategy concerning software license issues, will more likely lead to satisfactory results for this particular problem. This is most often done by involving the IT Procurement Team in order to see if a satisfactory solution with the software vendor can be found. Of course, possible additional costs for this aspect must be considered in the scenarios if the software vendor is not cooperative.

If the IT in question is outsourced, negotiation of a transition period with the service provider will likely prove necessary. This period must then be negotiated within the share purchase agreement, including the service provider. Alternatively, the selling company can guarantee the service providers its willingness to support the IT systems during the transition period. It is often an advantage to agree upon a fairly short transition period (dependent on the IT strategy) and agree upon possible extensions of this period. This will put some pressure on the in-house IT to push a migration project forward while at the same time provide the security, that at the end of the transition period, the service provider will not simply turn off the power. These costs also must be calculated into the potential total cost for the migration project.

Key personnel are always important when looking at IT. Maybe even more so, when combining two IT environments. Resources familiar with their respective systems are key to any successful integration project. It is, therefore, often good advice to try to identify and keep these key resources so that the migration project can run more smoothly. Relevant clauses can, and should be, incorporated into the share purchase agreement (to some extent) but often labor laws prohibit binding individuals within such restrictive contracts. Other alternatives need to be explored, be they stay on incentives or possible career advancement for the most essential key individuals. Again, these costs naturally must be considered in the overall analysis. Since the planning of the integration scenario is such a key element of a successful IT-DD, it will now be detailed further.

# Definition of Integration and Post-merger Scenarios

The IT-DD should look at the target's, and its own IT, from several viewpoints:

1. The strategic fit of customers, markets, products, and so on.
2. The potential new customers and markets for existing products (cross-selling-potential).
3. The synergies resulting from overlapping business models.

With the acquisition, the buyer normally articulates a vision on how the new business shall act in regard to the market, customers (new and existing) and how the business shall develop. IT, as a supportive function for most processes today, will also face different challenges such as how it will incorporate more customers in its customer relationship management system (CRM), administer more products or personnel, or support other (perhaps up to now unknown) processes and functions.

Depending on the post-merger integration scenario and the strategic fit/overlap of the two IT environments in question, the resulting integration projects will vary considerably in difficulty, resource intensity and timelines. Normally, the first order of business is to generate quick wins to show success as early as possible. In addition, in some industries (banking, energy, insurance) regulatory requirements might force some fast, and sometimes quite complex, adjustments to IT. However, these quick wins and necessary projects should not take the place of a carefully-planned and professionally-executed transition phase.

The most significant potential synergies normally involve personnel, systems and applications, procurement and project work. Some of these synergies can obviously be achieved faster than others. For instance, a project landscape of both IT environments, put into a matrix, will readily identify redundant projects or even projects which may contradict each other. It can also be that one IT environment already has functionalities in place the other is currently developing with an expensive project on its own. The identification of, and consequent abandonment of these redundant projects, will result in faster and easier ways to realize synergies. The consolidation of procurement contracts (hardware, licensing, consulting services, network services, and so on) can also result in accelerated cost savings and a short-term reduction of suppliers. See Figure 7.5 for the executive summary of IT Value Proposition with experienced figures in per cent.

The larger synergies, such as system or data center consolidation, will normally take a longer time due to the complexity of the issues but will also potentially bring bigger rewards. One factor in determining the complexity of these projects can be the degree of standardization of the two IT environments. Normally, the more standardized the IT environments are, the easier the integration will be. This needs to be identified, and discussed, in order to get a grip on the tasks ahead. In a worst case scenario (from the view of synergies) it might be the best possible solution to connect the two environments via interfaces and to start with parallel running systems before prematurely jumping head over heels into a large consolidation project which nobody has properly planned beforehand.

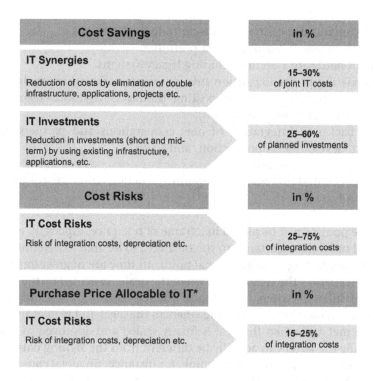

**Figure 7.5    IT Value Proposition to Merger and Acquisition Projects**

A carefully planned transition can be a special challenge when differing company and IT cultures meet head on. There might also be a difference in general company culture or a difference in the level of maturity or skills between the two IT organizations. If, for instance, a CMMI[2] level five certified organization meets up with a lesser certified one, this can create tensions and problems regarding approaches for projects. One of the major challenges, in this instance, will be to quickly transform the part of the organization lacking the relevant certification and bring it up to par with the other one. An additional cost to be considered here is that many personnel may need to be recertified.

Along the strategic guidelines dictated by the future strategy after an acquisition, the M&A team needs to concentrate on a small number of relevant scenarios during the DD-phase. The future IT environment will be determined by the business model emerging from the acquisition and its resulting changes for markets and customers but also the processes, system complexity and required capacity. All of these will ultimately determine the way in which the IT will be planned, built and maintained. Considering these issues, typical scenarios which should be looked at during a DD-process are:

2    CMMI: Capability Maturity Model Integration.

114 Value in Due Diligence

1. Migration scenarios for central and de-centralised IT systems.
2. Migration of customer and/or product portfolios.
3. Migration of hardware systems including legacy systems.
4. Scenarios relating to the expansion into different markets (national/international), products (new and extension of existing products etc.) and customers (a larger number, new target groups, and so on).
5. Front and back end integration of new cooperations and partners, for instance, distribution, development, production, and so on.
6. Integration and IT compliance.
7. Integration of central processes and reporting functions (finance, controlling, human resources, and so on).

All of the above points must be placed in a frame of reference, especially within a correct time frame and order of importance to the business, to be able to determine correct and adequate transition timing. Two additional points in time are of great importance for an IT post-merger scenario – the closing date when the deal is executed by the parties and the effective date (if different) when, for instance, financial consolidation and so on, will take place. The former marks the point in time when all the legal and regulatory requirements will have to be met and when the deal is finally sealed and approved by the regulatory authorities[3] while the latter can actually be different from the signing date and can lie in the past or the future. From this point in time, for instance, financial consolidation needs will shift to the buyer meaning that the IT will have to be in place accordingly.

All of the scenarios mentioned above have to be considered not only in the short term but also mid and long term regarding their impact on the profit and loss statements, balance sheet, and so on, in order to determine their true cost to the company (for instance: investment schedules, personnel reduction or the need to increase personnel and so on).

Here it is imperative to balance the speed to achieve these synergies with the complexity and the risks involved in such projects. To be able to quantify these synergies a project team, consisting of experts, needs to be set-up which concentrates on these issues:

1. A decision on the most important scenarios to be looked at (max. 3).
2. A determination of restrictions in a framework set by the M&A transaction.
3. A calculation of the impact on financial statements.
4. A recommendation, from an IT view, on the most viable scenarios (which do not have to be the most economical ones).
5. An impact of these findings into the final binding offer and possibly the purchasing agreement.

---

3    This is normally not the signing of a purchasing agreement due to the fact that regulatory /antitrust authorities still must affirm the deal. After this affirmation the deal is said to be 'closed' and all the stipulations in the purchasing agreement become valid.

# Content of the Final Assessment

After choosing the relevant IT post-merger scenarios (a maximum of three is recommended) these scenarios are now looked at in-depth regarding future business development and requirements, potential synergies but also compatibility with the existing IT systems. Each scenario must follow specific guidelines which will determine its overall attractiveness within the M&A transaction. Assumptions must be developed and assigned to each examined scenario:

1. Limits and framework of the specific scenario relating to the goals of the whole M&A transaction.
2. Necessary investment for each respective scenario.
3. Risk assessment of each scenario including possible ways to mitigate the risks – a risk assessment visualization could look something like Figure 7.6.
4. Detailed descriptions the pros and cons of each scenario.[4]
5. Detailed use of resources (time, skill, money) for each integration scenario.
6. Detailed analyses of the budgets needed in the future for each scenario (personnel, running costs, development costs).
7. Comparison of all scenarios especially regarding risk, time of implementation and resulting effects on financial statements.
8. Recommendation of one of the scenarios which best represents the requirements set by management for IT.

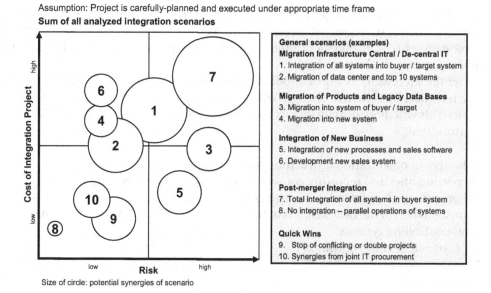

**Figure 7.6   Risk Assessment Integration Scenarios**

---

4    Best done in a way that shows all the scenarios together for comparability purposes.

After this analysis, the results are then put into a presentation showing the respective outcomes and consequences of choosing one or any of the other scenarios. Connections to other aspects like strategic goals, human resources, etc. also need to be highlighted and discussed. The goal of this final assessment should always be a well- balanced recommendation with precise input for the binding offer, contract negotiations, etc.

## TYPICAL MISTAKES

There are a couple of typical mistakes associated with IT integration scenarios most of which are centered on the cost and time requirements for relevant projects:

1. Financial risk is not considered.
2. Depreciation is not considered when integrating integration IT infrastructure.
3. Assumptions for system integration regarding investments, time, personnel and skills needed are often too low.
4. Costs to integrate legacy systems are budgeted too low and their continued usage can lead to operational risk and increased running costs.
5. Reduction in personnel can lead to compensation costs.
6. Time needed for integration of individual application is considered too short.
7. Key personnel and the risk of losing knowledge are not properly accounted for.

# IT and the Post-merger Situation

Having reached the post-merger situation now is the time for all the theoretical work to be applied. Chosen strategies will need to be projected and implemented ranging from a possible data center consolidation project right down to possibly updating the inventory number at every work station.

After the successful closing of an M&A transaction there are several areas, besides the purely technical ones, where changes will occur irrespective of the chosen post-merger scenario. This will more heavily impact the IT environment which, in the end, will likely be consolidated:

1. Changes in organizational structure (teams, management and so on).
2. Reporting lines and reporting content including adapting reporting systems.
3. IT procurement and vendor management.
4. Consolidation of the new business in the companies finance, investment management and controlling systems.
5. IT controlling and reporting.
6. Human resources regarding IT.
7. Project landscape.
8. Skills needed (some skills might become redundant or outdated over time).

Not all systems can be integrated at once so other strategies need to be looked at, such as, temporary workarounds or parallel running of systems and connecting them only via the relevant interfaces.

One factor that is often forgotten is the staffing of necessary projects. The existing IT environments obviously need as much attention as before the M&A transaction. However, in addition to 'business as usual', now integration projects and staff reductions may need to be undertaken. This can lead to a major increase in work load for all people involved and bottlenecks for special skills or key resources. These need to be addressed beforehand in order to react to the specific requirements of a post- merger situation. Much can be done by a professional project management office which coordinates all the necessary projects to determine the bottlenecks and allocates the relevant people to the tasks at hand.

A plan for the first 100 days after a merger has proven to be a good tool to keep an overview over all necessary activities regarding project work. These points should be addressed in such a plan:

1.  Project management office and its staffing.
2.  Project planning and use of tools.
3.  Definition and implementation of the new IT organization and management team.
4.  Definition of a communication strategy (how, when, where, what to communicate).
5.  Definition of all post-merger projects including project plan, staffing, time frame and costs and the parallel start of relevant projects.
6.  Calculation of synergies for each project and a comparison with overall synergy targets.
7.  List of projects (examples):
    – Vendor management and supplier contract consolidation (potential quick win)
    – Project matrix of all current (legacy) projects and decision on which projects to continue and which to stop (potential quick win)
    – In-depth analysis of existing systems and architecture and detailed project planning for consolidation by the use of infrastructure, application and system roadmaps (for instance: data center consolidation, consolidation of application landscape, consolidation of infrastructure and so on)
    – Definition and implementation of processes, determination of short-term or interim processes – interim processes can include: budgeting, evaluation of product portfolio, procurement, human resources, and so on.
8.  Detailed risk analysis for each project and activities to mitigate these risks.
9.  Involvement of social partners when discussing reduction or integration of personnel.
10. Development of human resources strategies to avoid brain drain due to unsatisfactory situations of people within the new IT organization.

From experience, the biggest risk-free quick wins can be achieved not by pure personnel reduction – this always incurs a risk as to remaining skill sets – but by stopping all ongoing projects which do not fit into the new IT strategy or which are actually being pursued by both companies involved. Other synergies, for instance, data center consolidation might promise higher savings in the future but need to be projected more carefully and will take a longer time to achieve. The use of a potentially higher purchasing power can also yield high, risk free returns by reducing purchasing prices ranging from infrastructure, software licensing or consultancy services.

## Conclusion

All in all, an IT-Due Diligence, during a M&A transaction, poses many challenges for the IT organization be they the short time frame, the analysis of a foreign and complex IT environment, or the handling and need to prioritize the massive amount of available information in a data room. With adequate preparation and the right people dedicating themselves to the task, this due diligence, and the following post-merger integration, can be handled in a successful and, more importantly perhaps, profitable manner. The benefits of a well-executed IT DD will show immediately in a well defined and realistic view on potential synergies and IT post-merger integration evaluation – and these are the factors that will primarily assist in evaluating a possible binding offer for the examined target. At the end of the day, the success or failure, as determined by management of a transaction, will probably not solely hinge on IT. Nonetheless, IT can, does and should play a significant factor in making or breaking most M&A deals today.

Successful (IT) Due Diligence is also one of the most rewarding projects to be undertaken. The learning curve can be tremendous in the first projects and probably will not change noticeably in subsequent ones. Why? Because each project is different, each IT poses its own unique challenges and opportunities and each post-merger integration broadens the view on how IT can be built to accommodate today's challenging and ever-changing business environments. For many businesses today, IT might not be considered as a competitive advantage but, without an almost perfectly working IT environment, most businesses today would probably not exist in the way they do.

# 8 Due Diligence on Young Companies: A Case Study

DR GORDANA KIERANS AND PROFESSOR RONALD GLEICH
*Strascheg Institute for Innovation and Entrepreneurship (SIIE)*
*EBS Business School International University, Wiesbaden, Germany*

THOMAS HASSELBACH
*MikroForum Technology Site, Wendelsheim, Germany*

## Introduction

The seemingly ever increasing number of corporate mergers and acquisitions (M&A) in recent years has widened and improved the overall knowledge and awareness of due diligence for both industry and research. In the past, due diligence investigations focused primarily on financial, legal and tax aspects prior to the merger of two companies. Based on industry experience and reports, and due in a great part to the poor track record of most recent M&A activities, management and researchers are now necessarily expanding their focus beyond these traditional aspects of due diligence.

Thus, many of the more recent M&A activities include an examination of other criteria for due diligence scrutiny and many of these alternative areas are eloquently discussed in detail in this book. Naturally perhaps, most of this research focuses on due diligence for the larger, most well-known and newsworthy corporate marriages. In contrast, this chapter will question what happens when relatively unknown, young companies are targeted for acquisition.

Before proceeding, it might be sensible to be to clarify, at the outset, what is meant herein by the term 'young' company. According to our view, and that of Audretsch (1999), they are often agents of change and for this reason they are frequently acquisition targets by larger, more well-established firms. It follows then, logically, that these 'young' companies have something promising to offer in terms of product, service or other unique propositions, or otherwise, they would not likely be either acquisition targets or agents of change. Moreover, the term 'young' implies that they are likely in their infancy, or at least early development. Therefore, it should be noted that the term 'a young company' excludes considering 'a small company' for obviously, although 'young' companies maybe 'small', small companies may not be young.

Unfortunately, when it comes to issues of traditional due diligence considerations, at such an early stage of development, many of these young companies cannot always provide sufficient financial statements to demonstrate their potential. Moreover, according to Bing (1996), in particular for these companies, the non-financial factors very often more reliably predict the future structure, viability and, indeed the worth, of these young companies. This circumstance then obviously has created a need for alternative criteria and approaches when evaluating these young firms as acquisitions.

Much of this chapter's content is based on a real-life checklist developed for the assessment of young companies. This 'case study' checklist, using unique criteria to evaluate young companies, was developed and refined at the MikroForum Technology Site, a technology park, near Mainz, in Germany. The criteria used have evolved based on hands-on experience using this checklist. The first part of the chapter briefly describes some background research about due diligence with respect to young companies and also provides a definition of technology parks. Subsequently, the next portion of this chapter presents MikroForum Technology Park, as a case study, relating its experiences to the previously presented theory. Finally, a practical checklist of due diligence criteria for evaluating young companies is presented and the chapter finishes with a conclusion and recommendations for further research.

# Theoretical Background

## EXPANDING THE HORIZONS OF DUE DILIGENCE

As all of the other chapters in this book expound, due diligence is an essential element in a merger and acquisition process. Its primary goal is simply to reduce risk. Therefore, its objective is to not only audit past performance but to also identify potential vulnerabilities or opportunities. Due diligence is initiated after the parties have decided that the deal is financially reasonable and after a preliminary understanding is reached, but before a binding contract is signed (Puranam, Powel and Singh 2006; Bing 1996).

The process of due diligence might be considered by some business representatives as a waste of time due to the onerous task of tediously gathering information that is likely already known (Howson 2003). Nonetheless, the numerous failures of many corporate marriages have shown that if companies had had a more sound and comprehensive due diligence mind-set and policies many of the pre- and post-merger M&A problems might have been better anticipated and resolved beforehand. Again, the other chapters in this book illustrate what some of these specific procedures and policies ought to have been.

In addition to a classic M&A, there are also other occasions when due diligence can be useful, and some of these are of particular importance for young companies: (Rankine, Stedman and Bomer 2003):

- Entering a joint venture agreement
- Granting, or requesting, a loan
- Investing in the shares of a company
- Entering into a major agreement with a supplier or a customer
- Starting a new business or entering a new market.

The above list is not exhaustive. For example, it can also be useful to apply due diligence when, as will be seen in this chapter, a technology park screens its corporate tenants who apply for space *and* capital as these parks oftentimes also offer capital and/or other incentives to start-up or young companies. Experience has shown that an adequate checklist of important criteria can help paint a clearer picture of the tenant's likelihood of success in future. This is critical to technology parks, such as MikroForum, as profitable tenants help, in part, to finance the growth of these parks.

## CHARACTERISTICS OF A TECHNOLOGY PARK

As many may not be fully-versed in the concept of technology parks, it is perhaps prudent to offer a brief background. A 'technology park' is often commonly referred to as an 'incubator' but admittedly there is some confusion about the role of these institutions. One of the reasons for this uncertainty could stem from a lack of clarity within industry itself. However, another, and more obvious reason, is that both an 'incubator' and a 'technology park' frequently offer similar services.

To help clarify the distinction, the role of a business incubator is to offer start-up companies (Bergek and Norrman 2008; Barrow 2001; Voisey *et al.* 2006) some of the following:

- Shared office space often under very favourable conditions
- A wide pool of services in order to reduce overhead costs
- Professional business support
- Network provisions
- Accountancy expertise
- Marketing advice including website design and exposure.

A technology park, on the other hand, offers many of these same services, but normally to more mature, albeit still young, companies instead of start-ups. Understandably then, this subtle difference is why most of the literature does not provide a clear distinction between these two concepts. This chapter will focus specifically on technology parks, although many of the aspects can apply for an incubator as well.

### Historical background

The first business incubator was established in 1959 as the Batavia Industrial Center in Batavia, New York (Lewis 2002). A large real-estate developer, Joseph Manusco, had been failing to find an anchor tenant for his 79,000 $m^2$ property so he decided to subdivide the space into smaller premises (Hackett and Dilts 2004). This subletting was not an instant success but by opening its doors to smaller, and in some cases even start-up companies, it did help the landlord earn some revenue to cover overheads and continue with necessary restoration. One of the early tenants, from Connecticut, actually operated an incubation business for chickens. Once when asked what he was doing with his building, Joseph Manusco answered that he was incubating chickens (Barrow 2001). Additionally, although he had other tenants who had, as with the chicken incubator, also requested business advice and/or assistance from Mr. Manusco with raising capital, the term incubator stuck. Within only a decade thereafter, business incubators had spread out all over the country.

The concept of technology parks, as described, is similar but, in addition to focusing exclusively on more mature young companies, they have a more narrow focus wherein common tenants likely share many of the same business interests, such as for example, IT or technology. Additionally, to exacerbate this incubation versus technology park confusion, there has evolved a third well-recognised variation of this business model known as science parks. They are often located close to a university, or are directly related to the universities themselves, and are often heavily funded by government finance (Link and Scott 2003).

The success of business incubators in America inspired other countries to initially adopt and then adapt the concept. The UK established regional innovation centres across the country (Westhead and Storey 1995; Siegel, Westhead and Wright 2003). Japan, Australia, Singapore, The Netherlands, Ireland, the Scandinavian countries and Germany followed similar approaches (Barrow 2001). Moreover, perhaps surprisingly, incubators or technology parks have not become a phenomenon exclusive to the wealthy industrialised countries. For example, The United Nations Fund for Science and Technology Development has helped initiate business incubation projects in China, The Philippines, Trinidad and Tobago and Nigeria (Barrow 2001).

In Germany, a number of variations of the incubator concept can be found. For example, Entrepreneurship Centres parallel the British version of incubators and, thus, accommodate mostly start-up companies. In contrast, as mentioned, the technology parks in Germany shelter and nurture young companies which are often between two and six years old. And again, as opposed to the United States, or other countries, where incubators are property-based initiatives (Colombo and Delmastro 2002), these parks are often government or regional development programmes. One of the exceptions in Germany is MikroForum Technology Site, our case study, which, as we will see, has developed a rather unique and successful variation of the technology park concept.

## Motivation behind the technology park

The implicit idea behind an incubator, or indeed a technology park, is to bring new businesses together in order to increase the probability of success (Lumpkin and Ireland 1988). Sharing premises alone does not guarantee success, but belonging to such a network does offer many other advantages, not the least of which is the indirect advantage of operating in an environment where the anxiety of starting a new business is dramatically reduced. Additionally, according to Allen and McCluskey (1990) incubators and parks also became, at the same time, a place where entrepreneurs overcame the loneliness of entrepreneurship (Allen and McCluskey 1990).

For most incubators and technology parks, it is very common to find that they serve specific industry segments (Lumpkin and Ireland 1988). The focus on a specific sector helps the park provide industry-tailored services and, thus, nurture and facilitate the growth of young, comparably like-minded companies. This also means that the park's management has to screen the new tenants and that management needs a certain framework to be better able to identify and evaluate potential in young companies. Not surprisingly, research shows that parks with less screening have lower occupancy rates (Lumpkin and Ireland 1988). This research clearly underscores the urgent need for management at incubators and/or technology parks to have a due diligence instrument to more accurately evaluate the potential of their prospective tenants.

Incubators and technology parks evolve, just like any other enterprise, and follow their own business life cycles. Therefore, the methods used to screen tenants also need to be adapted and correlated to the respective life cycle stage of the incubators. In the early stages of an incubator or technology park, the main objective is to attract initial tenants.

Therefore, the incubator or park's management is more often inclined towards simply finding tenants that can pay rent rather than seeking promising start-ups or promising young companies. After a critical number of tenants are housed within the premises, the attention then shifts from simple real-estate occupancy levels and development towards searching for added value. At this point, in addition to the existing on-premise services already offered, external consultants for additional advisory assistance are often engaged. Furthermore, at this stage of the development, the tenants that have remained a going concern have likely matured and profited from synergies derived from their relationship with other tenants. All of these aspects contribute to the high reputation of a park and, as a consequence, the technology park can now begin to selectively pick and choose its tenants and, indeed, may even have a demand that exceeds the space available. At this mature stage of the park's business life cycle, it can become one of the most important entities in its own business neighbourhood by providing numerous service jobs for its nearby communities. As a result, and in turn, the park can more closely scrutinise future tenants, thereby ensuring an even higher quality of tenant, and/or choose to expand its operation by building new facilities (Allen and McCluskey 1990; Barrow 2001).

Allen and McCluskey (1990) also observed that at the certain stage of their development, incubators and parks may start to follow increasingly quite divergent objectives. The authors summarise these observations as follows:

- The 'for-profit' property developers focus their intentions on capturing real estate appreciation.
- The 'non-profit' development corporations focus on creating jobs and improving the environment for young enterprises.

Additionally, these authors distinguish between four different institutions and their different objectives, as listed in Table 8.1.

Two additional models of incubators and parks not mentioned in Table 8.1, are public–private partnerships and corporate incubators. First, the public–private partnership is a hybrid model of two, or more, of the above-described organisational types and this combination and/or overlap of organisations produces quite different interests and, thus, this makes it impossible to form a specific distinct model. Second, corporate venture incubators/parks pursue the goal of adding back economic value to the partner company in form of new products and services (Barrow 2001). Therefore, hereto, this type of institution has also been excluded.

The institution to be presented in the remainder of this chapter, namely our case study MikroForum Technology Site near Mainz in Germany, contains many of the characteristics described above. It offers very innovative and architecturally unique premises, as do many other incubators, technology parks and science parks worldwide. All of these varied sites, however, are quite naturally highly influenced by their own country's culture, regional development, political stability and available government funding. Furthermore, each single incubator or technology park has undergone its own unique development, has sheltered different companies and has provided divergent services targeting different tenants.

**Table 8.1    Incubator and Technology Park Objectives**

| | For-profit Property Development Incubator/Parks | Non-profit Development Corporation Incubators/Parks | Academic Incubators/Parks | For-Profit Seed Capital Incubators/Parks |
|---|---|---|---|---|
| Primary Objective | Real-estate Appreciation | Job Creation | Faculty-Industry Collaboration | Capitalisation Investment Opportunity |
| | Sell proprietary services to tenant | Positive statement of entrepreneurial potential | Commercialise university research | |
| Secondary Objectives | Create opportunity for technology transfer | Generate sustainable income for organisation | Strengthen service & instructional mission | Product development |
| | Create investment opportunity | Diversify economic base | Capitalise investment opportunity | |
| | | Bolster tax base | Create good will between institution and community | |
| | | Complement existing programs and utilise vacant facilities | | |

*Source*: Allen and McCluskey (1990)

# Case Study: A Technology Park

## THE MIKROFORUM TECHNOLOGY SITE

As the only privately-held technology park in Germany, MikroForum Technology Site shelters young companies at different stages of their development. The site, founded in 1999, consists of 8,500 m² of office and laboratory space where approximately 16 young companies do their work and research. The park has two main clusters: life science and micro-technology and mainly profits from offering an existing infrastructure available to tenants, such as, telephone, internet, reception, janitorial and maintenance services, parking and even restaurant facilities. Furthermore, the tenants can access consulting services like marketing, branding, law and banking advice. Additionally, they get special purchasing rates and discounts on management seminars. All of the laboratories are equipped with state-of-the-art technology and media resources. Protecting the latest propriety research results is vital for the livelihood of any young company today, but for the life science and micro-technology segments it is absolutely critical. Assessing and securing the latest information for these innovation driven sectors is a 'do or die' necessity. Thus, another service offered to the tenants is the constant surveillance, protection and security offered on the premises that help to safeguard the respective achievements and intellectual property requirements of the tenants.

Today, MikroForum has become a mature site and is the biggest employer in the region of Wendelsheim. This successful track record helped the site to forge a private–public partnership with the German State of Rhineland-Palatinate. One of alluring amenities of the park is its pastoral setting, however, this is also a drawback as the neighbourhood is scarcely populated. Fortunately, offsetting this, the location does profit from excellent highway connections to some major urban centres such as Mainz to the north, or Kaiserslautern and Ludwigshafen to the south. As the immediate neighbourhood region does not provide enough skilled labour by itself, these connections are a life-blood advantage. In addition to these highway infrastructures, Frankfurt Airport is only a 45 minute drive and, therefore, MikroForum is connected with the rest of the Europe, and the world. MikroForum also encourages the tenant companies to follow a global strategy instead of concentrating on only the domestic, regional, German-wide or European marketplaces. As Goldstein and Luger (1990) have stated, a region's long-term economic prospects will depend on its ability to generate and sustain a concentration of enterprises capable of developing new products that can penetrate national and international markets. The same can also be said for MikroForum.

Although MikroForum is a private technology site, it does not fall completely within the 'For-Profit Property Development' classification of parks described previously. Its main objectives are, naturally, management of a private real-estate property, but also investment opportunities. The main focus of investment is not on an immediate high return but rather on the long-term development of the site itself. Additionally, the site collaborates with nearby universities, most notably one of Europe's leading business schools, EBS Business School in Wiesbaden, and also forges alliances with leading industries in order to learn, innovate and profit from these exchanges. Furthermore, the private–public partnership with the State puts job creation and regional development more on the front line. This job creation focus correlates with the site's goal of long-term development. As opposed to some incubators, but as with other private entities, it does not require its tenants to leave the facility after they have reached a certain size or spent a certain time period within the park. As Allen and McCluskey (1990) found out, these privately-held incubator institutions don't have explicit exit or graduation criteria.

Being a private technology site also means that venture capital, as required, can be more likely provided. Indeed, some companies have been able to finance their growth strategies and thereby, in return, contribute to the overall growth of the park. MikroForum's management is certainly keen to keep the park fully sublet, but the primary focus is to select tenants that will contribute to the long-term development of the park. At this stage of development, where MikroForum and its tenants have earned a unique role in the region by providing 250 jobs for its nearby communities, it is now planning an expansion of its facilities by an additional 2,400 m². Accordingly, the screening for new tenants has become, and will remain, even more detailed and focused in that prospective tenants now can be housed in either one of the micro-technology, or life science, clusters. Additionally, there is a category of young companies that may apply for space *and* for venture capital. In the past, the process of selection for these tenant candidates had not always been well-structured or executed but this has now changed. For all tenants, but especially for the companies that apply for venture capital, the park has implemented a clearly-defined due diligence process. This allows the park to 'screen' prospective young companies before investing capital and, thus, clearly this illustrates why MikroForum has been singled out as a relevant case for study on the topic of due diligence on young companies.

## Due Diligence in Practice

The due diligence criteria checklist used by MikroForum to evaluate its tenants, and its applicants for capital, was developed by a faculty at EBS Business School, one of the park's strategic partners. The specific idea behind the criteria was not only to identify young companies with a potential to earn a very high, albeit long-term, ROI (return on investment) but also to select tenants that could contribute to the long-term development of the park. As a private technology park, with no pre-determined, or otherwise, defined exit strategy for its tenants, MikroForum focuses on building a sound foundation of successful and highly-innovative companies. Young companies who wish to eventually continue their activities outside the park are able to pursue their own growth strategies elsewhere. Any terminations, as in any real-estate business, are simply defined by the lease contract.

The due diligence concept, and ultimately the developed checklist, as mentioned, also needed to focus on assessing young companies that are applying for venture capital offered by MikroForum's investors. In order to assess that a young company is indeed a promising investment *prior* to its entry into the technology site, the management required a simple but targeted assessment tool containing the most important key indicators (Gleich *et al.* 2009) that would help it make a better judgment of a young company's potential recognising that the company likely may not have had an established financial history. Assessing young companies with only a few years of financial statements, made it both clear and urgent that MikroForum could not focus only on tangible assets, but that it needed a list criteria that accurately evaluated other, and as mentioned perhaps more telling, intangible aspects.

Prior to this checklist being implemented, a proposed checklist concept was drawn-up and presented to a leading German venture capital company that had had no previous direct business relationship with the park. This venture capital firm's feedback helped to identify possible deficiencies in the checklist and assisted in refining the identified criteria. Subsequently, the checklist was given a test run with a potential applicant. This first-hand experience led to further final revisions defining more precisely the most relevant criteria. The checklist has now been implemented, and has evolved into its current form.

Although this due diligence checklist has been developed for a very specific screening process, namely in this case, evaluating a young prospective technology park tenant and/or an applicant for venture capital, this checklist, and its unique due diligence criteria, could also be used when a large company is acquiring a young company or when two young companies are merging. It is a very simple tool that can be conducted by a relatively small team of people and, therefore, at a relatively low cost benefit, for as Harvey and Lusch (1995) has pointedly stated in their research, there is a dollar sign on every issue during a due diligence process.

This chapter will now turn to highlighting the specific criteria that were developed at MikroForum. As mentioned, they are relevant for many other circumstances when due diligence on young companies maybe recommended and/or required. Two graphics

(Figure 8.1 and Table 8.2) will help illustrate both the overall due diligence process for young companies, and the checklist derived from this process, both currently in use at MikroForum. Recall that this checklist was developed in Germany specifically for screening innovation driven young companies and, thus, it reflects country and industry specific considerations. Nonetheless, this due diligence process criteria, and indeed the checklist itself, could be used to as a starting point in developing your own customised strategy for evaluating young companies.

Usually start-up or young companies, as mentioned previously, cannot always offer a suitable financial track record of success verified by accurate balance sheets and annual reports. MikroForum, prior to its specific due diligence criteria being identified, was limited to making judgement calls about the potential of these young companies based almost solely on the business plans offered to them. Figure 8.1 illustrates how this evaluation flow may have been undertaken. Acknowledging the obvious pitfalls of evaluating a company based on ever-changing business plans, where the ink often does not dry on paper before immediate changes are required, the development of alternative and relevant due diligence criteria for young companies became essential. Moreover, practical considerations deemed that a convenient and standardised across-management checklist would be extremely beneficial. Thus, by using the content headings Step 1 and Step 2 from Figure 8.1, a corresponding checklist was developed by following the same logical flow of information gathering and the exact same heading titles (that is, again Step 1 and Step 2 now used in both Figure 8.1 and Table 8.2) but obviously with the checklist detailing the specific criteria to be evaluated:

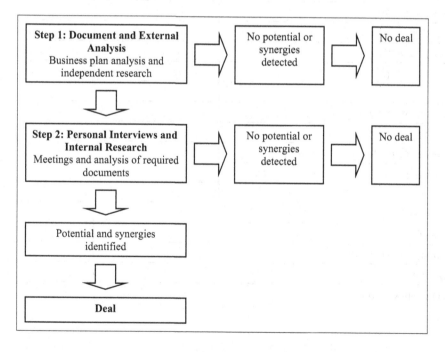

**Figure 8.1   Due Diligence Process for Young Companies**

*Source*: Own illustration

**Table 8.2  Due Diligence Checklist on Young Companies**

| Criteria | Step 1: Document and External Analysis | Step 2: Personal Interviews and Internal Analysis |
|---|:---:|:---:|
| Innovation and Product Analysis | | |
| *Sector and product details* | x | |
| *Current Research & Development* | x | |
| *Market potential (forecast)* | x | x |
| *Market development (review of the past development)* | x | x |
| *Technology audits* | | |
| *Product characteristics* | | x |
| *Production infrastructure required* | | x |
| *Suppliers' structure* | | x |
| *Environmental aspects* | | x |
| | | |
| Company Analysis | | |
| *Overall innovation strategy* | | x |
| *Quality of the business plan* | x | |
| *Competitor analysis* | x | |
| *Legal aspects* | | x |
| *Marketing materials* | | x |
| *Customer profile(s)* | | x |
| | | |
| Management Analysis | | |
| *Managing Director* | | x |
| *Experience of the Managing Director* | x | |
| *Other management and influential contributors* | x | |
| | | |
| Accounting Analysis | | |
| *Financial planning* | x | |
| *Profit and loss statements* | | x |
| *Equity ratio* | | x |

*Source*: Own Illustration

# The Due Diligence Checklist on Young Companies

With both the theoretical process flow seen in Figure 8.1 in mind, and the checklist in Table 8.2 in hand, MikroForum's management is now in a position to better evaluate prospective young company candidates utilising standardised, formatted criteria. To further explain their rationale for the items identified in this checklist, each heading and sub-heading will now be briefly addressed.

# Step 1: Document and External Analysis (as seen in Column 1 of the Checklist)

This step of analysis is based on information provided by the business plan and other documents to be externally analysed which, when taken together, should give any investors a good insight, albeit preliminarily, into the company and the corresponding market. Additionally, independent research is required to deepen the knowledge about the company prior to any personal interviews or meetings and internal analysis (see Step 2).

## INNOVATION AND PRODUCT ANALYSIS

### Sector and product details

The rationale behind identifying this criterion as a key determinant is that micro-technology and life science are the focus of the technology park. Thus, only when the new applicant company belongs to one of the two or related niches can the incubator offer its support and a lease agreement.

Furthermore, examining the product details gives the park an opportunity to assess the potential of the product. Being familiar with the market sector, the management can more easily judge if the product(s) are worth additional investment.

### Current research and development

Knowing the existing product(s), and those in the pipeline with their respective development stages, helps assess the potential of the company. If available, past results may also help to better judge and predict possible successes and/or probable failures lying ahead.

### Market potential (forecast)

The rationale behind forecasting market potential is perhaps obvious but if one looks closely this criterion is one of only two items that appears in both Step 1 and Step 2 on the Due Diligence Checklist (the other is the next item, also related to marketing). This underscores the urgency to paint a picture of what potential lies *ahead* for the young company. Although this information might also be provided by a business plan, it is highly-recommended that industry specialists be engaged to independently, and objectively, assess the market potential.

## Market development (review of the past development)

Despite the urgency to look ahead, history can teach us valuable lessons about the present and the future. It is therefore essential to review the historical trends in this market sector over the last few years. A volatile marketplace may be a forewarning of future major risks. It may also provide an indication (but not a guarantee) of how the market might develop in the future.

## COMPANY ANALYSIS

## Quality of the business plan

The first contact from a prospective young company usually happens when one receives a business plan. (Ironically, with respect to due diligence, it is likely that existing established businesses don't even have an updated business plan.) An extensive and detailed business plan should help to not only understand the company, but at the same time, also help to understand the depth of research the company has conducted and the level of commitment and enthusiasm the key management has for its concept. A word of caution is that the reader should not lose sight of the key unique selling proposition of the plan by being overly-impressed with a graphically fancy or well-presented plan. The devil is in the detail.

## COMPETITOR ANALYSIS

Not knowing the competitive landscape can lead to the early demise of any concept, regardless of how promising the concept may sound. If the market already has some key players, do not underestimate the competitive ruthlessness of any of them and, moreover, this increases the likelihood of any young company that shows promise to be acquired by one of these market sector leaders. Conversely, if the market niche is relatively unoccupied, the young company may have a significant first-mover-advantage and potentially reap great rewards. However, this might also indicate that there will be considerable challenges associated with developing an unknown market niche which could pose greater financial risks.

## MANAGEMENT ANALYSIS

## Experience of the Managing Director

As Lumpkin and Ireland (1988) also confirm, evaluating the Managing Director ought to be considered as one of the most important criterion to be examined. To underscore this point, the authors suggest that it would be more prudent to back and support an experienced 'A-class' manager who has a 'B-class product' that throw your weight behind a 'B-class' manager with an 'A-class' product. In evaluating a Managing Director, a successful track record of previous success is essential as are the practical skills accumulated in previous management experience. (In the case of MikroForum, it had to understand that exceptional scientific research conducted in laboratories was not always an indicator of good management nor will this experience indicate whether the Managing Director has the requisite leadership skills.)

## Employees and other management and influential contributors

Obviously few Managing Directors possess all of the individual qualifications, experience and skills to lead an enterprise. Be wary of those that proclaim they do. The key reason to focus on employees in general, and other members of the management team, is to assess if key holes in the Managing Director's CV are filled by these members. A review of the management team's capabilities should also include a check to see if there are any 'outside the team' experts providing counsel, such as, out-sourced accountants, lawyers, or perhaps Board Members, who are not necessarily on the payroll.

## ACCOUNTING ANALYSIS

### Financial planning

We have already mentioned that for many young companies this criterion will likely be the most inadequate. Nonetheless, a basic understanding and financial analyses are fundamentally essential to show that the young company can anticipate future costs and the potential development of the company. Obviously, the older the company, even if only two or three years, the more important this aspect becomes, for if there is a glaring lack, or perhaps even a hint, of financial management incompetence, clearly failure will be imminent.

# Step 2: Personal Interviews and Internal Analysis (as seen in Column 2 of the Checklist)

Now that the 'paperwork' part of the Due Diligence on young companies has been completed, and assuming that enough synergies and potential promise has been identified, the Due Diligence Checklist now guides management to move onto, and through, Step 2. It is now time to get personal. Following are the summarised rationales for each of these items:

## INNOVATION AND PRODUCT ANALYSIS

### Market potential (forecast) and market development (review of the past development)

As mentioned, these are the only two areas of investigation that are scrutinised in both Step 1 and Step 2. The duplication of these two items is deliberate and illustrates the absolute importance of these factors as either potential indicators of success, or omens of doom. Now that the face-to-face interviews have been initiated, it is now time to really test the mettle of the young company's management team by asking direct questions and expecting direct answers on all matters related to market potential and development.

## Technology audits

Even though an accepted tenant at a technology park will expect a high level of technological support through shared services, each company has its own unique technology requirements. It is therefore essential to press management in the interview to think comprehensibly about each and every piece of equipment that is required to purchase, or upgrade, to initially get the company off the ground and, thereafter, to keep it running. Negligently missing even one technological requirement at this stage can seriously lead to financial and cash problems and may mean that an essential piece of technology cannot be purchased or existing equipment cannot be upgraded.

## Product characteristics

This criterion is essentially related to assessing two principal concerns. First, does the product demonstrate a likely competitive advantage via a unique selling proposition or perhaps an intellectual property or patent advantage? Second, what are the production or development requirements, including initial and ongoing R&D, to get the product actually produced?

## Production infrastructure required

As itemised earlier, incubators and technology parks often provide state-of-the-art-laboratories and other production-related amenities for their tenants. If however, an applicant company requires, for example, a unique gas supply or environmentally incompatible (with the other tenants or prevailing regulations) disposal requirements, this may preclude a lease agreement. Anything required in this area, not supplied by the landlord, must be calculated as an anticipated budgetary expense.

## Suppliers' structure

This criterion raises issues of sourcing supplies required for making the product and/or assembling supplier-sourced components. A telling question to ask the young company's management in these interviews is how thoroughly they have sourced its suppliers in terms of quality, price and terms of payment. Additionally, if products are to be made by the young company, have supply chain and distribution channels been determined.

## Environmental aspects

This criterion is important in that it raises issues involved with measuring the ecological imprint the company's production processes may leave. In addition, it also may raise red flags with respect to onsite disposal of potentially hazardous materials and, possibly thereby, create health and safety concerns for employees, both those with the young company, and also the other tenants. However, there is another concern related to the environment that this criterion addresses. Should the young company be producing consumer goods, has the management thoroughly considered the consumers' perspective with regards to respecting and preserving the environment, and indeed, other social responsibility concerns, which are becoming more and more prevalent with each passing year, in the marketplace.

## COMPANY ANALYSIS

### Overall innovation strategy

This criterion sets out to explore the company's overarching and long-term innovation capabilities, philosophy and strategy. It is not intended to simply count the products in the R&D pipeline. As such, it asks the management of the young company to provide a picture of the whole company and its propensity to innovate and make necessary changes in the future for only the most highly innovative companies today will be here tomorrow to compete.

### Legal aspects

Patent litigations, or other intellectual property issues, can not only distract a company but can also siphon the company's cash reserves with needless legal, and frequently, endless expenses. The face-to-face interview allows the young company the opportunity to allay any concerns about potential litigation and here clearly the management evaluating the young company should not simply accept the young company's word or assurances on these issues. The interviewers should ask for, and expect, the young company to furnish all documents related with intellectual property rights, and indeed, any other significant contracts.

### Marketing materials

Professional design of marketing materials helps to reach more customers and extend the customer base. It is an important sales tool that very often gets neglected due to a 'DIY' or 'save money' attitude of the manager. A deficiency in this criterion may provide a hint of inadequate human resources or a lack of capital resources to meet an acceptable standard for its required professional marketing activities.

### Customer profile(s)

Closely related to the previous point, clearly-defined customer profile(s) are essential. It should reveal precisely who the primary and secondary customers will be and include structure, size, location, purchasing frequencies and relevant demographic and psychographic data. An inadequate picture of the customer profile will result in likely ill-fated marketing efforts or an indication that the market for the product has not yet been developed, or worse still, does not exist.

## MANAGEMENT ANALYSIS

### Managing Director

After studying the Managing Director's CV in Step 1, and following-up on any references, it is now important to meet the Managing Director in person. It is recommended that this meeting take place (if possible) at the manager's current office because this offers an opportunity to assess and verify them based on the credentials provided in the CV. This also affords an opportunity to witness, first-hand, the level of authority exhibited by the Managing Director in the active working relationships with other management and employees and 'feel' the overall atmosphere within the company. Seeing the managing director in this environment helps to judge how successful the 'leader' of the young company might perform in the future.

## INNOVATION ACCOUNTING

### Financial structure

Although a young company may not be able to furnish a comprehensive catalogue of detailed financial statements, it ought to be able provide insights in these face-to-face interviews about the management's financial acumen to manage financial matters. Moreover, if there are any financial instruments that are deemed essential to assessing the financial structure of the company, now is the time to insist that these documents are completed.

### Equity ratio

One of these essential financial documents that must be completed is an assessment of the relation between equity and borrowed funds. This is critical to judge the financial health of the company. It is also crucial information for an investor because it exposes possible risks.

### Profit and loss statement

For companies younger than five years these statements are not normally very reliable and, therefore, they don't play such a crucial role. Only after five years of operation would investors expect to make decisions based mostly on profit and loss statements (Kierans 2009). Nonetheless, it is recommended to take a close look at any available profit and loss statements. In the case of MikroForum, our case study, it does not evaluate start-ups as potential tenants, and therefore, recent P&L statements should be available and therefore must be furnished.

# Conclusions and Future Research

The objective of this chapter has been to present due diligence within the context of young companies and to offer a 'real life' case study of how MikroForum in Germany, has managed and developed a specific due diligence checklist to accomplish such a task. The first subsection dealt with some theoretical background regarding due diligence and thereafter the respective roles and definitions of incubators vs. technology parks were discussed. Making this distinction was necessary to set the stage for our case study on due diligence on young companies, as MikroForum was highly-successful technology park that, out of necessity, had developed a due diligence checklist specifically designed for the needs of this institution. However, anyone interested in evaluating young companies, be they potential suitors, investors, merger partners or venture capitalists ought to be able to adapt this checklist for their own purposes. To this end, this chapter includes the actual checklist and also a brief rationale for each of the selected criterion.

At the outset of this chapter, it was highlighted that many recent mergers and acquisitions have recently failed, with some of them actually earning newsworthy coverage. Due to this, it was mentioned that both academics and business professionals have broadened their traditional research focus, or business strategies, to become more aware of alternative methods of due diligence and thus mitigate likely M&A failures in the near future. Indeed, this is the principle aim of this book and the contributions our authors have offered to you the reader. With respect to due diligence on young companies, there is a certainly a void in research that needs to be filled. Thus, a lot of future research needs to address this unique due diligence niche. It should be remembered however, that due diligence, despite the advice presented in this chapter, and book, is a complicated endeavour and there will always remain some limitations. Every company, like every person, is unique and thus, although screening frames and due diligence checklists can provide a due diligence team with a general direction, and eventually a better-defined strategy, the final outcome of whether a merger or acquisition will succeed is, in a great measure, determined by experience and sound judgement.

# References

Allen, D.N. and McCluskey, R. 1990. Structure, policy, services, and performances in the business incubator industry. *Entrepreneurship Theory and Practice*, Winter 1990, 61–77.

Audretsch, D. 1999. Small firms and efficiency. In: *Are Small Firms Important? Their Role and Impact*, edited by Zoltan J. Acs, Boston, Dordrecht and London: Kluwer Academic Publishers, 21–37.

Barrow, C. 2001. *Incubators: A Realist's Guide to the World's New Business Accelerators*, Chichester and New York: John Wiley & Sons.

Bergek, A. and Norrman, C. 2008. Incubator best practice: A framework. *Technovation*, 28, 20–8.

Bing, G. 1996, *Due Diligence Techniques and Analysis: Critical Questions for Business Decision*, Westport, CT: Quorum Books.

Colombo, M.G. and Delmastro, M. 2002. How effective are technology incubators? Evidence from Italy. *Research Policy*, 31 (7), 1103–22.

Gleich, R., Henke, M., Quitt, A. and Sommer, L. 2009. New approaches in performance measurement: Methods for specification and operationalisation within the context of supply management. *International Journal of Business Excellence*, 2 (2), 105–23.

Hackett, S.M. and Dilts, D.M. 2004. A systematic review of business incubation research. *Journal of Technology Transfer*, 29, 55–82.

Harvey, M.G. and Lusch, R.F. 1995. Expanding the nature and scope of due diligence. *Journal of Business Venturing*, 10, 5–21.

Howson, P. 2003. *Due Diligence: The Critical Stage in Mergers and Acquisitions*. Hants: Gower Publishing.

Kierans, G. 2009. Bewertung von jungen Unternehmen: ein innovativer Lösungsansatz. In: *Perspektiven des Innovationsmanagements 2008*, edited by R. Gleich and P. Russo, Berlin: LIT Verlag, 179–96.

Lewis, D.A. 2002. *Does Technology Incubation Work? A Critical Review of the Evidence*, Athens OH: NBIA Publications.

Link, A.N. and Scott, J.T. 2003. U.S. Science Parks: The diffusion of an innovation and its effects on the academic missions of universities. *International Journal of Industrial Organization*, 21 (9), 1323–56.

Lumpkin, J.R. and Ireland, D.R. 1988. Screening practices of new business incubators: The evaluation of critical success factors. *American Journal of Small Business*, Spring, 59–81.

Purnam, P., Powell, B.C. and Singh, H. 2006. Due Diligence failure as a signal detection problem. *Strategic Organization*, 4 (4), 319–48.

Rankine, D., Bomer, M. and Stedman, G., 2003, *Due Diligence: Definitive Steps to Successful Business Combinations*. Harlow: Financial Times Prentice Hall.

Siegel, D.S., Westhead, P. and Wright, M. 2003. Assessing the impact of University Science Parks on research productivity: Exploratory firm-level evidence from the United Kingdom. *International Journal of Industrial Organization*, 21 (9), 1357–69.

Voisey, P., Gornall, L., Jones, P. and Thomas, B. 2006. The measurement of success in a business incubation project. *Journal of Small Business and Enterprise Development*, 13 (3), 454–68.

Westhead, P. and Storey, D.J. 1995. Links between higher education institutions and high technology firms. *Omega, International Journal of Management Science*, 23 (4), 345–60.

# Deal Negotiation and Post-Merger Integration

# 9 Redefining Due Diligence to Jump Start Effective Integration

PROFESSOR TIMOTHY J. GALPIN
*University of Dallas Graduate School of Management, United States*

Although often justified as a means of improving company performance, extensive research shows that most mergers and acquisitions (M&As) do not realize their intended goals (Papadakis 2005; Marks and Mirvis 2001; Agrawal and Jaffe 2000; LaJoux and Weston 1998). Likewise, considerable empirical evidence supports the premise that poorly conducted M&A integration efforts are the primary cause of underperformance (Larson and Finkelstein 1999; Pablo 1994; Chattergee *et al.* 1992; Datta 1991). Beyond the research, numerous case examples demonstrate the setbacks that mismanaged integration efforts create. For example, Daimler's acquisition of Chrysler (Edmondson *et al.* 2005), the merger of Sprint and Nextel (Taylor 2006), the marriage of Time Warner and AOL (Joyce 2003), and the merger between Citicorp and Travelers (Guerrera 2009) all encountered significant problems due to poorly conducted integration efforts. The following chapter presents the case that effective M&A integration and deal success begins not after the deal is done, but well before the deal is closed. Furthermore, deal success is enhanced by management expanding its definition of due diligence to include strategic, cultural, and human capital risks.

## Integration Begins with Due Diligence

Both M&A researchers and practitioners alike agree that deal-makers must make certain that the people in charge of the integration are fully-aware of the information uncovered during due diligence which can impact integration and ultimately deliver success, such as, cultural fit, strategic fit, key talent and so forth. For example, in their discussion of the factors which enhance M&A integration efforts, Schweiger and Goulet (2000) assert that ensuring continuity among those who conduct due diligence, with those who manage integration efforts, positively impacts deal performance. However, the authors also note that there is limited empirical evidence to support their claim and refer to Haspeslagh and Jemison (1991) and Jemison and Sitkin (1986) as two sources of research into the topic. Moreover, M&A practitioners (Galpin and Herndon 2007; LaJoux and Elson 2000) testify that one of the most important parts of making a deal successful, after you complete it (during integration), is what you do before you complete it (during due diligence).

Conscious of the crucial links between due diligence, enhanced integration and deal performance, experienced acquirers are redefining the process of due diligence. They are not only ensuring transparent communication between members of the due diligence team and members of the integration team, but knowledgeable deal makers are also beginning to employ a structured approach to assess both traditional (that is, financial and operational performance) and non-traditional aspects (that is, the strategy, culture, and talent) of potential partner and target companies. This expanded approach to due diligence has a central critical objective – to facilitate an effective integration process ultimately leading to deal success. Companies can mitigate integration risk by approaching their mergers and acquisitions process more comprehensively and treating due diligence and integration as a continuous process. Galpin and Herndon (2007) identify six stages of the M&A process:

1.   Formulate: Setting the firm's M&A strategy.
2.   Locate: Identifying potential target companies that may fit the firm's M&A strategy.
3.   Investigate: Completing detailed analyses of a target company.
4.   Negotiate: Reaching a definitive agreement between the two firms.
5.   Integrate: Combining the companies' people, processes, and systems.
6.   Motivate: Engaging the workforce to achieve both short and long-term performance of the newly formed company or 'NewCo'.

An effective integration effort encompasses each of these six deal stages, starting when management establishes the firm's M&A strategy, locates companies which fit that strategy and this process continues well into the integration and workforce motivation phases of the deal process.

# Due Diligence throughout the Deal Process

## FORMULATE STAGE 1

To begin the deal process, management needs to define a clear growth strategy based on sound data. This strategy formulation effort entails identifying what the external market opportunities and threats are for the company, along with the internal strengths and weaknesses of the organization to take advantage of the external market (Wheelen and Hunger 2008). This strategic 'self due diligence' provides the firm with specific criteria to not only describe what a viable target company for acquisition looks like, but subsequently identify and assess a target's strategic fit. Strategic acquisition criteria can include market share, geographic access, new products or technologies, customer segments, financial structure, organizational culture, workforce talent, and so forth. Having done the necessary 'self due diligence' during the strategy formulation stage, the company now has a solid foundation from which to conduct a thorough due diligence of target companies throughout the rest of the deal process. Furthermore, this provides a clear road map for how acquired firms will be integrated into the company's business processes, technology, and human resources.

## LOCATE STAGE 2

After the strategic template has been set as a result of the 'self due diligence' conducted during the previous stage, locating firms for acquisition can follow a focused and logical path. During this stage, initial high-level financial, operational and organizational analyses will lead to introductory discussions between the executives of the acquiring and target firms. These initial conversations include identifying potential cost and growth synergies that could result from a combination of the two organizations, based on the strategic criteria set in the Formulate Stage. The high-level due diligence conducted within the Locate Stage will be clarified in greater detail by more specific due diligence later on in the deal process. Given continued interest from both parties, initial deal parameters, terms and conditions can, during this stage, be defined and submitted as a part of a letter of intent (LOI) and a non-disclosure agreement.

Most letters of intent do an adequate job of describing desired deal objectives and also provide an overview of the proposed financial and operational aspects of the transaction. However, sophisticated acquirers have learned that it is necessary (by means of broader due diligence during the Locate Phase) to identify within the LOI key guiding parameters for the integration process. Broader letters of intent often include such aspects as: the governance structure of the NewCo, the overall process to be used for determining organizational structure and staffing decisions, agreement on the basic steps and provisions of the integration process to be used (for example, formation of integration teams, integration planning protocols, and leadership roles) and a high-level approach to reconcile major discrepancies between the two firms (for example, executive compensation, employee benefits and incentive plans) that can all hinder the integration effort.

## INVESTIGATE STAGE 3

The third phase of the deal flow model entails much more granular due diligence than is the case for the Locate Phase, in order to explore every possible facet of the target company, in as much detail as is practical, prior to finalizing the definitive agreement. Therefore, during this stage, detailed due diligence must be done pertaining not only to the traditional financial, legal, environmental and operational aspects, but also with regard to the non-traditional strategic, cultural, and human capital characteristics of the target firm. Key findings in all areas examined should be summarized for the acquiring management team to review and any potential 'deal killers' should be identified. The detailed due diligence findings are then used to set negotiating boundaries, determine deal pricing, and just as importantly, provide a basis for the subsequent integration effort.

## NEGOTIATE STAGE 4

This stage of the deal process involves steps and requirements for successfully reaching a definitive agreement. Negotiation team members develop the final negotiating strategy for all terms and conditions of the deal. Considerations include price, performance, people, legal protection and governance. An aspect of many negotiations that is particularly important to successful integration is gaining agreement on the terms and conditions of transition services for various functions, such as, information technology, financial reporting, payroll, benefits administration, and so forth. Those involved in the Negotiate Stage will utilize information gained from the due diligence conducted in the previous stages to achieve the best price and deal terms.

## INTEGRATE STAGE 5

Once negotiations are complete and the transaction is 'closed', this stage entails the actual process of implementing and running the NewCo's processes, people and systems. Moreover, during the actual implementation of planned integration activities there is still much more due diligence to occur. In order to determine how to resolve the numerous issues that inevitably arise at this stage, the combining organizations must continue the task of due diligence regarding each other in even more painstaking detail than had been done during the previous deal stages. From addressing travel policies to obtaining office supplies, an exhaustive due diligence learning process needs to take place during the Integrate Stage providing the combined management and employees of the NewCo with the requisite knowledge needed to run the day-to-day business.

## MOTIVATE STAGE 6

The sixth stage of the model is geared toward maximizing the long-term value of the NewCo. Once major integration activities are complete, and many of the projected deal synergies have been realized, management's responsibility now shifts to the demands of guiding the organization forward in order to achieve on-going performance improvements. In his discussions of creating long-term workforce motivation, Jon Katzenbach (2000, 2003) makes a clear case that management must identify, and act on, the sources of motivation for each employee. This type of 'individual due diligence' is necessary throughout the combined organization for two key reasons. First, what motivates one person is often different to what motivates another. Some employees are more motivated by extrinsic rewards such as pay, title, perks, and so forth, while the primary motivator of others is intrinsic rewards such as challenging work and continuous learning. Second, only when individual differences in motivation are identified through individual manager-to-employee due diligence across the workforce will the performance of the NewCo be sustained over the long-term.

The six deal stages are represented here as linear. However, the reality of deals dictates that all six stages are interconnected. From formulating a M&A strategy, through integrating the companies acquired as part of that strategy, to motivating the workforce of combined entities, due diligence of various scope and detail must be conducted to help ensure deal success. Table 9.1 summarizes who should be involved in due diligence at each stage of the deal process, and also identifies what information is needed during each stage. Keeping due diligence as a primary activity during each stage of the process will help to ensure that there is a high probability of both short- and long-term deal success.

**Table 9.1   Due Diligence during the Six Stages of the Deal Flow Model**

| Deal Stage | Parties Involved | Due Diligence |
|---|---|---|
| Formulate | Senior management team, M&A/ Strategy or Business Development department | Organizational 'self due diligence' including external opportunities and threats, and current internal organizational strengths and weaknesses. Identification of desired target company characteristics that will complement current strengths and weaknesses. |
| Locate | Senior management team, M&A/ Strategy or Business Development department, Operations, Technology, Human Resources | Analyses of industry and public domain information to identify candidates for serious target consideration. Broad synergy identification, assessment, validation and quantification leading to letter of intent. |
| Investigate | Senior management team, M&A/ Strategy or Business Development department, Operations, Technology, Human Resources, Integration Manager | Thorough review of target's core assets, business processes, technology, policies, and human capital leading to valid estimates of cost and top-line synergies and potential integration issues. |
| Negotiate | Senior management team, M&A/ Strategy or Business Development department | Utilize knowledge gained about target and synergy opportunities to achieve best price and deal terms. |
| Integrate | Senior management team, Operations, Technology, Human Resources, Integration Manager, Integration Teams | Granular detail about target organization and synergies leading to specific integration design and implementation. |
| Motivate | Senior management team, Human Resources, all managers throughout the combined organization | Manager to employee 'individual due diligence' to understand personal motivators for each employee. |

# Expanded Components of Due Diligence

## DETERMINING STRATEGIC RISKS

The first expanded component of due diligence is that of determining strategic risks. This assessment establishes the overall integration strategy in light of the general strategic rationale of each deal, and provides answers to two key questions:

* What are we buying and why?
* What level of integration is needed to achieve the key value-drivers?

Most deals have an overarching strategic rationale such as consolidation, product line or geographic expansion, the acquisition of R&D or talent, or industry convergence. Having a strategic rationale for each merger or acquisition also requires having a corresponding integration strategy in order to capture the desired value and synergies of each particular deal. This requires that any organization first clarify its own strategy and identify the gaps in capability that can be filled by merging or acquiring with other entities. Only then can management determine both the overall degree of integration required, as well as, what to integrate or not integrate.

## STRATEGIC DUE DILIGENCE

The strategic 'self due diligence', identified in stage one above, is typically conducted as a four part analysis that can be completed for any size organization in any industry. SWOT is an acronym commonly used to describe the particular Strengths, Weaknesses, Opportunities, and Threats that are important to a company's future. Although there are numerous approaches to, and frameworks for, conducting a strategic analysis (see for example, Nolan *et al.* 2008; Aaker 2001; Napier *et al.* 1998; Porter 1998), throughout the years, the SWOT analysis has endured as a primary analytical approach to determining a firm's strategy (Glaister and Falshaw 1999). Through an internal analysis, determining a company's strengths results in identifying the capabilities and resources it currently possesses which can be used to the firm's future competitive advantage. Likewise, identifying the company's weaknesses highlights the capabilities and resources that the firm currently lacks. Examples of these internal capabilities and resources that can be either strengths or weaknesses include the company's: technology, operational processes, culture, workforce talent, training, patents, R&D and so forth. Once the company's strengths and weaknesses are clearly identified and prioritized, management can then begin to determine the types of capabilities and resources that target companies should possess to augment the firm's strengths and supplement its weaknesses. Furthermore, determining and prioritizing the potential external opportunities and threats to the company is also critical to identifying target companies. External opportunities and threats include such variables as: new technologies, changing government regulations, improved competitor capabilities, demographic and population shifts, changing economic conditions and so forth. Taken together, the strengths and weaknesses of a firm along with the external opportunities and threats enable management to craft a viable M&A strategy.

### Determining the overall degree of integration

Once a thorough strategic 'self due diligence' has been conducted and the desired characteristics of potential target companies are identified, management can then determine the integration priorities required for each deal they conduct on a case-by-case basis. Knowledgeable acquirers know that this determination depends less on the scale, the business cycle, or the industry than on the desired capabilities to be obtained and the business goals to be achieved from each deal.

An effective approach to determining desired integration priorities for a particular deal is for the acquirer to identify and document the primary integration areas and potential risks to be considered based on the strategic fit between the target company and the acquiring firm. This documentation should include not only potential functional integration issues such as financial reporting, sales and marketing, but also potential organization-wide risks such as combining major business processes, technologies, or the brands of both firms. For each target company, the investigation team must identify the business goals (including initial numerical synergy estimates) associated with integrating each priority area of the target. Once this strategic fit analysis is completed, a target company should then be placed into one of three broad categories identifying the level of integration required for obtaining the desired deal results: full integration of all businesses processes across the entire acquired company; moderate integration of certain key functions or processes (for example, R&D, sales, or manufacturing); and, minimal integration of few, if any, of the acquired firm's functions or processes. This categorization will help management and others involved with integrating the two organizations understand the amount of effort required and strategic risks associated with the integration of a target. Full integration requires the most effort, and presents the highest risk, as more operational and organizational changes need to be managed. Likewise, full integration creates significant difficulties when 'unwinding' the combined entities should that be required later on. Moderate integration takes less effort and creates medium risk. Whereas, minimal integration takes the least effort and presents the lowest risk as fewer operational and organizational changes need to be managed, and 'unwinding' the combined entities is much less difficult.

## ASSESSING CULTURAL RISKS

The importance of cultural due diligence cannot be overstated. For example, Sales and Mirvis (1984) studied the impact of culture on M&A integration over a three-year period. The cultural dimensions they examined were: company philosophy, values and interpersonal and business behaviors. The researchers found that, during the first year after deal close, cultural disparity between combining organizations resulted in polarization, negative evaluations of the other company and anxiety and ethnocentrism between members of the combined firms. Moreover, the authors found that after three years these negative aspects diminished somewhat, but were still evident across the combined entity. The significance of organizational culture's impact on deal performance is also demonstrated in the findings of Greenwood et al. (1994). In an examination of the combination of two professional services firms, these investigators found that cultural differences led to conflict during integration even though the combination presented a good strategic fit for both firms. Several other studies have also demonstrated that cultural differences have a significant impact on both increasing the turnover of senior management and decreasing the financial performance of deals (Stahl and Voigt 2008; Lubatkin et al. 1999; Weber et al. 1996; Chatterjee et al. 1992). The findings of these studies raise an important question: If organizational culture has such an important impact on deal performance why then is 'cultural fit' not given more importance during due diligence? The answers to this might be that management likely became overly captivated with the strategic fit presented by a potential combination, or that the impact of culture on deal performance is far too often underestimated by management (Schweiger and Goulet 2000).

Although culture has been shown to have a significant impact on deal performance, organizational culture is not so easily defined. This is demonstrated by the numerous descriptions of organizational culture that have been put forth ranging from what a firm's management and employees consider appropriate business practices (Schein

1985), to the way an organization and its members think about what they do (Bower 2001), to organizational norms, values, beliefs and attitudes (Goulet and Schweiger 2006). This situation makes conducting the second expanded component of due diligence – a comprehensive assessment of the *cultural risks* associated with each deal – extremely difficult. What is required is a pragmatic cultural analysis framework enabling an unambiguous comparison of the combined companies' cultures. This analysis should focus on identifying the inevitable discrepancies and similarities between the organizational cultures of combining companies and determining whether these issues will be manageable during a cultural integration process. Table 9.2 illustrates ten cultural 'levers' that form the foundation of a comprehensive, pragmatic, and rapid cultural comparison diagnostic. Conducting this assessment will provide answers to the critical questions about the amount of effort and time it will take to integrate the cultures of the combined organizations.

The ten levers identified above in Table 9.2 taken together form an interrelated set of processes that make up a firm's culture. Moreover, examining which strategy and values are reinforced by each lever, along with how a firm has designed and implemented the ten levers, provides a pragmatic and actionable description of an organization's culture (Galpin 1996). By answering the questions presented in Table 9.2, those conducting due diligence can quickly compare the cultures of organizations involved in M&As. This comparison can be done in as much, or as little, detail as desired. However, a more detailed comparison will provide a better road map for eventual cultural integration of the organizations. A reasonably detailed comparison across the ten levers can be completed by human resources staff, and a few operational managers representing the two combining organizations, within a day-long session. As a practical matter, management in charge of a company's M&A efforts will find that allocating the time to conduct a cultural diagnostic (like the one presented in Table 9.2) during due diligence significantly helps to mitigate the cultural risk associated with combining organizations. It should be noted that finding considerable cultural differences between two firms should not necessarily be used as a reason to discontinue a potential merger or acquisition. Rather, a pragmatic cultural comparison provides transparency to an often murky aspect of due diligence, enabling management to clearly understand the complexities, actions and timeframes needed for effective cultural integration of the combining organizations.

**Table 9.2    Cultural Comparison Diagnostic**

| Cultural 'Levers' | Key Questions |
| --- | --- |
| Staffing and Selection<br>Communications<br>Training and Development<br>Goals and Measures<br>Rewards and Recognition<br>Organizational Structure<br>Decision-making<br>Rules and Policies<br>Ceremonies and Events<br>Physical Environment | What organizational strategy and values does each organization reinforce with each lever?<br>How is each lever currently designed and implemented within each organization?<br>What is common between the two firms for each lever?<br>How can similarities be underscored and strengthened?<br>What is different between the two firms for each lever?<br>How can differences be bridged?<br>What are the short, medium, and long-term cultural integration actions to be taken for each lever?<br>Who should be involved in culture integration efforts? |

## IDENTIFYING HUMAN CAPITAL RISKS

In addition to assessing the strategic and cultural risks of a proposed deal, the third expanded due diligence component is a comprehensive assessment of the *human capital risks*, answering the key questions:

- Who are the 'key talent' individuals in both organizations?
- What is the risk of not retaining them?
- How can we retain them and 're-recruit' their commitment to the new organization?

### Retention

A major component of human capital risk is the retention of key talent, which has been found to have a significant impact on deal performance (Brahma and Srivastava 2007; Salame 2006; Krug 2003; Schuler and Jackson 2001). Moreover, data from the American Management Association indicates that 25 per cent of top performing employees in an organization leave within 90 days of a major change event such as a merger or acquisition, despite the fact they still have a job (Withenshaw 2003). The reasons people leave a newly formed organization include: uncertainty about their role in the organization (Brahma and Srivastava 2007), a feeling of inferiority on the part of acquired employees and a loss status (Cannella and Hambrick 1993) and poor communications between the combining firms (Schweiger and DeNisi 1991). Although keeping key talent from leaving the NewCo is important to M&A success, simply retaining them is not enough.

### Re-recruitment

Going beyond retention, 're-recruitment' refers to regaining the commitment and engagement of employees to their work and the overall success of the NewCo. Employee engagement is vital to the success of M&As as it has been shown to have a significant relationships with productivity, profitability, employee retention, safety, and customer satisfaction (Buckingham and Coffman 1999; Coffman and Gonzalez-Molina 2002).

A key due diligence tool for evaluating human capital risk is the retention and re-recruitment assessment shown in Table 9.3. This aspect of due diligence enables management to identify the key talent within each organization, as well as, catalogue the actions associated with both retaining that talent and, additionally, 're-recruiting' their commitment to the success of the NewCo. Completing the retention and re-recruitment assessment involves three main steps: 1) identify key talent; 2) understand individual and group engagement factors; and 3) develop an action plan to address these factors.

**Table 9.3    Retention and Re-recruitment Assessment**

| Name | Area/ Expertise | Criticality | Engagement Factors | Retention/Re- recruitment Actions | Sponsor |
|---|---|---|---|---|---|
| Names of key individuals and teams | Areas, expertise, and/or functions that they work in | What the organization would lose if these people or groups left | The identified factors that engage the key people or groups identified | The retention and recruitment actions that will be taken | The person(s) responsible for acting on the retention and re-recruitment actions |

## Identifying key talent

The first major step in conducting the retention and re-recruitment assessment is to identify key people or groups, that is, those whose departure would have significant a detrimental effect on the organization. People or groups can be considered 'key' for various reasons, but the business impact of losing them should be the factor that deems them essential. The first three columns of the assessment call for: generating a list of the key employees and groups within the combining organizations; identifying the area of the business they work in and the expertise they possess; and then discovering what the impact of their departure would be on the business (for example, the loss of a key client or customer, important innovation abilities, knowledge of a core product or service offering, considerable project-management skills and so forth). If the loss of these or other critical organizational capabilities would occur when someone leaves the firm, then the person or group can be considered 'key talent'.

## Understanding what engages employees

The second main step in conducting the retention and re-recruitment assessment is to understand what engages individuals and groups. At a macro or organization-wide level, employee commitment and engagement is reinforced by the presence of a clear set of human resource management practices supporting the firm's desired strategy and core values (Dessler 1999). These practices include: hiring people based on their 'fit' with the organization's strategy and values, training linked to strategy and values, incentive pay, information sharing, participation in decision making, skills training and development, cross-utilization and cross-training, tradition-building symbols and ceremonies, extensive two-way communications, putting in place the right leaders (who demonstrate a commitment to people development) and promotion from within (Pfeffer 2005; Dessler 1999). Moreover, how employees are let go from an organization can have as much, if not more, impact on workforce engagement than the firm's hiring and workforce development practices. When layoffs occur, during the integration of combining firms for example, more than just the exiting employees pay attention to how the process of separation is conducted. People remaining in the organization view how separations were addressed as a clear indicator of the value a firm places on its workforce.

In this regard, Dessler (1999) stresses the need for management to demonstrate what he terms as 'organizational justice'. He contends that fair procedures, regarding employee separation for example, play a key role in fostering employee commitment. Conducting employee separations in a manner that demonstrates both respect for the individual and the integrity of the organization leaves people who are exiting the firm with a sense of fairness. Likewise, management fosters a sense of engagement and commitment among those employees who remain in the organization as they also recognize the separation process as having been fair.

Taking into consideration the observation that 'employees don't quit companies, they quit managers' (Buckingham and Cunningham, 1999) in combination with the fact that an employee's primary contact with an organization is through his or her direct supervisor and the job itself (Griffin 1980), micro-level engagement practices can be even more important than the macro practices described above. One of these micro-level, manager to employee, practices is transformational leadership. Transformational leadership has consistently been linked to high levels of employee and organizational performance (Whittington *et al.* 2004; Hater and Bass 1988; Yammarino and Bass 1990; Howell and Avolio 1993) has been found to increase employee commitment to the organization (Whittington *et al.* 2004; Bycio *et al.* 1995) and build trust in the leader (Podsakoff *et al.* 1990). Transformational leaders demonstrate one or more of the following characteristics: inspirational motivation, intellectual stimulation and individualized consideration (Bass and Riggio 2006; Avolio 1999; Bass and Avolio 1994). Inspirational motivation occurs through envisioning and articulating an attractive future that provides meaning and challenge for followers (Bass 1985). Intellectual stimulation is created by the transformational leaders' questioning of assumptions, reframing of problems and approaching existing situations from a fresh perspective (Bass 1985). Individualized consideration refers to the transformational leaders' mentoring role and also paying special attention to each individual's need for achievement and personal growth (Bass 1985).

Another micro-level engagement practice is job enrichment. Enriched and motivating jobs have been found to have five principal dimensions: task variety, task identity, task significance, autonomy and feedback (Hackman and Oldham 1976). Furthermore, the presence of these core dimensions results in a variety of positive individual and organizational outcomes such as motivation, engagement, high quality of work performance, satisfaction at work and low levels of absenteeism and turnover (Saks 2006; Hackman and Oldham 1976).

In addition to transformational leadership and job enrichment, a third important micro-level engagement practice is goal setting. The process of goal setting begins with a high level of challenge in the form of specific, difficult goals. It has been demonstrated that challenging employees with difficult goals and providing them with ample feedback results in higher performance, satisfaction, commitment and high intentions to remain in the organization (Locke and Latham 1990; Mento *et al.* 1987).

## Developing an action plan

Once management has identified the key talent, and has identified the factors that are important to retain and re-recruit these people, the third major step in conducting the assessment is to develop an action plan. Retention and re-recruitment actions should address both the macro-level (organization-wide human resources practices) and micro-level (manager to employee) engagement factors discussed above. Addressing these two levels through a series of coordinated actions establishes a robust retention and re-recruitment plan that has a high probability of success. For example, at the macro organization-wide level, management must ensure that key talent are fully aware of, and included in, the core human resources practices of the NewCo such as: the hiring and selection of new employees; training linked to the NewCo's strategy and values; incentive pay programs; decision-making; cross-training; recognition during company ceremonies; and, extensive two-way communications (Pfeffer 2005; Dessler, 1999).

Beyond involvement in the macro-level human resources practices of the NewCo, management must also address micro-level (manager to employee) engagement practices for each of the critical individuals, or groups, identified in the assessment. Micro-level retention and re-recruitment actions can include: increases in base and/or bonus compensation; enhancements in title, roles, and/or responsibilities; interesting and challenging job content; assignment to high profile projects; greater autonomy; changes of location; changes in the reporting manager; personalized communication; additional perks such as membership payments, office size, location; frequent coaching and feedback; regular positive reinforcement; and, addressing a work/life balance including flexible schedules or working remotely (Galpin and Herndon 2007; Ford 2004; Heinen and O'Neill 2004; Jamrog 2004). Each of these practices separately may increase key talent retention and engagement during M&As. However, when applied in combination these actions will help increase the likelihood of retaining and re-recruiting those people who are deemed 'key' to the NewCo's success.

## Summary

The expanded view of due diligence thus far presented bridges the gap between theory and practice across the disciplines of corporate strategy, M&A integration, organizational culture and human capital management. Conducting due diligence throughout all stages of a deal regarding the strategic, cultural and human capital risks of a potential combination is vital to M&A success. Assessing these areas requires a fundamental redefinition of traditional due diligence. Beyond redefining *what* is included in due diligence efforts (that is, the content), a fundamental redefinition is also needed in *how* due diligence processes should be conducted and *who* should be involved.

Too often executives perceive due diligence to be a one-time endeavor, yet, practical experience dictates otherwise. Due diligence must be done and redone, at ever-deeper levels of detail involving greater numbers of people at each level as the transaction progresses and through each deal stage. Beyond senior management, determining the strategic risks associated with a potential deal, human resources practitioners – skilled in M&A activities – should be involved from the early phases of due diligence to provide a focused assessment of the human capital risks of deals including cultural comparisons and retention and re-recruitment risk assessments. Doing so will generate more thorough and robust due diligence information, establishing the foundation for a well-planned and executed integration effort, ultimately leading to both short and long-term deal success.

# References

Aaker, D.A. 2001. *Developing Business Strategies*. 6th edition. New York: John Wiley & Sons.

Agrawal, A. and Jaffe, J.F. 2000. The post-merger performance puzzle. In *Advances in Mergers and Acquisitions*, edited by C. Cooper and A. Gregory. New York: JAI Press, 7–42.

Avolio, B. 1999. *Full Leadership Development*. Thousand Oaks: Sage.

Bass, B. 1985. *Leadership and Performance Beyond Expectations*. New York: The Free Press.

Bass, B. and Avolio, B. 1994. *Improving Organizational Effectiveness Through Transformational Leadership*. Thousand Oaks: Sage.

Bass, B. and Riggio, R. 2006. *Transformational Leadership*. 2nd Edition. Lawerence Erlbaum and Associates.

Bower, J.L. 2001. Not all M&As are alike – and that matters 'performance'. *Harvard Business Review*, 79(3), 93–101.

Brahma, S.S. and Srivastava, K.B. 2007. Communication, executive retention, and employee stress as predictors of acquisition performance: An empirical evidence. *ICFAI Journal of Mergers & Acquisitions*, 4 (4), 7–26.

Buckingham, M. and Coffman, C. 1999. *First, Break All The Rules: What The World's Greatest Managers Do Differently*. New York: Simon & Shuster.

Bycio, P., Hackett, R. and Allen, J. 1995. Further assessments of Bass's (1985) conceptualization of transactional and transformational leadership. *Journal of Applied Psychology*, 80, 468–78.

Cannella, A.A. Jr. and Hambrick, D.C. 1993. Effects of executive departures on the performance of acquired firms. *Strategic Management Journal*: Special Issue, 14, 137–52.

Chatterjee, S., Lubatkin, M.H., Schweiger, D.M. and Weber, Y. 1992. Cultural differences and shareholder value in related mergers: Linking equity and human capital. *Strategic Management Journal*, 13, 319–34.

Coffman, C. and Gonzalez-Molina, G. (2002). *Follow This Path: How the World's Greatest Organizations Drive Growth by Unleashing Human Potential*. New York: Warner Books, Inc.

Datta, D.K. 1991. Organizational fit and acquisition performance: Effects of post-acquisition integration. *Strategic Management Journal*, 12, 281–97.

Dessler, G. 1999. How to earn your employees' commitment. *Academy of Management Executive*, 13 (2), 58–67.

Edmondson, G., Welch, D., Thornton, E. and Therese Palmer, A. 2005. Dark days at Daimler. *BusinessWeek* [online, 15 August] Available at: http://www.businessweek.com/magazine/content/05_33/b3947001_mz001.htm [accessed: 13 March 2009].

Ford, R.L. 2004. Ways to retain a diverse work force. *Public Relations Tactics*, 11 (6), 6–6.

Galpin, T. 1996. Connecting culture to organizational change. *HR Magazine*, 41 (3), 84–90.

Galpin, T. and Herndon, M. 2007. *The Complete Guide to Mergers and Acquisitions: Process Tools to Support Integration at Every Level*. 2nd edition. San Francisco: Jossey-Bass.

Glaister, K.W. and Falshaw, J.R. 1999. Strategic planning: Still going strong? *Long Range Planning*, 32(1), 107–16.

Goulet, P.K. and Schweiger, D.M. 2006. Managing culture and human resources in mergers and acquisitions. In *Handbook of Research in International Human Resource Management*, edited by G. Stahl and I. Bjorkman. Northampton, MA: Edward Elgar, 405–32.

Greenwood, R., Hinings, C.R. and Brown, J. 1994. Merging professional service firms. *Organization Science*, 5 (2) 239–57.

Griffin, R. 1980. *Task Design*. Glenview, IL: Scott, Foresman and Company.

Guerrera, F. 2009. Flawed conception. *Financial Times* [online, 16 January] Available at: http://www. ft.com/cms/s/0/8e4875e4-e401-11dd-8274-0000779fd2ac.html [accessed: 13 March 2009].

Hackman, J. and Oldham, G. 1976. Motivation through the design of work: Test of a theory. *Organizational Behavior and Human Performance*, 16, 250–79.

Haspeslagh, P.C. and Jemison, D.B. 1991. *Managing Acquisitions: Creating Value through Corporate Renewal*. New York: The Free Press.

Hater, J. and Bass, B. 1988. Superiors' evaluations and subordinates' perceptions of transformational and transactional leadership. *Journal of Applied Psychology*, 73, 695–702.

Heinen, J.S. and O'Neill, C. 2004. Managing talent to maximize performance. *Employment Relations Today*, 31 (2), 67–82

Howell, J. and Avolio, B. 1993. Transformational leadership, transactional leadership, locus of control, and support for innovation: Key predictors of consolidated-business-unit performance. *Journal of Applied Psychology*, 78, 891–902.

Jamrog, J. 2004. The perfect storm: The future of retention and engagement. *Human Resource Planning*, 27 (3), 26–33.

Jemison, D.B. and Sitkin, S.B. 1986. Acquisitions: The process can be the problem. *Harvard Business Review*, 64, 107–16.

Joyce, E. 2003. Time Warner Nixes AOL From Nameplate. *ClickZNews* [online, 18 September] Available at: http://www.clickz.com/showPage.html?page=3079621 [accessed: 13 March 2009].

Katzenbach, J.R. 2000. *Peak Performance: Aligning the Hearts and Minds of Your Employees*. Boston: Harvard Business School.

Katzenbach, J.R. 2003. *Why Pride Matters More Than Money: The Power of the World's Greatest Motivational Force*. New York: Crown Business.

Krug, J.A. 2003. Why do they keep leaving? *Harvard Business Review*, 81 (2), 14–15.

Lajoux, A.R. and Elson, C.M. 2000. The Art of M&A Due Diligence: Navigating Critical Steps & Uncovering Crucial Data. New York: McGraw-Hill.

Lajoux, A.R. and Weston, J.F. 1998. Do deals deliver post-merger performance? *Mergers and Acquisitions*, 33, 34–7.

Larsson, R. and Finkelstein, S. 1999. Integrating strategic, organizational, and human resource perspectives on mergers and acquisitions: A case survey of synergy realization. *Organization Science*, 10, 1–26.

Locke, E. and Latham, G. 1990. *A Theory of Goal Setting and Task Performance*. Englewood Cliffs: Prentice-Hall.

Lubatkin, M., Schweiger, D. and Weber, Y. 1999. Top management turnover in related M&As: An additional test of the theory of relative standing. *Journal of Management*, 25 (1), 55–67.

Marks, M.L. and Mirvis, P.H. 2001. Making mergers and acquisitions work. *Academy of Management Executive*, 15, 80–94.

Mento, A., Steel, R. and Karren, R. 1987. A meta-analytic study of the effects of goal setting on task performance: 1966–1984. *Organizational Behavior and Human Decision Processes*, 39, 52–83.

Napier, R., Sidle, C. and Sanaghan, P. 1998. *High Impact Tools and Activities for Strategic Planning*. New York: McGraw-Hill.

Nolan, T.M., Goodstein, L.D. and Goodstein, J. 2008. *Applied Strategic Planning: An Introduction*. San Francisco: Pfeiffer.

Pablo, A.L. 1994. Determinants of acquisition integration level: A decision-making perspective. *Academy of Management Journal*, 37, 803–36.

Papadakis, V.M. 2005. The role of broader context and the communication program in merger and acquisition implementation success. *Management Decision*, 43, 236–55.

Pfeffer, J. 2005. Producing sustainable competitive advantage through the effective management of people. *Academy of Management Executive*, 19 (4), 95–106.

Podsakoff, P., MacKenzie, S., Moorman, R. and Fetter, R. 1990. Transformational leader behaviors and their effects on followers' trust in leader, satisfaction, and organizational citizenship behaviors. *The Leadership Quarterly*, 1, 107–42.

Porter, M.E. 1998. *Competitive Strategy: Techniques for Analyzing Industries and Competitors*. New York: The Free Press.

Salame, R. 2006. Why do mergers fail? *Key Strategy* [online, January] Available at: http://www.peoplemix.com/documents/articles/Why%20Do%20Mergers%20Fail.pdf [accessed: 1 April 2009].

Sales, A.L. and Mirvis, P.H. 1984. When cultures collide: Issues in acquisition. In *Managing Organizational Transitions*, edited by J.R. Kimberly and R.E. Quinn. Homewood, IL: Irwin, 107–33.

Saks, A.M. 2006. Antecedents and consequences of employee engagement. *Journal of Managerial Psychology*, 21 (7), 600–19.

Schweiger, D.M. and DeNisi A.S. 1991. Communication with employees following a merger: A longitudinal field experiment. *Academy of Management Journal*, 34, 110–35.

Schweiger, D.M. and Goulet, P.K. 2000. Integrating mergers and acquisitions: An international research review. In *Advances in Mergers and Acquisitions*, edited by C. Cooper and A. Gregory. New York: JAI Press, 61–91.

Schuler, R. and Jackson, S. 2001. HR issues and activities in mergers and acquisitions. *European Management Journal*, 19, 239–253.

Schein, E.H. 1985. *Organizational Culture and Leadership*. San Francisco: Jossey-Bass.

Stahl, G.K. and Voigt, A. 2008. Do cultural differences matter in mergers and acquisitions? A tentative model and examination. *Organization Science*, 19 (1), 160–76.

Taylor, P. 2006. Sprint Nextel in shake-up of senior staff. *Financial Times* [online, 22 August] Available at: http://www.ft.com/cms/s/33404e74-31fc-11db-ab06-0000779e2340.html [accessed: 13 March 2009].

Weber, Y., Shenkar, O. and Raveh, A. 1996. National and corporate cultural fit in mergers/acquistions: An exploratory study. *Management Science*, 42 (8), 1215–27.

Wheelen, T.L. and Hunger, J.D. 2008. *Concepts in Strategic Management and Business Policy*. 11th edition. Upper Saddle River, New Jersey: Pearson Education, Inc.

Whittington, J.L., Goodwin, V.L. and Murray, B. 2004. Transformational leadership, goal difficulty, and task design: Independent and interactive effects on employee outcomes. *The Leadership Quarterly*, 15 (5) 593–606.

Withenshaw, J. 2003. Successful termination. *Canadian Manager*, 28 (3), 20–4.

Yammarino, F. and Bass, B. 1990. Transformational leadership and multiple levels of analysis. *Human Relations*, 43, 975–95.

# 10 Integration Due Diligence: Setting the Stage for Value Creation

PROFESSOR L. JAY BOURGEOIS III AND HENNING HOEBER
*Tayloe Murphy International Center, Darden School, University of Virginia, United States*

## Integration – M&A's Favorite Trip Wire

Mergers and acquisitions (M&A) are an important ingredient of a company's broader corporate strategy and can be a major contributor to growing the business. However, they are quite complex in nature. A typical corporate acquisition process consists of several interrelated steps, including M&A strategy development, target identification, due diligence, valuation analysis, deal negotiation and post-merger integration (PMI).

Each of these steps is geared towards the creation of shareholder value *via* business combinations that provide cost reduction, revenue enhancement, or otherwise improved competitive position. Value creation in this context means 'increasing the expected free cash flows of the combined entities beyond current expectations',[1] so that, in the end, the gains exceed the transaction costs. However, it is not until the PMI phase that the sought-after synergies can be realized, which makes PMI a critical step in a M&A transaction. This is where value is actually captured, while all the other steps are primarily a necessary preparation for closing the deal.

PMI is also the trickiest part of a merger. If the buyer is not able to cash in on a deal's synergies and fails to make the combined entity worth more than its original components, the transaction is generally considered unsuccessful. And indeed the number of unsuccessful M&As is alarmingly high. Approximately 65 to 85 per cent of all mergers fail to create value.[2] While there are a myriad of reasons why mergers are not successful, in many cases the reason is simple: a failure to develop and execute an appropriate PMI strategy.

But why do so many well-intended and promising acquisitions flounder on PMI? Part of the problem is that this area simply tends not to get the attention it deserves and the consequences can be devastating in terms of value destruction.

This is where due diligence can help, by x-raying a prospect merger candidate in detail. Until recently, this process was generally associated with supplying information for the assessment of strategic fit and valuation analysis. But the information collected in the due

---

1    Goedhart, M., Koller T. and Wessels, D. 2005. *Valuation: Measuring and Managing the Value of Companies.* 4th Edition. Hoboken: John Wiley & Sons, 432.

2    Sirower, M.L. 1997. *The Synergy Trap: How Companies Lose the Acquisition Game.* New York: Free Press, 145–166.

diligence process can also help to assess the target's integratability and the potential deal breakers associated with the PMI process. However, only few corporations take advantage of their data collection and the results of target investigation to actually synthesize them to evaluate, in advance, if merger value can be achieved during integration, and, if so, what steps and level of effort will be required.

Against this background, our chapter aims at providing the reader with a basic understanding on how to conduct integration due diligence in order to increase the chances of value creation. Armed with detailed upfront insights into the challenges and requirements of post-merger management, a buyer is more likely to hit the ground running on Day 1.

## The PMI Pyramid

In business combinations, there are four areas that cause the majority of a merger's challenges, and therefore, require special attention during the pre-closing due diligence. We label theses areas as strategy, architecture, plumbing and wiring, and culture. Together they make up what we call the PMI Pyramid, as shown in Figure 10.1. The pyramid's components should be the focal points of integration due diligence, and their analysis can tell the buyer where to focus the firm's efforts in the integration process.

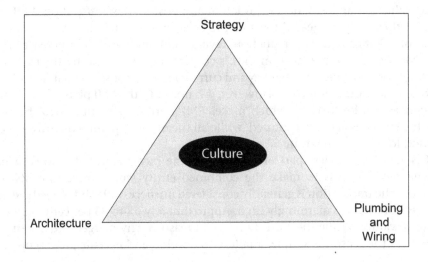

**Figure 10.1 The PMI Pyramid**

### STRATEGY

Strategy should be the guiding light of any M&A transaction. Determining what a corporation wants to buy should be deeply rooted in an understanding of the current business(es) it operates or plans to operate, the basis of competition and value drivers of the respective industries and the acquirer's existing overarching strategies.[3] This understanding is critical for adjusting a current, or finding a new, strategy for the combined entity that contributes to the achievement of post-acquisition value.

All M&A transactions need a broad roadmap that highlights the objectives of each deal. The PMI then must assure the strategic interplay of the two companies to reach these goals. In this context, the pre-closing due diligence is often the only chance to evaluate the viability of a corporation's M&A strategy and its chances for realizing value creation.

Mergers can take a variety of forms and understanding what kind of merger a firm is undertaking can help in the formulation of an appropriate integration strategy. One of the ways in which a target can be classified strategically is according to the degree of its relatedness to the acquirer's core business. Figure 10.2 categorizes acquisitions in terms of closeness to the buyer's current business. These classifications represent ideal or pure forms; different deals may include different elements of each category, but the spectrum may help one get a sense of where a particular deal falls. In addition, if buyers have completed other mergers, or plan to complete additional deals, they can assess what is being gained by locating those deals on this spectrum.

These classifications provide a broad-stroke understanding of what types of mergers there are, and they may help identify some general challenges to expect after completing a deal.

## Buying the competition

The mergers that aim at altering the industry structure in a way that is favorable to the buyer are mostly found in mature and capital-intense industries, which suffer from slow growth, limited possibilities for organic expansion and a high degree of rivalry and

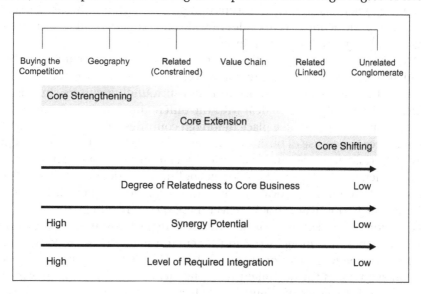

**Figure 10.2 Acquisitions by Degree of Relatedness to Core Business**

3     Harding, D. and Rovit, S. 2004. *Mastering the Merger: Four Critical Decisions That Make or Break the Deal.* Boston: Harvard Business School Publishing, 35.

overcapacity. As a consequence, the acquirer tries to gain scale, improve pricing, or take capacity out of the market. The buyer is usually very familiar with the terrain and the targets available. If the buyer is simply acquiring assets (factories) or locations (retail) and consolidating capacity, as opposed to intellectual capital, the PMI can be a straightforward asset consolidation with relatively little concern for human capabilities or culture. If, however, the buyer is acquiring labor-intensive competitors (for example, banks), it may be difficult to integrate a well established competitor, with its own corporate culture, values and objectives, which all tend to be deeply embedded in both the target's operating procedures and workforce. Both are likely to be changed and/or reduced, so an acquirer should be prepared for resistance. It is important to note that the amount of information supplied to the buyer in the pre-closing due diligence process may be very limited due to competitive concerns of the target or seller. This deal, therefore, entails additional challenges for the acquiring party.

Critical questions for the buyer's integration due diligence should include: Are the cultures of the firms likely to create rivalry? What is the target's basis of competition and under which business model do they operate? Do these two factors need fundamental adjustment? Will the target firm be upset about 'losing out' to a competitor? Is it useful to preserve the target's characteristics or absorb its operations completely? How will the buyer deal with overlaps in operations?

## Geography

Once a company has consolidated its position in the home markets and, as organic growth opportunities or promising local acquisition targets get scarcer, a next logical step is to pursue either adjacent domestic territory or international growth. In most cases of cross-border acquisitions in the same industry, the operating units remain local, usually due to local customer relationships, distribution or transportation issues. These deals are designed to bring the acquirer economies of scale and scope and are associated with the first steps in building international industry players.

In PMI, the overarching and streamlined processes of the acquirer can often be implemented right away, and the target may welcome any enhanced efficiency. But the buyer walks a thin line when it comes to issues surrounding culture. In this category, an acquirer may not only have to deal with the different corporate culture of the target. 'Geography' acquisitions can take place in foreign countries, and the local characteristics can also influence the course of business and pace of integration. The more dissimilar the countries' cultures, the more sensitively the integration team must approach its tasks, particularly when historical, religious or geopolitical considerations come into play. A thorough understanding of local customs and regulations is crucial for success. The staffing of an integration team should reflect these special requirements.

Key questions include: What local laws and regulations need to be considered? Does the buyer's business model work in that environment? How are local competitors different from the buyer's traditional competitors? How is the acquirer perceived in the foreign country? Who is the key talent with knowledge of the local markets? Can local management work together efficiently with headquarters? Will the integration team and any dispatched managers need special training? Is the buyer able to handle foreign exchange exposure?

Both the 'buying the competition' and 'geography' categories have a common underlying intent; they aim at strengthening the core business of a company.

## Related–constrained

These acquisitions consider targets with linkages to the buyer in markets, products and/or technology (MPT). An example for illustrating the logic of related-constrained expansion is BIC, a leading manufacturer of disposable low-cost plastic items, namely ballpoint pens, cigarette lighters and shavers. BIC started with an inexpensive, yet reliable ballpoint pen designed for mass production. After successfully marketing its product in Europe, BIC acquired US manufacturing capacity via the Waterman Pen Company. The two key components of the pens were injection-molded plastics (for the casing) and precision metal (for the tip and ballpoint). Instead of high-end stationery stores, drugstores were the primary outlets for the BIC pen. When BIC designed a non-refillable butane lighter, the product had linkages through markets and technology, as it was also sold in drugstores and made of injection-molded plastics and precision metal. The same proved true for BIC's disposable razor. With every new product introduced, BIC preserved the MPT linkages with its original ballpoint pen. But when the company tried to market disposable pantyhose through grocery stores, it failed, as not a single linkage to the core skills – plastic molding, precision metal manipulation and marketing through drugstores – existed.

The linkages of two firms must be clearly identified before a deal closes, as PMI leverages them for value creation. Therefore, issues that need to be addressed during integration due diligence are: Are the linkages sufficient in number and strong enough to justify the purchase? How does the buyer choose the best practices of each firm and apply them to the newly merged entity? How easily are the company's capabilities transferable to, or from, a target company? Where can the buyer lever its core skills in the business? Are the resources in place for applying a respective technology? Is the sales force capable of selling a different product to its existing clients?

## Value chain

Value chain acquisitions are relatively straightforward in their nature, but difficult to complete. In vertical transactions, bringing together two firms with different positions in the extraction, production, assembly and distribution chain can result in a more secure supply and efficient co-ordination of the different stages, while costs of communication, bargaining cost, costs of monitoring, compliance and enforcement costs decline in such a setting.[4] Apart from these cost-related issues, the buyer may also have simply detected that more value is added or appropriated in the 'upstream' or 'downstream' parts of the value chain. What makes these deals difficult is the fact that normally a supplier or customer of a firm operates in a different environment and with different technologies and business models. A car manufacturer may buy products from an electronics chip company on a regular basis, but that does not automatically mean that it is capable of running this supplier efficiently after a backward-integrating acquisition.

---

4    Arnold, G. 2005. *Handbook of Corporate Finance: A Business Companion to Financial Markets, Decisions & Techniques.* Harlow: FT Prentice Hall, 264.

Post-merger integration mainly has to deal with getting the interface of the two companies right. Integration due diligence should, therefore, answer the following questions: What does each respective firm need to learn about the new business it is entering? Is it more sensible to allow the target firm to operate as an independent business entity? What should and should not be integrated? Who will manage the interface of the companies? Is the buyer able to effectively monitor the target's operations and management? Will the target's relationships with other, competing customers be maintained? If not, how will excess capacity issues be addressed?

The related-constrained and value chain categories constitute an intent of extending one's core or supporting it.

## Related–linked

Related-linked acquisitions show some elements of conglomerate diversification, yet they are not completely unrelated to a company's original core business. These deals are more about pushing the business frontier further and further, based on a (loose) common thread. The reason these acquisitions form a separate category lies in their tempting nature. Management may justify deal-making strategies to unite several companies under one umbrella on the basis of common underlying theme. But there can be huge differences in the interpretation of a common thread and if management pushes the frontiers of this common thread too far, it may destroy value, because the acquisitions cannot be webbed into the corporate whole. Consider two examples of related-linked expansion for illustration.

A valid theme-based diversification strategy was implemented by easyGroup. Tracing back its origins to 1995, when the budget airline easyJet was incorporated, the group constantly pushed forward the low-cost thread and applied it to car rentals, internet cafés, cinemas, cruises, hotels and office space. easyGroup used its skills in yield management, cost structure improvement, business model transfer and branding ('easy' brand) to successfully expand operations based on a common no-frills thread.

Now take Yamaha, originally a musical instruments manufacturer with a strong focus on pianos. From its experience in piano-making, Yamaha developed capabilities in bending, manipulating and laminating woods (for piano cabinets), the engineering of sound (tones) and in marketing and distributing pianos.[5] Yamaha subsequently applied these to guitars and drums, both made of wood, and distributed them through its traditional channel, namely music retailers. The sound engineering skills associated with the manufacturing of acoustic musical instruments led the company to enter other electronic musical instruments businesses, such as keyboards and synthesizers. Following its success in musical instruments, Yamaha began to diversify by making a multitude of sideline products that shared unique materials or manufacturing techniques with its piano business, such as skis, tennis rackets, and furniture.[6] Similarly, from the relatively high-margin electronic-organ business, the company branched into the cutthroat competition of television, VCRs, and audio-equipment production.[7] With only manufacturing-

5    Bourgeois, L.J. and Spreadbury, A.W. 1994. *Yamaha Corporation and the Electronic Musical Instruments Industry.* Darden Case, UVA-BP-0348, 3.

6    Schlender, B.R. 1993. Yamaha: The Perils of Losing Focus. *Fortune*, 127 (10), 100.

7    Schlender, B.R. 1993. Yamaha: The Perils of Losing Focus. *Fortune*, 127 (10), 100.

related capabilities supporting these businesses, Yamaha Corporation did not fare well. Top executives, well-versed in the musical instruments market, were not able to move aggressively on less-familiar turf and Yamaha's diversity of operations grew to be a problem because independent-minded divisions failed to pool resources and expertise.[8]

Therefore, buyers can cross a risky threshold when it comes to related-linked acquisitions. They must know exactly what they are buying and how an acquisition with a greater distance from its core, will create value in the overall corporate portfolio. As a consequence, questions a buyer should ask when performing integration due diligence should include: What kind of relationship (direct or indirect) does this acquisition represent? How can we leverage this relationship during the PMI? Is the buyer moving too far away from its core business? Does the buyer (really) have the capabilities to compete in the new industry? Can management handle a new industry and deal with its competitive dynamics?

## Unrelated conglomerate

Most diversified corporations started off as single-business firms. As time passed, these firms ventured into related businesses and eventually added unrelated business units. Classic examples include American firms General Electric and Tyco International, German Siemens, Korean Hyundai or the Tata Group of India. With the expansion into other lines of business, the need arises for 'the overall plan for a diversified company' that 'makes the corporate whole add up to more than the sum of its business unit parts'.[9] In plain language this means corporate strategy has to create value. Unrelated acquisitions have to deal with problems similar to the ones found in the related-linked category. Only here, the synergy potential is even smaller, if existent at all. Integration is therefore often limited to the establishment of an adequate information flow between business units and headquarters, human capital development, capital budgeting issues and the channeling of resources into divisions.

PMI-related questions for due diligence include: Is there any need for (partial) integration? Should this acquisition be treated as a bolt-on? Does culture matter? How can the headquarters create value? Can the acquirer create more value than any other potential buyer? Does the buyer have enough qualified business unit managers to lead the new portfolio company? How will the unit be linked to other operations in the conglomerate structure?

Related-linked and unrelated conglomerate are part of a firm's intent to shift away from its core.

To know exactly where the deal is positioned on the grid is quite important. A buyer must be clear about the strategic objectives of an acquisition in order to check during the integration due diligence how viable it will be to achieve these goals. Otherwise, the merger will run into trouble later. Consider the merger of AOL and Time Warner. Although both firms conceived the merger as related-constrained (complementary products), in reality, the merger fell somewhere between value chain (one firm supplying another) and related-linked (establishing a platform in a new industry). AOL's main line of business

---

8    Bourgeois, L.J. and Spreadbury, A.W. 1994. *Yamaha Corporation and the Electronic Musical Instruments Industry.* Darden Case, UVA-BP-0348, 3.

9    Porter, M.E. 1987. From competitive advantage to corporate strategy. *Harvard Business Review*, 65 (3), 43–59, 43.

was the delivery of internet access, whereas Time Warner provided various forms of visual media and entertainment. Although they identified a number of opportunities for synergies and expansion, the two firms failed to recognize that value-chain integrations are among the most difficult to complete due to differences in technologies, differences in economic models, and by implication, differences in culture. These differences were glossed over, and unfortunately, both firms failed to gather sufficient information about the true business practices of the other firm. With an inadequate starting point for the deal, the integration efforts were focused on the wrong spots. A solid pre-closing due diligence process, with a focus on the strategic issues, would have prevented this merger failure.

As shown in Figure 10.2, from an acquisition's position on the line, generalized assumptions can be made in advance about the synergy potential and the degree of integration required. The further a buyer moves away from its core business, the lower the expected synergies. While one can achieve considerable economies of scale and revenue-enhancing synergies when buying a competitor, additions to a conglomerate's portfolio will generally exhibit few possibilities for cost savings. One's integration due diligence should locate where the value creation potential in each deal is located and how it can be unlocked in the PMI process.

The degree of integration required also decreases as one moves from the left to the right. To achieve the benefits of scale and scope, related businesses will have to be tightly integrated into the existing operations, as opposed to unrelated acquisitions that tend to be operated independently, mostly under a holding structure. These different requirements for autonomy should be reflected in the buyer's integration approach.

A commonly utilized framework in strategic due diligence are the 'Four Cs' of costs, customers, competitors and capabilities[10] which are used to assess the full potential of an acquisition.

A first step is to analyze a target's cost position relative to the competition and the buyer's own business. Integration due diligence determines the means required to achieve the potential cost synergies. For example, for an underperforming product line in the target, the integration team should be prepared for layoffs, internal employee replacements, their legal consequences, or – in the case of an entire division – a full-scale divestiture, preferably with a potential buyer already in hand.

A target's customers are the source for revenue-enhancing synergies and top-line growth. But there is a real threat of losing customers during the sometimes unavoidable disruptions of a merger. Once the target's most important customers have been identified during due diligence, the integration task force should contact key clients to pacify possible worries and explain the benefits of the merger to them.

Analyzing competitors is another essential step. A company should anticipate and counter how competitors will take advantage of any post-merger chaos. In the 'fog of the merger' the competition will try to capture market share or lure key talent away. To avoid these often irreversible side-effects, the integration team must disburden line managers, enabling them to maintain the firepower in the core business operations, and develop attractive employee retention plans.

---

10    Cullinan, G., Le Roux, J.-M. and Weddigen, R.-M. 2004. When to walk away from a deal. *Harvard Business Review*, 82 (4), 96–104.

Capability analysis is often the most overlooked factor in due diligence. A competitive advantage built solely on physical and tangible resources has a short half life. In contrast, organizational capabilities embedded in routines, tacit knowledge, customer and community relationships and intellectual capital provide more sustainable competitive advantages. But they are fragile. Therefore, it is an essential task of integration due diligence to determine what capabilities exist, which ones can be transferred to, or from, the target and what kind of capability transfer is the dominant source of value creation.[11] However, capability analysis can be much more difficult than the other three Cs, as these capabilities reside mostly within people. Therefore, one must detect, very early on, precisely where these critical capabilities are located. The PMI team then needs to prepare a detailed plan how to retain the key sources of the strategic capabilities and develop a blueprint on how to efficiently transfer them to, or from, the target without destroying them in the process. Failing on these issues of capability detection and retention may put at risk the benefits of an entire acquisition, especially in research-driven industries like biotechnology, medical devices or alternative energies.

The upper corner of the PMI Pyramid provides insights into the necessary strategic interplay of the two units, which is derived from the target's relationship to the buyer's core business and based upon the strategic intent of the transaction. Integration due diligence prepares this interplay that is ultimately achieved in the PMI process and checks how sustainable the business model and strategic positioning of the target are and how they will improve the acquirer's competitive abilities.

## ARCHITECTURE

In order to release the full potential of a combined entity, its former components have to be aligned properly. The architecture focus of integration due diligence provides information on which organizational arrangement is best suited to unlock merger value.

Once buyers have thought about where the deal falls on the larger map, they must dig a bit deeper and determine how much of the other firm should be integrated. One mistake many firms make is to assume that all parts of the target must be integrated into its new parent, or, conversely, that the target should be kept at arm's length. But not all acquisitions are alike. Figure 10.3 illustrates common organizational arrangements and highlights changes in target identity, as well as the type of relationship between firms that might emerge when differences in the acquisition strategy are considered.

The degree of integration must be tailored to the needs of the firms involved. For example, one would expect conglomerates or private equity firms to hold their various units separately, whereas in an industry-consolidating acquisition of a competitor, one would expect the absorption that accompanies taking excess capacity out of the system. However, finding the right arrangement cannot await Day 1 (closing). The integration team should use the time and information of the due diligence process to develop the appropriate integration approach and have the necessary action plans ready for execution on Day 1.

---

11    Haspeslagh, P.C. and Jemison, D.B. 1991. *Managing Acquisitions: Creating Value Through Corporate Renewal*. New York: Free Press, 142.

**Figure 10.3 Common Organizational Arrangements**

| Organizational Arrangement | Degree of Integration | Target Identity | Relationship to or with the Acquirer/ Parent |
| --- | --- | --- | --- |
| Hold | None: Maintain separate organizational entities/business units | Target remains autonomous; however, influence is exerted if necessary | Cash and information move between the respective firms |
| Retain/Preserve | Limited: Merge back office, install control systems, but keep separate product lines/ unique characteristics | Target's original identity remains to a large extent, but control and internal structures change | Transfer or exchange of best practices, financial and management support |
| Absorb | Full: Merge staff and field employees, impose the acquirer's standards and practices | Target identity is lost and replaced by the acquirer's identity | Takeover |
| Meld | Hybrid: Create a new organizational entity from the original companies | New identity is created for the combined entity | Partnership/ Amalgamation |

Standardized approaches of PMI are well-suited for matters of speed and efficiency, especially in the case of serial acquirers. But, however handy they may be, standardized integration does not mean 'let's make them look like us' and it surely does not exonerate a buyer from thorough integration due diligence.

A future organizational structure should reflect the company's basis of competition and the challenges associated with the industries it competes in. Management should not insist on old structures, but pick the organizational framework that will offer the most efficient management and ease in leadership on the one hand; while on the other hand, the new approach to organizing the company should match the new scale, reach and combined markets. If, for example, the products the new entity manufactures have a similar use across regions or countries, or if they are more specialized and have targeted user groups, management may opt for a product-based approach towards organization. In the case of varying consumer tastes, different forms of use and peculiarities across borders, which result in different sales methods, the integration team might want to propose a geography-based approach. In the first alternative, the product manager would have profit and loss responsibility, while in the latter, the country manager would be accountable for the results of the operations. A thorough due diligence that links organizational and market requirements is key to avoid picking the wrong institutional design for the corporation.

However, structures cannot live by themselves; they need to be filled with people to work. If the merger does require personnel reorganization or a shifting of responsibilities, integrators should identify and promote champions and supporters of the change, as well as, identify and remove detractors. For example, if a firm is acquiring another firm and the (obstructionist) CEO of the target wields a great deal of power and influence over his or her employees, the buyer CEO may need to remove him or her from a position of authority to get buy-in from those employees. Similarly, if there are executives within the buyer's own organization who are anti-merger or who are trying to undermine the shifts in power and influence, they may need to be removed. The integration due diligence must assess key personnel to the largest possible extent for their integrity and for their support of the acquisition.

Pharmaceutical giant GlaxoSmithKline, born from the merger between Glaxo Wellcome and SmithKline Beecham in 2000, learned the value of promoting pro-integration leadership after the first attempt to combine the companies failed in 1998. During the first round of negotiations, the two firms were unable to reach consensus on who should run the newly combined entity, resulting in a complete breakdown of the merger talks. In 2000, realizing their past mistakes, the CEOs of both firms agreed to a mutually-beneficial leadership transition plan to ensure successful completion of the merger. SmithKline's CEO, Jan Leschly, agreed to step down, allowing his second-in-command, Jean-Pierre Garnier, to become chief executive of the new company. At the same time, Glaxo Wellcome's CEO, Richard Sykes, agreed to become chairman of the newly-merged firm with the understanding that he would retire after two years. This plan allowed both firms' management teams to get what they wanted and complete the integration.[12]

When planning a PMI strategy, firms should emphasize urgency. For example, serial acquirer Cisco always ensures that integrations happen quickly so that political troubles and jockeying are avoided or minimized. Similarly, GE Capital warns against the dangers of slow change as uncertainty may lead to decreased morale and also compromise the likelihood that synergies will be realized.

The task of amalgamating two formerly independent businesses and reorganizing them for the maximum benefit of the combination is not easy, and – making the task even more challenging – the decisions made are often difficult to reverse. Providing a solid understanding of the new company's structural needs and human resources (HR) requirements is, therefore, a critical task of a buyer's integration due diligence.

## PLUMBING AND WIRING

Plumbing and wiring (P&W) concerns connecting the original entities of a merger to make them operational. But because of its unglamorous nature, the need for P&W due diligence often gets overlooked in the acquisition process. Processes of inbound logistics, manufacturing, distribution and support functions must be reviewed and checked for their compatibility. This is especially the case for deals that aim at core strengthening or core extension, as there can be significant process overlaps or the need to connect operations.

In addition, the best practices that the other firm brings to the table should be considered early for incorporation into the buying firm's strategy. Consider, for example CEMEX, a Mexican cement producer and well-oiled M&A machine. Having completed over 40 deals since the late 1960s, with each acquisition the company adopted new best

---

12    BBC News. 2000. Merger's Troubled History. [Online, 17 January]. Available at: http://news.bbc.co.uk/2/hi/ business/606677.stm [accessed: 3 February 2009].

practices from each of the target firms. CEMEX's interdisciplinary teams worked closely together with the target firm's employees and managers on a so-called 'business process gap analysis'.[13] After comparing the processes, the superior processes from the target were not only retained, but disseminated company-wide. Today, more than half of CEMEX's current standardized business processes have come from previously acquired companies.[14] This approach not only captures the benefits of faster integration and more rapid cost savings, if an acquisition is in fact undertaken, but also actively involves the target's workforce and values the company's legacy.[15]

Furthermore, integration due diligence must investigate what needs to be in place and ready to go on Day 1, so the merger can indeed happen and all stakeholders can understand what is happening. Will the merged firms need a completely new global directory so employees can contact each other? Will they need new signs and stationery so customers will know about the new corporate entity? Will the infrastructure need to be merged so e-mails and telephone lines work smoothly? How will titles be reshuffled? New corporate e-mail addresses, business cards and the occupancy of office space also fall into this area. Considerations such as these could easily fall by the wayside if not considered well in advance.

These issues may seem relatively insignificant at a first glance, but they must not be underestimated. Job titles are a favorite source of clashes and friction. Downgrading a Managing Director to an Executive Director or Vice-president under the new corporate structure can have severe impacts on the self-image of this employee and may lead them to leave the company. The same often goes for such prestige perks and benefits as company cars. Integration due diligence must check if any of these issues may become a major deal breaker.

Within the new organization, information must reach the intended audience to influence decisions. Furthermore, performance must be perceived and interpreted consistently throughout the combined entity in order to compare achievements and progress on an apples-to-apples basis. Therefore, an appropriate Management Information System (MIS) has to be in place, as soon after the acquisition as possible. Integration due diligence must take a close look at how difficult it will be to merge different systems and the amount of training required for employees to get acquainted with the new standards. In the broader IT area, hardware needs to be connected and system software must be aligned. Integration due diligence must estimate the degree of compatibility and the cost associated with system upgrades.

The same goes for reward systems, pension and benefit programs. As most employees process events and information through the WIFM (what's in it for me) filter, compensation issues must be resolved and communicated on Day 1 in order to prevent uncertainty among the workforce and to combat headhunting from competitors. Integration due diligence should review the target's policies in these areas as soon as possible in order to estimate any additional post-merger costs for the buyer or for the validation of compensation-based synergy estimates.

13    Casanova, L. and Hoeber, H. 2009. *CEMEX (A) – Building a Global Latina*. INSEAD Case, 308-380-1, 9.

14    Austin, M. 2004. Global Integration the CEMEX Way. TheDeal.com [Online, 15 February]. Available at: http://www.thedeal.com/corporatedealmaker/2004/02/global_integration_the_cemex_w.php [accessed: 8 May 2009].

15    Casanova, L. and Hoeber, H. 2009. *CEMEX (A) – Building a Global Latina*. INSEAD Case, 308-380-1, 9.

Operational, HR and organizational due diligence will supply a great deal of information on the P&W area of integration due diligence, but whenever possible, it should be complemented with interviews and conversations with the target's workforce in order to get a first-hand impression of the post-merger expectations. However, in the pre-merger phase, access to target employees may be limited.

To ensure that the pace of a possible integration is considered in advance, the acquiring firm should form timelines and map them out. The sequence of events may matter a great deal and formulating a timeline can help an integration team and senior executives keep track of progress, as indecision can be very expensive. There is value in executing decisions quickly with the information available rather than waiting to see if the choices made will be absolutely correct. In this context, integration due diligence should also already be thinking about the metrics that will be used to evaluate PMI performance. If the right work is done ahead of time, integration can be completed swiftly and successfully.

## CULTURE

Culture is in the center of the pyramid because it relates to all the other areas and is, concurrently, the most difficult area to observe and resolve. As PMI efforts focus on the nuts and bolts of integration strategy, such as the architecture of reorganization or the strategic interplay, one must not lose sight of the fact that the 'softer' areas of integration can matter a great deal as well. In fact, cultural mismatch can lead to very painful and dramatic failures. A critical part of the integration due diligence process is to truly understand how the organization with which a corporation is merging operates and to be aware of the values that drive its management and employees.

It can be difficult to evaluate culture, especially in the pre-closing phase, but much of the evaluation will come from candid conversations, interviews, and observations of the other firm. It is also important to consider how differences, and perhaps similarities, in culture will affect decisions at every level of the corporation. Integration due diligence must also evaluate the requirements of training and development for both cultural understanding, as well as functional understanding. If the cultures of the corporations mesh well, there is an increased likelihood that expected synergies will be realized sooner rather than later. Given the time value of money, this, of course, elevates the net present value of the synergies captured.

DaimlerChrysler provides an illustrative example of the problems that can arise from a culture clash among employees. The integration team invested much time and money trying to help employees understand the differences between American and German culture, but the firm's real problems seemed to stem from differences in management perceptions and business practices. The firms championed different values, had different compensation structures, and ultimately, had very different philosophies about how to brand their products.[16] Although there is no question that understanding the differences between cultures in the traditional sense is critical, it is also important to realize that culture also includes business practices and routines, firm values, and management and employee attitudes. A thorough integration-focused due diligence conducted before

---

16    Finkelstein, S. 2002. *The DaimlerChrysler Merger.* [Online: Tuck School of Business at Dartmouth]. Available at: http://mba.tuck.dartmouth.edu/pdf/2002-1-0071.pdf [accessed: 3 February 2009].

the closing may have detected the true sources and the entire scope of culture-related problems that Daimler, as the acquiring firm, eventually faced.

Cultural due diligence is a relatively new area of the due diligence process, as previously cultural issues had been neglected. In the facts-oriented world of takeovers, culture seemed somewhat displaced and too soft for serious consideration. But these soft factors can deliver a hard punch when it comes to value creation, or conversely, destruction. Integration teams should invest time conducting a thorough due diligence on the other firm's culture and ways of doing business. However, integration due diligence should also involve investigating one's own firm, culture and processes in order to determine if the buyer fits the target's needs. This is especially true in situations where the value of both companies resides in specific organizational capabilities, intellectual assets or human capital, which is often observable in professional-service industries, such as consulting, law or advertising.

One approach to consider is writing down both firms' Top 10 Decision Rules.[17] Most firms have some ingrained way of doing business that may not always be readily obvious or readily articulated. Taking the time to clarify the firms' implicit decision-making rules can help determine whether the buying firm's values are compatible with those of the target. Also, understanding one's own decision-making rules could help an integration team create a strategy that is customized for its stakeholders. In case the buyer cannot get the necessary information on the other firm's decision rules during the pre-closing phase, the integration due diligence should work with a best-guess approach based on observable behavior or other informal sources.

Another part of going to school on one's own firm is the evaluation of a company's M&A history and the implications these deals have had on the firm's culture, processes and strategies. If the buying firm has gone after other acquisitions and mergers in the past or shifted lines of business, it should consider mapping the strategies and moves employed in the past and essentially 'connecting the dots.' Very few intended strategies are actually realized, but in the process, new strategies emerge. Connecting emergent strategies and identifying patterns can help a company determine what is missing from its own organization, as well as what skills, products, and expertise are available to work with. This knowledge has direct implication for the integration due diligence.

## Integration Due Diligence: Another Function in the Company Screening Process?

In the course of an M&A process, the strategic acquisition justification or financial valuation analysis can paint an enticing picture of a takeover proposal, but at the end of the day, it is a target's integratability that makes or breaks the deal. Integration due diligence is about identifying the challenges and pitfalls of post-merger integration in the pre-closing phase.

But acquirers should not worry; they do not need a separate team for integration due diligence *per se*. Instead, an acquirer should put together a core team of experienced integration managers in the pre-closing phase that evaluates the critical issues for post-merger management in an integration due diligence, with a special focus on the PMI

---

17    Bourgeois, L.J. 1996. *Strategic Management: From Concept to Implementation*. Fort Worth: Dryden Press, 700–702.

Pyramid's components. During integration due diligence, the team can already detect potential threats in the four mentioned areas and their possible implications for the post-merger integration process. The PMI team must be informed of possible disturbances and sources of problems in advance to be able to deal with them once they surface. It is also important to avoid distracting surprises during the course of PMI in order to keep the edge in the daily operations. A buyer can simply not afford line managers to firefight avoidable post-merger problems. Potential stumbling blocks detected in an integration due diligence should be included in the integration plan in order to make a future transition as unobstructed as possible.

The team responsible for the evaluation of a target's integratability can draw on the information gathered in other areas of transactional due diligence. Strategic and operational due diligence are all about how, and where, to create significant value from the target in the future, or, in other words, how an acquirer will make more money from the business than the previous owner.[18] Organizational due diligence checks the institutional requirements and necessary framework for the future course of business, while cultural due diligence highlights the soft factors of business combinations. From this information, integration leaders can source what they need to prepare for post-merger integration and develop an awareness for the critical issues of a possible PMI process. After conducting integration due diligence, the PMI team will also be well-prepared for Day 1 and the actual integration implementation.

An acquiring company, therefore, just has to make sure that the integration team gets access to the information collected from the overall due diligence investigations. In this sense, integration due diligence is more an alignment of knowledge than another stand-alone function in the due diligence process, and it is critical that the buyer addresses PMI-related issues as soon as possible, in order to check if the merger value can be unlocked in the integration process at an affordable cost. In many successful acquisitions, members of the valuation team are on the PMI team and *vice-versa*.

18    Dickson, M. 2007. Where Diligence is Due. *Acquisition Finance Magazine* [Online], 5(12), 22–23. Available at: http://lek.skyworld.com/UserFiles/File/22_23ACQ_v5_12.pdf [accessed: 8 May 2009], 22.

# 11 *The Attributes of a Successful Acquisition Leader*

PROFESSOR ATHINA VASILAKI

*IÉSEG School of Management, Université Catholique de Lille, France*

## Background

This chapter investigates the leadership attributes and actions that can enhance post-acquisition organisational performance. It utilises an innovative and multi-disciplinary study initiative to identify and empirically investigate the effect that these attributes have on acquisition performance. Semi-structured interviews and questionnaires with chief executive officers that have undergone acquisitions were used to identify these leadership competencies and critical actions. This chapter, with this study as its foundation, contributes to the academic and practitioner communities in providing recommendations to chief executive officers and senior managers on the characteristics they should portray, and the actions that they should take, to ensure the success of the acquisition. It is among the first studies to place leadership in the context of acquisitions and hence, covers a gap in the literature. The results are of high importance to the due diligence process as chief executive officers and acquisition leaders will have an understanding of how they, through their personality, and the actions that they implement, can influence the success of the acquisition and thus, enhance the subsequent performance of the merger and/or acquisition strategy.

## Introduction

Acquisitions are an important vehicle for corporate profitability and growth. They enable firms to reduce their costs by achieving greater scale and they provide a mechanism by which firms gain access to new resources that produce operating efficiencies and increase revenues by changing the ways in which a firm operates (Anand *et al.* 2005). However, approximately 70 per cent of mergers and acquisitions (M&As) fail (Hitt *et al.* 2001). Previous research, has demonstrated that many M&As do not result in the benefits expected by the decision makers. In an attempt to understand the reasons for this high failure rate, M&A research has recently focused on managerial attributes and human resource activities (Datta 1991; Haspeslagh and Jemison 1991; Vaara 2002).

One of the reasons that M&As fail to achieve their intended synergies is lack of implementation skills, unclear vision and problematic leadership (Kay and Shelton 2000). This lack of skills is directly related to the due diligence process where organising for acquisitions takes place (Sudarsanam 2003). Most researchers agree that the success of the integration and implementation process starts with due diligence (Galpin and Herndon 2007). A due diligence process is an imperative process to ensure the success of the following stages of M&As (Galpin and Herndon 2007). In this process, a detailed investigation of the target company, as well as, plans for synergy realisation are developed. Due diligence supports valuation, negotiations, structuring and post-acquisition planning as investigators try to uncover as many risks as possible that could impede the success of the M&A.

One prominent issue in the due diligence process is the selection of the leader that will organise and implement the integration (Howson 2008; Schuler and Jackson 2003). This leader will provide the strategic direction, organise the resources for teams responsible for deal making and will direct these teams in order to deliver the firm's strategic objectives and shareholder value (Sudarsanam 2003).

The effect of leadership during M&As is a factor that can influence the acquisition's performance. Leadership plays a strategic role in organisational change designs as it demonstrates 'the ability to anticipate, envision, maintain flexibility and empower others to create strategic change as necessary' (Ireland and Hitt 2005: 63). In the case of M&As, it could be argued that effective leadership can lead to the success of the acquisition as the leader will be able to better manage any conflicts that may arise between employees, coordinate the integration of the two organisations, understand the organisational culture of the target organisation and try to integrate the departments and their respective policies and practices as smoothly as possible. Leadership due diligence allows an objective assessment of the qualities needed from senior managers to effectively implement the acquisition process. This process identifies a profile of individuals' capabilities against a range of general management competencies (Howson 2008) that could facilitate the value creation of the M&As.

However, the impact of leadership on the success of the acquisition has only been partially recognised by scholars and practitioners (Fubini et al. 2007). Although leadership, as a concept, is acknowledged in studies for acquisition performance, none of the scholars that have extensively studied acquisitions have investigated, articulated or explored the causal relationship between leadership and acquisition success (Sitkin and Pablo 2004). Therefore, there are inconsistencies and contradictions in the literature concerning the exact role leaders have in such a process and the influence that they have in managing change and achieving the harmonisation of the acquisition. Sitkin and Pablo (2004) argued that it would only be a slight exaggeration to suggest that scholars and practitioners have ignored the role of leadership in M&As success and failure.

Therefore, against this background, the present author initiated a study with the principle aim to investigate the attributes of a successful acquisition leader. In order to achieve this aim this study illustrated the relationship between different leadership attributes and subsequent acquisition performance. In doing so, this study aims to provide the attributes that a leader should have in order to implement a successful acquisition and to realise the expected synergies. There are two research questions that this study aims to address, namely:

1.  Which are the attributes of an acquisition leader?
2.  Which of these attributes enhance post-acquisition organisational performance?

In order to answer to these questions, this chapter first discusses the importance of leadership during the acquisition process and provides the justification for the significance of the study. Second, it describes methodology and data collection and finally, it provides a discussion of the results and the conclusion. It is important to point out that this study focuses on the role of acquiring leaders during the acquisition and the attributes and actions they should have in order to ensure the success of this process.

## Literature Review

Academics argue that acquisitions have not lived up to their potential in terms of increasing shareholder value and maximising wealth. Several researchers have found that less than half of all acquisitions meet their initial financial expectations (Covin *et al.* 1997; Hitt *et al.* 2001). The reasons attributed to the failure of the harmonisation of the acquisition, and the subsequent performance of the organisation, have been many and diverse.

Recent studies, however, point to the belief that human versus financial factors are among the root causes of acquisition failure (Covin *et al.* 1997; Marks and Mirvis 2001). The high degree of failures has been attributed to human-related problems (van Dick *et al.* 2006). Restructuring usually involves major organisational changes (such as shifts in corporate strategy) to meet new competition or market conditions, increased use of debt and a flurry of re-contracting with managers, employees, suppliers and customers (Gaughan 2002). This activity sometimes results in the expansion of resources devoted to certain areas, and at other times, in contractions involving plant closings, layoffs of top- and middle-level managers, staff and production workers and reduced compensation. Furthermore, conflicts of interests between employees of both firms may lead to loss of key talent, loss of productivity and, eventually, in a clash of management styles and egos between the two firms (Abedin and Davies 2007). As well, reasons such as loss of autonomy, self-interest and conflicting corporate cultures, in addition to, a lack of inspirational leadership have been attributed for causing failure (Haspeslagh and Jemison 1991; Sitkin and Pablo 2004).

An acquisition may also fail as acquirers often fail to plan and properly execute the integration of their targets, frequently neglecting the organisational, internal cultural (Lee and Alexander 1992) and human factors (Abedin and Davies 2007). The inability to manage the integration process results in the loss of opportunities for improving the performance by exploitation of the available synergies (Larsson and Finkelstein 1999). The task of integration, or achieving the organisational fit, encompasses several aspects. Datta (1991) found a very high correlation between the diversity of management styles and a poor post-acquisition performance. Thus, the managerial or organisational inability to manage and implement change, that is, to successfully integrate the two organisations can result in poor performance of the company and, eventually, failure to achieve the strategic objectives of the acquisition.

This organisational inability to manage the change process is attributed to a lack of inspirational leadership in the integration process. Haspeslagh and Jemison (1991) argued that problematic leadership, as well as, the lack of implementation skills of the acquiring leader can lead to difficulties in integrating the two organisations. Poor leadership during the acquisition process has also been associated with the poor integration of the management structures (Larsson and Finkelstein 1999), the failure to address cultural differences (Stahl and Voigt 2008) and poor communication (King *et al.* 2008). Fubini *et al.* (2007) argued that companies fail to acquire integration capabilities in order to achieve the acquisition objectives and this is due to poor leadership. Fubini *et al.* (2007) identified four common leadership challenges to be tackled for the achievement of 'corporate acquisition health', the most thorough and sustainable test of acquisition success, namely: communication, integration of the two organisational cultures, becoming an active champion for crucial external stakeholders and, lastly, continuous learning. Fubini *et al.* (2007) stated that if leaders fail to respond to these challenges, then the integration process will be complicated, with culture clashes and conflicts arising and the acquisition likely will not create the expected synergy. Similarly, Nemanich and Keller (2007) and Javidan *et al.* (2004) argued that most acquisitions fail to reach their objectives in the post-acquisition integration process due to the lack of charismatic and transformational leadership from the acquiring company. Therefore, clearly leadership is a challenge that should be taken into account when designing and implementing the integration process in order to reach the intended benefits of the acquisition.

Thus, leadership can be the key determinant or input influencing the outcome of a major strategic decision. Ashkenas and Francis (2000) argued that it is the leader's position of authority that facilitates the integration process. The role of leadership in acquisitions clearly draws upon particular sets of value- and knowledge-based capabilities that can help the organisation to be more effective (Sitkin and Pablo 2004). Kotter (1990) argued that leadership in acquisitions facilitates coherence and adaptability. Hitt *et al.* (2001) likewise argued that, with respect to achieving synergy, managerial actions are an essential foundation of the value-creation process.

Chief Executive Officers (CEOs) and other senior managers have an individual stock of skills, knowledge and resources that can shed light on the success of the post-acquisition performance. Kiessling and Harvey (2006) argued that leaders are viewed as critical to enhancing post-acquisition performance as they possess knowledge critical to ongoing business operations. Leaders can affect performance as they have the ability to motivate and direct these knowledge assets to their greatest potential. Finally, Goldman (2007) argued that acquisition success is also related to the strategic thinking capabilities of leaders. All these arguments point toward the important role of leadership in the acquisition context as it is vital to ensure acquisition success. Consequently, it is the leader that can successfully implement this change and it is imperative to investigate the attributes that help leaders to productively integrate the two organisations, the acquirer and the target. Overall, the leader's style is a central determinant of how a post-merger organisation will be managed. Therefore, it is important to investigate the attributes that make an effective leader, in this context, as effective leadership is clearly needed to effectively integrate two organisations.

Moreover, this study of leadership is of great importance for both the academic and practitioner communities. First, for the academic community, it places leadership in the context and process of acquisitions which, as mentioned earlier, had been previously underestimated or indeed ignored in the literature. Second, it provides guidelines for practitioners in order to develop the right capabilities and competencies to successfully implement and accomplish an acquisition strategy.

# Methodology

Two research questions, as discussed previously, have guided this study on leadership. The first research question investigates the attributes of an acquisition leader whereas the second explores the relationship between these attributes and post-acquisition organisational performance in order to test their effectiveness.

This first research question was investigated using semi-structured interviews. Twelve interviews took place asking CEOs, or other managers responsible for the execution of an acquisition, to describe the characteristics of a successful acquisition leader, as well as, the actions that this leader should take in order to ensure the smooth transition from a single company to a newly-combined organization. The semi-structured interviews lasted for approximately one hour and were conducted either face-to-face or over the phone (depending on the availability of the person interviewed). These semi-structured interviews were a very efficient way to allow the respondents to analyse and critique their own style, as well as, to talk about their experience as a leader who has undergone and completed an acquisition. The aim was for all interviewees to be given exactly the same context of questioning. According to Bryman and Bell (2006) all respondents should be given exactly the same interview stimulus as any other participant and this guideline would be strictly followed. The interviewees were given prompts or open questions that allowed them to describe the situation. Specifically, questions were asked about the events leading up to the acquisition, about the intentions, the implementation strategies and, finally, the synergistic benefits aimed for in the acquisition. For example, some questions were: 'How did you integrate the structure, systems and processes of the two organisations?'; 'How did you inspire commitment and sense of belonging to the new organisation?'; 'How did you manage cultural differences?'; 'How did you communicate with employees?'; 'What were the problems encountered during the acquisition?'; 'How were they solved?'; and, 'What actions did you take?'.

After the semi-structured interviews were completed, the researcher analysed the responses and identified the attributes and behaviours needed to ensure the success of the acquisition. This analysis investigated grouping similar items in different categories that included the interpersonal characteristics and demographics of the executives, as well as, the actions they took to ensure that the acquisition would be successful. The responses generated a list of 33 attributes and actions that were identified by the executives as critical success factors. These 33 attributes were later sent to a group of executives which had already undergone several acquisitions in order to conduct the pilot study. This pilot study enabled the researcher to establish the likelihood that the survey instrument would be completed by respondents in broadly similar circumstances to those of the pilot group and to establish that the questions were clear and easily understood.

This pilot questionnaire was forwarded to 20 CEOs. The researcher received twelve responses which were highly satisfactory given the nature of the research. Through the feedback received from the pilot questionnaire, the 33 items were further reduced to 20 as there were some redundant questions and some others had to be revised. This pilot study enabled the development of the final questionnaire instrument.

The next step was to identify potential respondents. The study's sample consisted of acquisitions made by British companies, with data collected via a postal questionnaire. To fully capture the creation of value in an acquisition and the synergistic benefits, as well as, the effect that specific leadership attributes have on acquisition performance, one should study acquisitions three to seven years after the completion of the transaction. Risberg (1999) argued that only then can the researcher ascertain if the acquisition was a success or not and measure the impact that it had on aspects of organisational performance. Therefore, only acquisitions that were completed between 2001 and 2004 were selected. This meant that the companies were almost fully-integrated, enabling the respondents to give a more detailed and objective account on the aspects of the post-acquisition integration process. This sample is of particular interest as it includes the latest M&As wave, which had not been thoroughly studied thus far.

The Bureau van Dijk database of acquisitions was used to search for the sample population. The search results indicated a total population of 1,056 companies that satisfied the selection criteria. The companies selected were from a variety of industries to increase external validity. Following further screening, out of the 1,056 companies, only 764 were finally selected. One crucial criterion was that the CEO of the acquiring company at the time of the acquisition was still employed at the same company. Several companies were responsible for more than one acquisition within this period. In order to avoid several questionnaires being sent to the executives of multiple acquirers, the single largest acquisition in terms of bid value for each acquirer was selected for inclusion in the survey sample. This was done from the data in FAME database that has information about the value of the deals and it was cross-referenced from the company's reports.

Usable responses were obtained from 139 acquisitions representing 18.7 per cent which is satisfactory given the sensitive nature of the questionnaire, the level of management queried and the low response rate in M&As survey research (Very *et al.* 1997). This response rate is consistent with those in other survey-based studies of post-acquisition strategy and performance.

The first part of the questionnaire asked the CEOs to rank the attributes and actions that foster the success of an acquisition. This part reflects the first research question. In order to analyse this data, descriptive statistics were used such as frequencies and means. To answer the second research question, CEOs were asked to express their satisfaction with post-acquisition organisational performance. In order to test the performance, both financial and non-financial indicators, were used. This research question was investigated using multiple regression analysis. The 20 leadership success factors identified in the earlier steps of the research were regressed against performance in order to find out which of these attributes were most significant in enhancing post-acquisition organisational performance.

## Results

Table 11.1 presents the results from the interviews and provides the answer to the first research question of this study, namely, 'Which are the attributes of an acquisition leader?'

It represents the 20 attributes and actions that leaders should take into account when executing an acquisition strategy. These items represent both characteristics of the leader, as well as, the actions that should take place in order to ensure the success of an acquisition. The items identified from the interviews can be divided in two categories: (i) the attributes of the leader; and (ii) the actions that should be implemented. Table 11.1 shows the attributes and actions listed according to their higher importance. Items 3,

5, 8, 12, 14, 17 and 18 refer to the leaders' characteristics, whereas the remaining items show the actions that they should take. From this table, it can be seen that the most important leadership attribute, in the context of acquisitions, is to provide clear vision, aims and guidelines for the acquisition, as well as, to set the example and become the role model for the employees to follow. As for personal characteristics, the most crucial is to be aware and sensitive to critical cultural differences and to be fair and objective while implementing a corporate acquisition strategy. The percentages represent the number of times these attributes and actions were mentioned by the CEOs as being imperative and critical for the acquisition success. It can be concluded that due to their high percentages, CEOs should demonstrate these characteristics and implement certain actions according to these guidelines in order for the acquisition to be successful.

The second research question investigated the impact that these variables have on post-acquisition organisational performance. Table 11.2 presents the regression results for the complete sample of 139 acquisitions. This regression analysis is exploratory in nature investigating which leadership attributes and actions are significantly associated with post-acquisition organisational performance. Out of the 20 items that were initially

**Table 11.1   Leadership Attributes**

| Leadership Attributes | % |
|---|---|
| Provide clear vision, aims and guidelines for the acquisition | 91 |
| Set the example, become the role model | 88 |
| Be aware of and sensitive to critical cultural differences | 87 |
| Promote a common identity and sharing logic | 85 |
| Be fair and objective | 83 |
| Motivate and empower employees | 82 |
| Establish clear communication channels | 81 |
| Have previous acquisition experience | 80 |
| Promote innovative and creative thinking to deal with complex post-acquisition tasks | 80 |
| Transfer resources between the two organisations | 77 |
| Encourage employee involvement | 73 |
| Develop strategic implementation skills | 72 |
| Encourage employees to accept change | 71 |
| Be flexible and willing to take risks | 67 |
| Build coherence with other members of the TMT | 67 |
| Coach and mentor employees | 65 |
| Have conflict management skills | 63 |
| Instill trust | 61 |
| Encourage team building and collaboration | 61 |
| Build relationships with other stakeholders | 58 |

identified through the interviews, and verified in the pilot questionnaire, only 10 were significantly associated with performance. The strongest associations are present in 'be aware and sensitive to critical cultural differences' ($\beta$ = 0.249, $p$ <0.001), 'provide clear vision, aims and guidelines for the acquisition' ($\beta$ = 0.290), 'motivate and empower employees' ($\beta$ = 0.312, $p$ <0.001) and 'encourage employee involvement' ($\beta$ = 0.430, $p$ <0.001). The other attribute, apart from being culturally aware and sensitive that was also significantly associated with performance is 'be fair and objective' ($\beta$ = 0.294, $p$ <0.05). As far as the actions are concerned 'promote a common identity and sharing logic' ($\beta$ = 0.167, $p$< 0.05), 'establish clear communication channels' ($\beta$ = 0.174, $p$ <0.05), 'transfer resources between the two organisations' ($\beta$ = 0.252, $p$ <0.01), 'set the example and become the role model' ($\beta$ = 0.242, $p$ <0.05), as well as, 'promote innovative and creating thinking to deal with complex post-acquisition tasks' ($\beta$ = 0.149, $p$ <0.05) were also significant indicators of post-acquisition organisational performance. $R^2$ is 62 or 0.62, which indicates that these variables account for 62 per cent of the variation in the post-acquisition performance. Overall, this regression model answers the second research question on the specific attributes and actions leaders can undertake that can enhance post-acquisition organisational performance.

**Table 11.2 The Effect of Leadership Attributes on Acquisition Performance**

| Leadership Attributes | B | (SE) | $\beta$ |
|---|---|---|---|
| Be aware and sensitive to critical cultural differences | 4.129 | 1.2130 | 0.249*** |
| Have conflict management skills | .884 | 1.254 | 0.061 |
| Develop strategic implementation skills | 1.134 | 1.296 | 0.073 |
| Have previous acquisition experience | 1.692 | 2.063 | 0.074 |
| Be flexible and willing to take risks | 2.249 | 1.989 | 0.104 |
| Be fair and objective | 6.209 | 2.178 | 0.294** |
| Instil trust | .619 | 2.144 | 0.030 |
| Build coherence with other members of the TMT | .712 | .958 | 0.059 |
| Encourage employees to accept change | .549 | 1.421 | 0.037 |
| Provide clear vision, aims and guidelines for the acquisition | 4.679 | 1.497 | 0.290*** |
| Build relationships with other stakeholders | .528 | 1.600 | 0.029 |
| Promote a common identity and sharing logic | 2.342 | 1.154 | 0.167* |
| Establish clear communication channels | 3.153 | 1.508 | 0.174* |
| Encourage team building and collaboration | 3.297 | 2.349 | 0.139 |
| Transfer resources between the two organisations | 4.426 | 1.686 | 0.252** |
| Motivate and empower employees | 4.974 | 1.363 | 0.312*** |
| Set the example, become the role model | 4.336 | 1.826 | 0.242* |
| Coach and mentor employees | .755 | 1.645 | 0.044 |
| Encourage employee involvement | 9.723 | 2.199 | 0.430*** |
| Promote innovative and creative thinking to deal with complex post-acquisition tasks | 3.386 | 1.926 | 0.149* |

Note: $N$ = 139, *$p$ <0.05, **$p$ <0.01, ***$p$ <0.001, $R^2$ = 0.62, $F$ = 9.41 ($p$ <0.001)

# Discussion

An analysis of the results demonstrated which leader attributes and actions are specifically important in managing and executing an acquisition strategy. The results of this study make an important contribution to available acquisition literature and practice as they point out what actions and characteristics a leader can use to enhance the success of the acquisition. This type of study has been generally neglected in the past and this study herein provides a telling, albeit partial, answer to the question of 'what constitutes an acquisition leader successful' which has been posed in the academic and practitioner literature but not directly or fully answered. The results indicate that in an acquisition, leaders should demonstrate behaviours such as be aware of the cultural differences, be fair and objective, as well as, have the appropriate implementation and management skills to enable the harmonisation of the acquisition and, thereafter, lead to higher acquisition performance.

Moreover, actions such as promoting innovative and creative thinking to deal with complex post-acquisition tasks will promote employees' intelligence, knowledge and learning so that they can adjust to the change process of the acquisition and be innovative in their problem solving and solutions to the continuous adjustments needed in acquisitions (Fubini *et al.* 2007). The results point out that transmitting a clear and shared mission, creating a feeling of belonging to the organisation and infusing purpose into the other members of the organisation, so as to alleviate any ambiguities during the acquisition, enhances acquisition performance. Acquisitions require implementation capabilities and a clear vision from leaders. Hence, their behaviour is critical for clarifying directions and for implementing change. Moreover, acquisition leaders, being responsible for change in the followers' thoughts, beliefs and values, thus have to also clearly communicate and articulate the desired goals and promote innovative ways to cope with challenges during the acquisition.

Marks and Mirvis (2001) discussed the importance of positive vision coupled with an articulation of the principles, values and priorities behind a merger or acquisition. Gadiesh *et al.* (2002) argued that the content of a post-acquisition vision must clearly specify its purpose and what the acquisition plans to achieve. Through this articulation, the leader will ensure the harmonisation of the integration process as a clear framework of integration and tasks be achieved will be present. Ashkenas and Francis (2000) stated that guiding the integration process takes a new type of leader, someone who can solve complex situations quickly, relate to many levels of authority smoothly and bridge gaps in culture and perceptions. Most theories conclude that effective leaders ought to be able to influence their followers towards achieving a goal (Ireland and Hitt 2005; Stahl and Voigt 2008) and that leaders should provide vision and inspiration to their followers and, additionally, create a structure and a culture that will enable and facilitate various positive behaviours (Nemanich and Keller 2007) specifically those needed for integrating two organisations.

Other behaviours and attributes are also relevant concerning CEO leadership capabilities to enhance post-acquisition organisational performance. The results of the study confirm previous statements in literature regarding the importance of leadership in acquisitions. Morosini *et al.* (1998), as well as, Sitkin and Pablo (2004) stressed the importance of leading by example at various hierarchical levels so as to build trust and influences and to achieve the intended objectives. Gadiesh *et al.* (2002) argued that continuous, enthusiastic 'crusading' is needed to get the vision across, implying that the CEO should stay engaged in the process of maintaining good relationships, delegating responsibilities and communicating to subordinates every decision being made in this change process. Morosini *et al.* (1998) argued that CEOs should provide clear, motivational vision that energises individuals and focuses them on what is expected in terms of a desired end state, as well as, a conciliatory process. Clear vision is essential in the post-acquisition integration process in order to ensure the ultimate integration of cultures. Leaders responsible for implementing an acquisition strategy should raise subordinate's awareness of the importance and value designated outcomes, get employees to transcend their own self-interests for the sake of the group or organisation and change or increase subordinates' needs. Through such means, employees' motivation and self-confidence are enhanced.

By defining the need for change, creating new visions, mobilising commitment to these visions, leaders can ultimately transform the organisation (Den Hartog *et al.* 1997). According to Bass (1985) this transformation of followers can be achieved by raising the awareness of the importance and the value of a designed outcome, getting followers to transcend their own self-interests by altering or expanding the followers' needs. Strong leadership positively affects satisfaction and performance of individuals, teams and organisations (Arnold *et al.* 2001). Leadership has also been found to result in higher levels of organisational commitment and is highly-associated with business unit performance (Arnold *et al.* 2001). In this present study of leadership, empowering and motivating employees has been found to have a positive effect on post-acquisition organisational performance. Hence, leadership in acquisitions will, in turn, increase commitment to the new organisation, higher job satisfaction and lessen the negative behaviours that employees might feel during an acquisition. It is important to communicate the new vision to the employees and encourage them to participate in the change process required for a successful acquisition. Leaders in the due diligence process should be aware of these issues in order to ensure that the implementation will be successful and will lead to the expected benefits and synergies.

One of employees' major concerns is the loss of identity (Covin *et al.* 1997). Employees can experience a powerful sense of loss when changes in the organisational routines occur and employees may experience shock, anger, disbelief, depression and helplessness before, during and after the acquisition (Schweiger *et al.* 1987). Ullrich *et al.* (2005) found that organisational identification is associated with the degree of continuity in the practices of the organisation. They argued that if neither projected, nor observable, continuity is given, deep structure identification would likely be very difficult to maintain or achieve (Ullrich *et al.* 2005). Similarly, Amiot *et al.* (2006) assessed organisational identification based on job satisfaction, event characteristics and situational appraisals about the organisational change, as well as, the coping strategies used by employees to deal with mergers. The results here demonstrated that job satisfaction and organisational identification are highly dependent on feelings of self-efficacy. If employees perceived that the post-acquisition integration process had been implemented in a positive manner, they reported stronger feelings of self-efficacy than those that perceived when the process had not been properly implemented.

Van Dick *et al.* (2006) found that post-M&As identification was positively related to job satisfaction and organisational citizenship behaviour and, conversely, negatively related to turnover intentions. If employees do not show organisational identification with the new entity, then this can have a negative effect on the social integration process as it disrupts the creation and maintenance of relationships in the organisation (Meyer and Altenbord 2007). This, in turn, can have a negative impact on employees' commitment, identification and job satisfaction which, in turn, can have an effect on performance. Significantly then, there are two critical conditions that ought to be met in order to achieve post-merger identification. These are communication and involvement in post-merger integration process (Barterls *et al.* 2006).

It is well-accepted that communication is the key tool within any change process (Kanter *et al.* 1992). This lack of communication may lead to high uncertainty levels among employees. Schweiger *et al.* (1987) suggested that communication during a merger process, in the form of a realistic merger preview, can help the employees get through the process. Their results also indicated that the absence of a coherent communication program can lead to significant increases in stress, perceived uncertainty and absenteeism and significant declines in job satisfaction, commitment and perceptions of the company's trustworthiness. Dooley and Zimmerman (2003) found that effective communication facilitates the integration process as it provides a safe space for substantive differences and conflicts to surface and to be addressed.

The results of this study confirm many of the discussed topics above, including the role of leaders. The study points out that establishing clear communication channels is imperative in M&As. It argues that communication should minimise uncertainty and ambiguity among the stakeholders involved in the process and, most importantly, among the employees of the organisation. Moreover, communication is also associated with the employees' and management's intention to stay with the organisation after M&As. Galpin and Herndon (2007) mentioned that up to half of the executives leave the organisations within three years of the acquisition. Therefore, early and detailed information about the new vision and strategy of the organisation, as well as, about the plans to integrate the operations of the two organisations should be available and communicated to senior managers, as well as employees, to avoid confusion and negative behaviours against the M&As.

Furthermore, the results point out that it is important to involve employees in the process of M&As. This can happen either by providing them with detailed information about the process or by delegating important tasks to them. Leaders should carefully listen to employees' concerns about the acquisition and involve them at every possible stage. This will, in turn, as the results highlight, increase post-acquisition organisational performance. Thus, employees will be more satisfied about the process and be more willing to co-operate with the proposed new changes, hence minimising the negative reactions that they might have towards the acquisition process. Employee involvement will increase the identification with the new organisation as a shared logic and belongingness is communicated to them. The results also point out that promoting a common identity and a shared logic among the employees will increase the probability of the success of M&As as it will lead to higher performance levels.

Employee involvement and participation in M&As is a key that characterises successful acquisition implementation (Amiot *et al.* 2006) as it empowers employees and provides them with a sense of agency and control. Researchers have tested the importance of employee participation during major organisational changes. Employees who participated during the implementation of changes reported higher job satisfaction and commitment to the organisation. As employee commitment is closely linked with identity in the organisations, it could be argued that employee involvement should be encouraged in M&As. To support this, Bartels *et al.* (2006) found that employees who were involved in the integration process demonstrated higher commitment levels as they were able to identify themselves with the new entity. Van Dick *et al.* (2001) stated that involvement means identification with the job. In the M&As context, this implies that employees who are involved in the M&As process will demonstrate higher levels of identification when compared with employees that were indirectly involved. These then are, of course, other factors that leaders need to comprehend.

The above results also highlighted that transfer of resources is an important indicator of post-acquisition organisational performance. Although this action is more linked with the strategic intent of the acquisition, it is important for leaders to devise a plan during the due diligence process regarding the type of resources they need to exchange between the two organisations in order to realise the synergy potential. Most importantly, leaders should pay attention to the knowledge and intellectual capital available to both the companies and set out plans in order to make full use of the talent present in the new combined entity.

## Conclusion

The results pointed out above in this chapter, in the various studies, reveal the attributes and the actions that leaders should have, and take into consideration, to ensure the success of M&As. The results present an ex-post assessment of these attributes based on the performance of completed acquisitions. This provides an insight on the issues that CEOs should pay attention to during all stages of the M&As. It could be argued that this is of high importance to the due diligence process where all the information about the transaction and the integration of the two companies takes place. Leaders and CEOs should be ready to face the difficulties that lie ahead in the integration process and should develop the right capabilities in order to deal with these difficulties more coherently and systematically.

This chapter, and its highlighted study, has proposed these attributes and actions as a proposal of the most important qualities as they were generated by interviews and validated by the questionnaires. It should be pointed out that these attributes and actions should be received as guidelines but CEOs should not be limited to these factors alone. Every M&A is a unique phenomenon which is managed differently depending on the circumstances and different needs of each person involved in the process. Nonetheless, these attributes and actions can help alleviate the negative reactions of the members of the organisation and enable CEOs to implement the integration process more smoothly, however, CEOs should not ignore other potential dynamics that are unique to their organisations.

This study makes a significant contribution to the M&A literature. It has placed leadership in the context of the acquisition process and has provided a basis that can be used during the due diligence process so leaders can more successfully manage the later stages of the M&As. The results have revealed the range of leader attributes, as well as, leader actions that can enhance post-acquisition organisational performance. This study is among the first that has investigated the leaders' attributes and linked them to the subsequent acquisition performance. Therefore, this study has built upon the existing

M&As literature and the critical issues of the due diligence process by adding leadership attributes and actions into this context. As highlighted, it is also very important for practitioners due to the ex-post nature that has been covered. The attributes and actions investigated in this study were assessed, against subsequent acquisition performance, in order to measurably determine if they are actually contributing to increased performance or not.

However, it should be noted, that there are certain limitations of studies of this kind. Although both qualitative and quantitative methods were used to establish the attributes of the successful acquisition leader, more in-depth research is needed. As acquisitions are dynamic processes more investigation of these attributes should be carried out. This study did not take into account, for example, the demographic variables of the leaders nor their cross-cultural competence and intelligence. Future research should include the above characteristics when assessing the attributes that make an acquisition leader successful. Moreover, this study focused on CEO attributes and actions, without taking into account that in M&As other management is also involved in the process. Although the choice of CEO for investigating the relationship between leadership and subsequent acquisition performance is valid in the literature, M&As leadership is more complex and dynamic, involving people from different levels of the organisation. Therefore, future research should take a more broad focus on leadership.

# References

Abedin, S. and Davies, G. 2007. Pre-merger identification: Ties with the past bind us to the future? *Advances in Mergers and Acquisitions*, 6, 17–36.

Amiot, C.E., Terry, D.J., Jimmieson, N.L. and Callan, V.J. 2006. A longitudinal investigation processes during a merger: Implications for job satisfaction and organisational identification. *Journal of Management*, 32, 552–74.

Anand, J., Capron, L. and Mitchell, W. 2005. Using acquisitions to access multinational diversity: thinking beyond the domestic versus cross-border M&A comparison. *Industrial and Corporate Change*, 14, 191–224.

Arnold, K.A., Barling, J. and Kelloway, E.K. 2001. Transformational leadership or the iron cage: Which predicts trust, commitment and team efficacy? *Leadership and Organisation Development Journal*, 22 (7), 315–20.

Ashkenas, R.N. and Francis, S.Z. 2000. Integration managers: Special leaders for special times, *Harvard Business Review*, 78, 75–9.

Bartels, J., Douwes, R., de Jong, M. and Pruyn, A. 2006. Organisational identification during a merger: Determinants of employees' expected identification with the new organisation, *British Journal of Management*, 17, S49–67.

Bass, B.M. 1985. *Leadership and Performance Beyond Expectations*. New York: The Free Press.

Bryman, A. and Bell, E. 2006. *Business Research Methods*. Oxford: Oxford University Press.

Covin, T.J., Kolenko, T.A., Sightler, K W. and Tudor, R.K. 1997. Leadership style and post-merger satisfaction, *Journal of Management Development*, 16, 22–33.

Datta, D.K. 1991. Organisational fit and acquisition performance: Effects of post-acquisition integration. *Strategic Management Journal*, 12, 281–97.

Den Hartog, D., Van Muijen, J.J. and Koopman, P.L. 1997. Transactional versus transformational leadership: An analysis of the MLQ. *Journal of Occupational and Organisational Psychology*, 70, 19–34.

Dooley, K.J. and Zimmerman, B.J. 2003. Merger as marriage: Communication issues in postmerger integration. *Health Care Management Review*, 28, 55–67.

Fubini, D., Price, C. and Zollo, M. 2007. *Mergers: Leadership, performance and corporate health*. New York: Palgrave Macmillan.

Gadiesh, O., Buchanan, R., Daniell, M. and Ormiston, C. 2002. The leadership testing ground. *Journal of Business Strategy*, 23, 12–17.

Galpin, T.J. and Herndon, M. 2007. *Mergers and Acquisitions: Process Tools to Support M&A Integration at Every Level*. London: John Wiley.

Gaughan, P.A. 2002. *Merger, Acquisitions and Corporate Restructurings*. New York: John Wiley and Sons.

Goldman, E. 2007. Strategic thinking at the top. *Sloan Management Review*, Summer 2007, 75–81.

Haspeslagh, P.C. and Jemison, D.B. 1991. *Managing Acquisitions*. New York: The Free Press.

Hitt, M., Harisson, J.S. and Ireland, D.R. 2001. *Mergers and Acquisitions: A Guide to Creating Value for Stakeholders*. Oxford: Oxford University Press.

Howson, P. 2008. *Checklists for Due Diligence*. Aldershot: Gower Publishing.

Ireland, R.D. and Hitt, M.A. 2005. Achieving and maintaining strategic competitiveness in the 21st century: The role of strategic leadership. *Academy of Management Executive*, 19, 63–77.

Javidan, M., Pablo, A.L., Singh, H., Hitt, M. and Jemison, D. 2004. Where we've been and where we're going. In *Mergers and Acquisitions: Creating Integrative Knowledge*, edited by A.L. Pablo and M. Javidan. Strategic Management Society Series. Oxford: Blackwell Publishing.

Kanter, R. M., Stein, B. and Jick, T. 1992. *The Challenge of Organisational Change*. New York: Free Press.

Kay, I. and Shelton, M. 2000. *The People Problem in Mergers*. New York: Watson Wyatt.

Kiessling, T. and Harvey, M. 2006. The human resource management issues during an acquisition: the target firm's top management team and key managers. *International Journal of Human Resource Management*, 17, 1307–20.

King, D.R., Slotegraaf, R. and Kesner, I. 2008. Performance implications of firm resource interactions in the acquisition of R&D intensive firms. *Organisation Science*, 19, 327–40.

Kotter, J.P. 1990. What do leaders really do? *Harvard Business Review*, 68, 103–11.

Larsson, R. and Finkelstein, S. 1999. Integrating strategic, organisational and human resource perspectives on mergers and acquisitions: A case survey of synergy realisation. *Organisation Science*, 10, 1–26.

Lee, D.S. and Alexander, J.A. 1998. Using CEO succession to integrate acquired organisations: A contingency analysis. *British Journal of Management*, 9, 181–97.

Marks, M.L. and Mirvis, P.H. 2001. Making mergers and acquisitions work: Strategic and psychological preparation. *Academy of Management Executive*, 15, 80–92.

Meyer, C.B. and Altenborg, E. 2007. The disintegrating effects of equality: A study of a failed international merger. *British Journal of Management*, 18, 257–71.

Morosini, P, Shane, S. and Singh, H. 1998. National culture distance and cross-border acquisition performance. *Journal of International Business Studies*, 29, 137–58.

Nemanich, L.A. and Keller, R.T. 2007. Transformational leadership in an acquisition: A field study of employees. *The Leadership Quarterly*, 18, 49–68.

Risberg, A. 1999. *Ambiguities Thereafter: An Interpretive Approach to Acquisitions*. Malmo: Lund University Press.

Schuler, R. and Jackson, S. 2001. HR Issues and activities in mergers and acquisitions. *European Management Journal*, 19, 239–53.

Schweiger, D. Ivancevich, J.M. and Power, F.R. 1987. Executive actions for managing human resources before and after acquisition. *Academy of Management Executive*, 1, 127–38.

Sitkin, S.B. and Pablo, A.L. 2004. The neglected importance of leadership in mergers and acquisitions. In *Managing Culture and Human Resources*, edited by G. K. Stahl and M. Mendenhall. Stanford: Stanford University Press

Stahl, G.K. and Voigt, A. 2008. Do cultural differences matter in mergers and acquisitions? A tentative model and examination. *Organisation Science*, 19, 160–76.

Sudarsanam, S. 2003. *Creating Value From Mergers and Acquisitions: The Challenges*, London: Financial Times Prentice Hall.

Ullrich, J., Wieseke, J. and van Dick, R. 2005. Continuity and change in mergers and acquisitions: A social identity case study of a German industrial merger. *Journal of Management Studies*, 42, 1549–69.

Van Dick, R., Ullrich, J. and Tissington, P.A. 2006. Working under a black cloud: How to sustain organisational identification after a merger. *British Journal of Management*, 17, S69–79.

Vaara, E. 2002. On the discursive construction of success/failure in narratives of post-merger integration. *Organisational Studies*, 23, 211–48.

Very, P., Lubatkin, M., Calori, R. and Veiga, J. 1997, Relative standing and the performance of recently acquired European firms, *Strategic Management Journal*, 18, 593–614.

# 12 *Post-Merger Growth Due Diligence*

MEHDI FARHADI AND PROFESSOR GEORGE TOVSTIGA
*Henley Business School, University of Reading Greenlands,*
*Henley-on-Thames, United Kingdom*

## Introduction

During the 1990s, companies looked inward to increase shareholder value, extend size and boost their market power through mergers and acquisitions (M&A). From those external growth efforts, along with a focus on shrinking bottom line costs through synergies, companies hoped to achieve greater shareholder value. This trend resulted in a number of mammoth transactions.[1]

Most companies consider external (inorganic) growth through M&A as one of the quickest ways to increase market share. However, experience has shown that growth following an M&A deal ultimately depends on the:

1. post-acquisition leadership capabilities;
2. employees' identification with the post-merger firm;
3. strategic deployment of post-deal innovative capabilities;
4. mobilisation of an entrepreneurial culture within the combined organisation.

For these reasons, we suggest this chapter's content suggests that post-merger growth has less to do with achieving cost synergies and improved efficiencies, for example in corporate sourcing or production, but more with the right strategic growth rationale, selection and combination of assets and capabilities. A company that goes through a M&A deal has to consider and comprehend that 'intangibles' – the merged enterprise's stock of intellectual capital – and not necessarily its 'tangibles' drive and determine value following an M&A transaction. By focusing on post-merger organic growth enabled through combined assets and capabilities, companies are better able to:

1. achieve shareholder value;
2. build a position of sustainable competitive advantage;
3. consistently exceed the value perceptions of customers.

---

1    The terms 'transactions' and 'deals' in this paper refer to 'mergers' and 'acquisitions'. The authors acknowledge that any deal has its own unique challenges and success factors. This contribution, however, focuses mainly on the overriding challenges and success factors of both mergers and acquisitions.

To initiate and sustain internal growth following an M&A transaction, executives need to appraise their post-merger growth strategies on the basis of the merged firms' combined resources, assets and capabilities. This chapter will introduce a novel approach to the strategic management of M&A that emphasises due diligence reviews and post-merger performance planning.

## The Growth Dilemma

To sustain competitive standing, companies must go through continuous growth (Ansoff 1957). Executives strive for growth to gain larger market share and turnover. Growth is pivotal to the well being of businesses. M&A represent one of the more popular strategic options for achieving fast track sales and short-term profit growth. However, they are also more highly prone to failure.

Planning and implementing post-merger growth is easier said than done. Experience suggests that inorganic growth through M&A transactions does not always improve companies' competitive standing vis-à-vis their rivals. A prominent example is the Schaeffler-Continental deal in 2008. Schaeffler KG, based in Bavaria, Germany launched a hostile USD 18 billion bid to purchase its much larger rival Continental AG. The deal positioned the combined group third behind Germany's Bosch and Japan's Denso among the global suppliers to the automotive sector. Schaeffler successfully secured approximately 36 per cent of Continental's stock through a series of swap deals mainly leveraged by investment banks. The deal was finalised in August 2008 (Farhadi and Tovstiga 2008b). In the ensuing economic downturn, however, Schaeffler's high debt and shrinking sales forced the once solid and cash-rich family-owned company to petition the Federal Government of Germany for financial aid. Did Schaeffler erode its competitive standing through consummating a highly leveraged M&A deal? As the Schaeffler case suggests, acquiring another firm can be a very complex process that potentially is fraught with risk. Indeed, extant research reveals that M&A transactions are seldom successful. In the recent decade, most M&A activities have failed to meet their initial strategic objectives: Three out of four M&As fail to achieve their financial and strategic objectives (Marks and Mirvis 2001).

Practitioners and researchers tend to blame merger mishaps on the:

1. lack of strategic fit (for example, inappropriate deal rationale);
2. rising price-to-book values (for example, acquisition premium);
3. mode of the acquisition (for example, friendly or hostile);
4. poor post-merger integration (for example, cultural misfit).

Another frequently cited reason for merger failures is the inherent complexity in materialising synergies – leading to failure to achieve anticipated synergies. Planning and implementing synergies is one of the major topics associated with external growth. However, overemphasis on synergies tends to distract transacting companies from achieving post-merger growth (also see Farhadi 2007; Rothenbuecher and Schrottke 2008).

This chapter argues that post-merger success measured through shareholder value return (for example, dividend or stock price) ultimately occurs only as a result of a continuous internal growth of the combined post-merger organisation after the successful integration of the acquirer's and acquired resources, assets and capabilities. Successful M&A deals are more likely to lead to sustainable, feasible and acceptable internal growth after the post-merger integration phase.

Successful deals typically (1) generate value for both companies and their shareholders; (2) extend the customer base and enhance customers' perceived value; (3) improve competitive standing; and notably (4) increase operational effectiveness. Together, these are the key determinants for organic growth. Figure 12.1 portrays the post-merger 'growth dilemma' faced by many corporations in the context of corporate mergers. The hypothetical growth curves represent sales growth for three companies: pre-merger, 'Company A' (or purchaser) and 'Company B' (or target) and post-merger, the combined organisation 'Post-Merger Company' (amalgamated company after the consummated deal). Both companies are in a position to grow at different shapes before their involvement in the hypothetical transaction. The illustration suggests that the acquirer has been growing slower than the target. The target company is, therefore, an attractive candidate to the acquirer. The hypothetical case implies two post-merger scenarios: (1) a consistent post-merger growth or (2) a value-eroding decline following the post-merger integration phase.

Consider the following example to illustrate this point: the Germany-based market leader in the Enterprise Resource Planning Software industry, SAP, has always pursued an organic growth strategy, which has been fostered by innovative software products and customer-focused services. At SAP, continuous improvement of products and services has resulted in enhancing customer value. For this reason, SAP has been able to consistently achieve organic growth in the past decade. In 2008, SAP announced its intention to consummate the acquisition of Business Objects, a French company. The deal was rationalised by the complementary product portfolio of Business Objects covering a wide range of new and existing end customers. Indeed, the transaction was designed

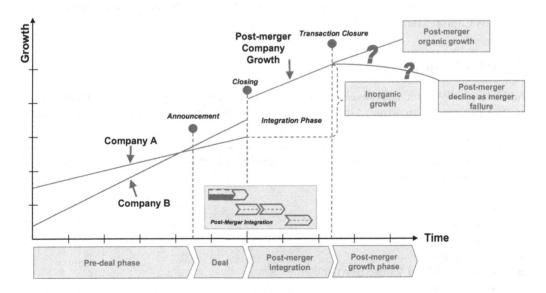

**Figure 12.1 Post-Merger Growth Dilemma**

as an injection to fill an existing gap in the SAP product portfolio and to generate competitive advantage for both, the customers and the Germany based software house SAP Aktiengesellschaft. Early on in the merger process SAP became aware of doubts raised by analysts about SAP's lack of deal experience to fully integrate and absorb business objects' resources, assets and capabilities. SAP, therefore, declared its intention to run and maintains Business Objects as an independent asset. Synergies were focused, to some degree, on software integration between the different product sets, only if to increase cross-sell opportunities with existing customers. As it turned out, the consummated deal, in the end, neither distracted SAP from innovation nor misguided the worldwide ERP market leader through overly daring synergistic goals.

By contrast, the USD 38 billion merger of relative equals in 1998, Daimler and Chrysler, significantly diminished post-merger growth. Initially, Daimler and Chrysler were motivated to get together because of huge opportunities, such as economies of scale through larger size, complementary strengths, geographic coverage and design/ engineering competencies. Although an annual revenue enhancement of USD 1 billion had been estimated at the beginning of the deal, the merger ultimately failed to achieve this objective (Rynbrandt and Bruner 2000). Prior to the Daimler-Chrysler merger, both firms had been performing at levels above the automotive industry standard. At that time, Chrysler was the most profitable American automaker. Daimler-Benz was the leading global brand with highest reputation for engineering, design, quality, and customer value. There was widespread expectation that the merger would be successful (Cook 1998). Everyone expected significant benefits from the combined capabilities of Daimler and Chrysler and cost savings from the merger synergies. However, following the merger, the stock price felt significantly (Rynbrandt and Bruner 2000). Evidence suggests that internal growth was not the highest priority for DaimlerChrysler; rather, the focus was on materialising fiscal synergies (Meyer *et al.* 2002). Ultimately, in 2007, after a ten-year corporate marriage, Daimler corrected its inorganic growth strategy by the divestiture of its 80.1 per cent stake in Chrysler Holding LLC in a USD 7.44 billion deal (about USD 30 billion less than premium paid in 1998) with the New York based private equity house, Cerberus Capital Management.

## Growth Definition

According to Webster's Revised Unabridged Dictionary (1913) 'growth' can be interpreted as 'the process of growing'. Growth may also be understood in terms of an outcome achieved.

There has been an ongoing debate on the nature of growth and its measurement. In the schools of economics and audit/accounting, growth is explained by a number of financial proxies, such as:

1. sales;
2. market share;
3. assests;
4. productivity;
5. Economic Added Value (EVA);
6. free cash flow;
7. shareholder value return (stock price and dividend).

Conversely, in the schools of human and intellectual capital (with origins in the resource-based theory of the firm) and in knowledge and innovation management, growth is defined through intangible assets, such as human capital, intellectual properties, brand, corporate culture and capabilities, for example, innovative competencies, learning curve and research and development expertise. Moreover, Tobin's Q, as a financial measure, has been applied in the context of intangible growth as a broad indicator of the contribution of intangibles to the firm's market value.

Growth has also been classified as internally and externally driven. Organic (or internal) growth focuses the firm's efforts to develop, nurture and build its internal portfolio of resources and capabilities. In contrast, inorganic (or external) growth comes with a merger or an acquisition of third party assets/capabilities and the transformation of two stand-alone companies into a single post-deal organisation. Additionally, mergers and acquisitions are often considered to be interchangeable. In fact, they are quite different. A merger happens when two companies decide on joining forces in their respective fields of business – they may be identical, similar, or totally different. Both their shareholders and management agree on surrendering their shares and revaluing and re-registering them under the new company. In acquisitions, the acquiring company assumes ownership of the target company's shares or asset and liabilities. Also, acquisitions almost always result in a change in the target company's management; and more often than not, in favour of the members of the acquiring company.

Because of the inherent complexity involved in monitoring and measuring corporate growth based upon intangibles, academic studies and business writings have, in the past, mainly focused on tangible measures, predominantly on financials and sales. In this context, 'revenue' as a proxy, dominates the active debate on growth. Prominent strategic management and business administration models, for example, BCG Growth Matrix, thus represent corporate growth by sales.

For example, Raisch and von Krogh (2007) suggest two types of corporate growth and distinguish between (1) minimum and (2) maximum growth. In their proposed model, they also measure growth through turnover. Minimum growth is driven by: (1.1) Competitive growth based upon assets and capabilities; (1.2) shareholder growth expectations; and (1.3) productivity growth which has to do with the capability growth. Companies' maximum growth strongly depends upon: (2.1) financial assets; (2.2) managerial capabilities; and (2.3) market conditions. To assess turnover growth, Weston (2004: 284) suggests applying discrete compound annual growth rate of sales or continuously compounded annual growth of revenues. Louis (2004) suggests that purchasing assets causes negative abnormal share return. Accounting literature makes earnings management via accruals, immediately before acquisition responsible for this underperformance. Koller *et al.* (2005: 655) create a link between corporate growth – measured by periodic revenues based upon: (1) innovative products; (2) customer base; and (3) distinctive technologies. Porter (2004: 362) suggests a strong relationship between corporate growth and relative market share based upon two proxies: (1) cash use; and (2) cash generation. Porter, therefore, links corporate growth with working capital efficiencies and effectiveness. Lee (2004) accentuates that 'since excess resources can provide services at zero marginal cost, they motivate entrepreneurs to apply them to new activities, engendering growth and diversification.' As seen, all of these studies focus mainly on 'tangible' assets.

Contrary to the studies emanating from the schools of accounting, numerous academic papers emerging from the school of economics suggest that revenue growth is not an appropriate proxy for measuring corporate growth; instead, other alternatives ought to be taken into account, for example, free cash flow (FCF) for monitoring corporate performance because of the effects of different currencies and ongoing changes in accounting rules and creative accounting (Koller *et al.* 2005; Hess 2007). Notably, Sirower and O'Byrne (1998) address several shortcomings of FCF as a financial measure for monitoring periodic performance. They argue that FCF subtracts the entire cost of an annual investment rather than spreading the cost of the investment over the life of the asset that has been acquired. As an alternative, they suggest the concept of Economic Value Added (EVA®): 'Unlike FCF, EVA effectively capitalizes, instead of expensing, much corporate investment and then holds management accountable for that capital by assigning the capital charge just described.'

To review the above, it could be argued that shortcomings related to: (1) the definition of growth based solely on financial measures; (2) an overemphasis on cost synergies in a merger game; and (3) a strong shareholder value orientation may have caused the majority of merger mishaps over the recent decades.

## Merger Process

The M&A value chain consists of: (1) a preliminary phase; (2) a transaction phase; and (3) an integration phase (Farhadi and Tovstiga 2008a). In the preliminary phase, merger or acquisition-fuelled growth generally sets the stage for an appropriate growth strategy, which begins with the search for a suitable candidate. The transaction phase includes diverse due diligence reviews and post-merger integration planning, business valuation and the actual transfer of liability and control over the company or the shareholding (closing). The closing marks the transition from planning mode to execution mode. In the post-merger integration phase, the target's resources, assets and capabilities, identified during the transaction phase, are integrated into the new post-merger organisation.

Due diligence provides the pre-condition for smooth integration. Notably, while M&A practitioners are apparently routinely engaged in financial, tax and legal due diligence activities, they simply fail to appraise the organic growth potentials of the combined organisation and mastermind post-merger internal growth strategies and plans.

## Post-merger Growth Due Diligence

After facing near-bankruptcy in 1971 and subsequent intervention by the British government, Rolls-Royce was split into Rolls-Royce Motor Cars (automobiles) and Rolls-Royce PLC (airplane engines) in 1973. The British armaments manufacturer Vickers acquired the automobile manufacturer Rolls-Royce Motor Cars in 1980 and divested itself of the luxury brand in 1998. Vickers had originally planned to sell Rolls-Royce Motor Cars to BMW, but Volkswagen came up with a more attractive offer and acquired Rolls-Royce Motor Cars for approximately USD 800 million. However, while the Wolfsburg-based automobile manufacturer assumed that it was acquiring Rolls-Royce Motors, with all that this entailed, it realised only after the deal that the rights to the Rolls-Royce trademark remained in the possession of Rolls-Royce PLC. Hence, while Volkswagen now assumed ownership of Rolls-Royce Motor Cars, including the manufacturing plant, it did not own the brand name Rolls-Royce. This error in due diligence was to haunt Volkswagen, particularly when the rights to the Rolls-Royce trademark were transferred from Rolls-Royce PLC to BMW AG. After the Rolls-Royce and Bentley trademarks were separated in 2003, Volkswagen acquired Bentley and BMW received the rights to use the Rolls-Royce trademark. As a result, VW currently builds Bentleys in Crewe, while BMW manufactures hand-made Rolls-Royces in Goodwood.[2]

The case of Volkswagen Rolls-Royce poses a telling question. Did the parties involved overlook the importance of differentiating assets in their deal? Or, perhaps, did they simply fail to consider the transferability and integrability facets of the target's intangible assets? If the latter is indeed more accurate, was this an unusual occurrence? Hardly.

## WHAT IS DUE DILIGENCE?

The case of Volkswagen-Rolls-Royce does underline the substance of assets but also both their transferability and integrability in the acquirer's organisation. In due diligence practices, we often come across unexpected gaps of this sort. In practice, the stakeholders involved in M&A deals seldom employ a holistic approach to the 'evaluation' and 'combination' of growth assets and capabilities. Lawyers tend to focus on reviewing and managing structural and regulatory issues and accountants – if they consider post-acquisition growth at all – look, due to the difficulties of valuing intangibles, solely at tangible assets, for example, quality of earnings according to the generally accepted accounting principles. Indeed, even in the companies themselves, the post-merger integration teams are rarely familiar with the full range of post-deal growth issues, such as, management vision, objectives and strategies.

In the context of an M&A, the phrase 'due diligence' refers to the survey of the status quo of the target company (or the part of an entity) that is considered for a sale and the critical examination of significant issues relating to the transaction. Thus, presumably, a thorough examination of the target's assets and capabilities should pinpoint the risks and integration potential.

In M&A transactions, a target is traditionally valued on the basis of its working capital, fixed capital, intangible assets and intellectual properties (Smith 2002). Due diligence audits are designed to have a significant role in determining the purchase price, which can perhaps be the decisive factor for continuing a M&A transaction.

In addition to M&A deals, due diligence investigations are also usually performed during management buy-outs (MBO), leveraged buyouts (LBO), in an initial public offering (IPO), when raising debt and equity capital, restructuring, outsourcing and the privatization of public enterprises. Figure 12.2 illustrates the course of due diligence actions along the M&A events from the early bid to deal closing. It highlights the required input, scope of activities and the output of due diligence reports including the list of imminent challenges / risks and recommendations (Farhadi et al. 2008).

---

2    The Volkswagen/Rolls-Royce case has been discussed at length in the press and in several studies. The authors of this article have compiled information from several studies and sources and present them here. For more information please refer to Handelsblatt (2003), 'Limousine soll englisch bleiben – BMW baut jetzt Rolls Royce' and Valoir and Dai (2006),'Intellectual Property Due Diligence – A Cautionary Tale' p. 17, IP & Technology Programme (BNA). More details on this case are also available in the company profiles of the abovementioned companies on the internet (for example, www.wikipedia.com).

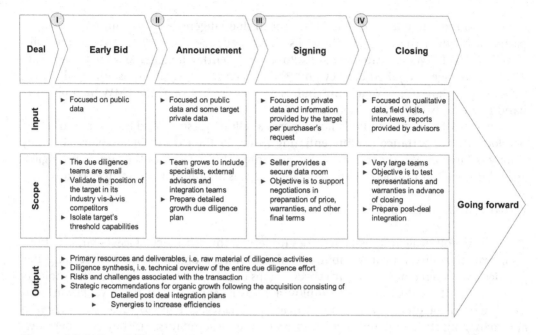

**Figure 12.2 Due Diligence Process**

## PURPOSE

The parties to a M&A process, be they – buy-side or sell-side – have to carry out a series of due diligence investigations with due care. In a buy-side due diligence, the buyer ensures that there will be no surprises after the purchase agreement has been signed. The main objective is to help acquirers decide whether to embrace or kill a deal. In a sell-side due diligence, vendors endeavour to have selected growth assets and capabilities transferred to a potential buyer in order to underpin the desired value or price of the assets. By and large, conducting due diligence reviews has become one of the most integral parts of corporate transactions.

M&A professionals are generally adept at conducting commercial, operational, financial, tax and legal due diligences. These investigations, however, neither portray the big picture of a transaction nor tell the whole story about the deal (Adolph *et al.* 2006). A post-merger growth due diligence aims to:

1. identify existing facts on the target's growth platform, including resources, assets, capabilities and appraised by the growth drivers respectively;
2. uncover relevant risks and challenges associated with the durability, replicability, sustainability, transferability of the target's growth platform;
3. prepare strategic options for risk management, as well as, potential post-merger integration problems and challenges;
4. secure evidence underpinning the investigations, determining the asset price (transaction value) and estimating the cost of post-merger integration efforts (transaction cost).

A post-merger growth due diligence audit also enables a systematic analysis of the targets' future growth potential for the buyer within the scope of a combined business. In hostile takeovers, conducting a growth due diligence may prove to be a difficult task to accomplish, as the purchaser would need to gain access to confidential data on the operational and financial performance of the target.

## ANALYSIS

As a classic reference, Penrose (1959) argues that companies seek their full potential through the effective and efficient application of all available resources. Relying on the resource-based and economic theories, a company's performance hinges on its resources and distinctive capabilities. Indeed, researchers agree that differentiation from rivals takes place because of the sustainability of resources and capabilities (for example, Grant 1991; Barney 1991; Peteraf 1993; Mahoney and Pandian 1992; Prahalad and Hamel 1990; Stalk *et al.* 1992; Collis and Montgomery 1995; Amit and Shoemaker 1993; Porter 1991). It should be noted here, that resources can also be classified, for example, into tangibles and intangibles (Collis and Montgomery 1995) or assets and competencies (Hall 1992).

The difference between resources and capabilities emerges from the fact that capabilities are built upon consistent learning of how to apply, combine and make best use of resources, people and processes, or in other words, the effective and efficient combination of resources in day-to-day business activities. An illustration is Dell Computer which has achieved unprecedented growth by combining manufacturing and delivery for customer-tailored personal computers. Through the internet, Dell has significantly increased its presence in the market place. Dell's growth drivers have considerably enhanced its ability to combine assets, people and processes (Thomson and Martin, 2005). Dell's major assets today are its brand, reputation for inexpensive personal computers, end-customer relationships and its accelerated time-to-market capability.

The relationships among the value determining factors for the pre-merger growth through mergers and acquisitions, their influence on acquiring and combining the required assets and capabilities and, notably, prolonging organic growth after the integration phase. Each category includes its respective growth drivers. For those companies that decide to implement external growth through acquisitions and establish internal growth following the post-merger phase, it is vital to not only assess and evaluate the target's assets and capabilities but also their post-merger transferability and integrability in the post-merger organisation.

Therefore, M&A practitioners need to evaluate (see also Porter 1991; Zahara and Das 1993; Collis and Montgomery 1995; Grant 1991; Prahalad and Hamel 1994) the value of assets and capabilities by asking key questions and conducting six key appraisals:

1. A competitive superiority appraisal; do the acquired assets and capabilities systematically lead to the acquirer's post-merger differentiation and if so, how?
2. An appropriability appraisal; is the acquirer able to improve competitive advantages through the acquired assets and capabilities? Are they appropriate?
3. An imitability and scarcity appraisal; can rivals easily imitate the acquired and post-merger combined resources and capabilities? What are the barriers?

4. A durability appraisal; do the acquired assets and capabilities add value over time? What is the life time and financial value of the purchased assets measured through depreciation?
5. A sustainability appraisal; how difficult is it for new entrants and existing rivals to substitute the acquired and combined post deal resources and capabilities?
6. A transferability appraisal; can the assets and capabilities be transferred to the new organisation? Are there any legal boundaries, such as patents or licences? Is the target the owner of the intellectual properties? Can the acquired assets and capabilities be integrated in the new post-merger organisation? How can they generate superior value for the stakeholders?

## THE PROCESS

The post-merger growth due diligence process, consisting of six appraisal steps, should be run as a project within the due diligence phase of the transaction. Other due diligence work streams may start simultaneously or slightly later. The due diligence should not be run in vacuum. The project is prone to exchange information with other investigations such as commercial, financial, legal and operational due diligence projects.

The first step in a growth due diligence investigation is to understand the purchaser's strategic rationale of the deal and how it would boost post-closing growth. Furthermore, the growth strategies of the target company need to be isolated and investigated. Transactions are most often designed to fit with the inorganic growth strategy. If the due diligence team does not understand the purchaser's rationale and inorganic growth strategy it will not be suitably placed to conduct the due diligence investigations and analyses.

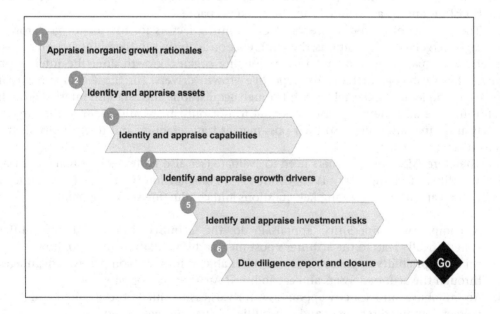

**Figure 12.3 Post-Merger Growth Due Diligence Audit**

The second and third steps are about evaluating the target's assets and capabilities. The appraisals at this stage include the superiority, appropriability, imitability, durability, sustainability, transferability and integrability tests. The fourth phase focuses on identifying and evaluating the growth drivers, that is, the major components of the business that enable organic growth after the integration phase. The fifth step focuses on isolating the risks, challenges and opportunities associated with the M&A and post-merger growth drivers. At this stage, the scenario planning technique can be applied to simulate growth. Finally, step six consists of all required activities to prepare a report including the due diligence findings, open issues, red flags and recommendations on future growth.

## Appraise inorganic growth rationales

The central thrust of this chapter is that a company's post-merger growth precisely depends on its distinctive assets and differentiating capabilities acquired and combined in a M&A deal. External growth options – strategically designed to obtain new resources (assets) and capabilities (competencies) – are prone to be faced with a number of challenges and risks relating to planning and implementing. Reliable evidence and experience from previous deals show that the success of an inorganic growth is dominantly influenced by: (1) its strategic rationale; (2) the size of the target company; (3) the deal experience of the purchaser; and (4) the financial resources applied in the transaction, for example, transaction value. Alongside these, intercultural factors, such as cultural diversity among employees, are expected to play a major role in the initiation and successful implementation of a merger or acquisition. As commonly accepted, the transaction mode (i.e. hostile versus friendly takeovers) and industry relatedness are also important variables shaping the success and enabling growth performance following an M&A deal.

Rothenbuecher and Schrottke (2008) propose seven growth rationale types for mergers and acquisitions in their unique empirical study of post-merger performance of 175 mergers and acquisitions:

1. volume extension;
2. regional extension;
3. product-oriented extension;
4. horizontal integration of competency;
5. vertical forward integration;
6. vertical backward integration;
7. business extension or diversification.

They suggest that the foremost cause of post-merger financial slowdown is 'treating all mergers alike.' They recommend tailoring post-merger integration approaches and strategies based upon the requirements of the strategic deal rationales.

Procter & Gamble, for example, has always defined its acquisition strategy with the objective of sensibly complementing or expanding its product range through M&A transactions. Procter & Gamble acquired leading established global brands (Oil of Olay facial cream or Pantene shampoo in 1985, Blendax AG for the dental care product Blend-a-Med in 1987, Noxell Corporation for Noxema and Cover Girl and Gillette in 2005), as well as, newly developed products. As a result, its beauty division generated just under half of the revenue and more than half its profit in one year (also see Procter &

Gamble company profile, Data Monitor 2007). Data reveals that distinctive post-merger integration approaches of the purchased assets were used by Procter & Gamble.

Post-merger growth due diligence has to appraise the M&A rationale of the purchaser and verify whether an acquisition can inject new differentiating assets and capabilities to the purchaser's business. Practitioners need to address strategic questions such as does the M&A transaction create long-term value to the purchaser, its employees and customers?

When companies are involved in a M&A, the first question concerning the post-merger growth is how well is the acquisition aligned with, and valuable to, the purchaser's growth strategy. To answer this, companies must identify both the target's internal growth strategy and its alignment with the purchaser's inorganic growth strategy. Companies need to determine whether the target's growth strategy fulfils the target's value requirements. In addition, the performance objectives for the target need to be understood. Notably, the acquisition rationale has to offer credible benefits to justify the deal.

## Identify and appraise assets

However, justifying M&A rationales and crafting bold strategies are not enough for achieving sustainable growth. They must be translated into measurable and feasible activities to acquire and combine distinctive assets and capabilities. When a company is involved with new assets and capabilities, it will be faced with a chain of difficulties and uncertainties. Through mergers and acquisitions, companies have to appraise the value and potential contribution of the assets and capabilities to the post-merger growth.

As discussed, assets can be classified into tangibles and intangibles. Easy to measure tangibles are measurable and physically existing resources with immediate impact on the business: long-term fixed assets (real estates, machinery or plants) and working capital (financial assets). Some difficult to measure intangible assets are, for instance, human capital, intellectual property rights, culture and organisational knowledge and competencies. Intangibles in M&A deals can be difficult to value and manage. In an automotive assembly line, for example, if a robot produces error and does not behave based upon the functional algorithm, it will be instantly replaced or repaired. Inversely, in case of post-merger cultural misfit – a cultural error - organisational value may be destroyed latently.

It's virtually impossible to imagine the modern business world, or indeed today's society, without intangible assets. Their economic and social impact is without question. Numerous academic and professional studies have advised companies of the dangers of ignoring or underestimating the role and importance of intangible assets in M&A. Thus, the essence of a deal, that is, the price of the targeted acquisition, more often than not hinges on both tangible *and* intangible assets. This holds true for transactions involving large established companies as it does for technology start-ups. Particularly in the case of technology acquisitions, intellectual assets are often the prime motivation for the acquisition. Cisco CEO Jon Chambers has been quoted as saying that:

> Most people forget that in a high-tech acquisition, you really are acquiring only people. That's why so many of them fail. At what we pay, USD 0.5–2m for an employee, we are not acquiring current market share. We are acquiring futures.

Cisco, over the years, has pursued an extraordinarily successful acquisition strategy. With his statement, Chambers underlines the importance of intellectual assets in a transaction. Intangible assets – sometimes referred to as the firm's intellectual capital – manifest themselves in a variety of forms. These might include, for example, the firm's human and relational and/or structural intellectual capital. In short, to a large extent, intangibles constitute the firm's intellectual assets.

Danzon *et al.* (2007) examined the determinants and effects of M&As in the pharmaceutical and biotechnology industry using SDC data on 383 firms from 1988 to 2001. The evidence unearth suggests that mergers of larger pharmaceutical and biotechnological companies are a response to expected excess capacity due to patent expirations and gaps in a firm's product pipeline. Therefore, assets, such as patents, underpin the growth.

An acquisition can be considered then as: (1) selection of right assets and capabilities; and (2) a smooth combination of the acquired assets and capabilities. A post-merger growth due diligence investigation, consisting of the six sustainability tests discussed earlier must, therefore, identify and appraise the quality of acquired (and combined) assets. Do the assets lead to the post-merger growth? How can the acquired assets generate competitive advantage? Can the rivals copy these resources? Are resources and assets protected by intellectual property rights? Do the acquired assets and capabilities add value over time? What is the life expectancy of the purchased assets? How difficult is it for new entrants and rivals to replace the post-acquisition assets? Can the assets be transferred to the new post-closing organisation? Is the target the owner of the assets' intellectual property rights, for example, trade mark, copy right? Can the acquired assets be combined with the existing resources? How can they get combined to best support a superior internal growth?

## Identify and appraise capabilities

Minnesota Mining and Manufacturing (3M), a globally operating multi-technology corporation established in 1902, and perhaps best known for its Post-It and Scotch brands, has a stringent strategy to develop and combine new capabilities inorganically. According to their own information, 3M produces more than 50,000 different products based on 40 different technology platforms. Research and development capabilities play a leading role in this US conglomerate's business strategy. The group first formulated its objective of inorganic development of capabilities by way of acquisitions in 1982. Since then, this global player has turned its attention to acquiring innovative companies with large research and development budgets. This is 3M's response to the growing challenges of globalization and increasingly stiff competition (Lamb 2006). This strategy has evidently built the M&A capabilities of 3M. To date, the company has developed M&A capabilities that enable 3M to select targets and to smoothly integrate valuable assets. Data shows that M&As to 3M are business as usual.

Based upon Kay (1994), the distinct post-merger architectural capabilities consist of: (1) the combined networks of contractual relationships within and around a firm (suppliers, employees and customers); (2) the dissemination of information across the post-merger company to support combined logistics of manufacturing and delivery; and (3) the management of post-merger intellectual properties through combined product/

service design and aggressive public relations and advertising attempts aimed at target market.

An effective combination of the assets and architectural capabilities of the purchaser, and those of the target company, leads to exceptional post-merger organisational knowledge and core competencies and, therefore, strengthens growth, for example, annual turnover and profitability. Combining capabilities are expensive and time-consuming because of the inherent complexity of their implementation and associated costs. Once established, however, they add considerable value to the growth of the combined firm.

One key capability is managing brands for they contribute to company's reputation and are one of the major assets of a company, for example, for providing quality, good value for money, guaranteed delivery times, choice of products, employer of choice, fun place to work, team incentives, or flexible working. Another significant capability concerns the ability of the combined organisation to consistently innovate resulting in new products/services and enhanced customer value. Such capabilities are risky, hard to sustain, and not seldom a commercial failure.

In combining capabilities, companies need to conduct due diligence investigations to configure processes, technologies, financial and human resources of the organisation and manage regulatory implications, the degree of management commitment and organisational ownership. Post-merger growth due diligence should provide reliable answers to important questions such as what gaps exist between the skills and capabilities of the acquiring and target organisations? What post-merger human performance gaps will exist (for example, competency, skills, organisation behaviour)? What R&D intensive and technological gaps will be filled through the M&A (for example, product, process, information)? How will competitors respond to the inorganic growth and retaliate? What mechanisms are in place to monitor and evaluate competitive performance and to respond when necessary?

## Identify and appraise growth drivers

Growth drivers reflect the performance of the acquiring firm after the merger with the target directly linked to the combined assets and capabilities, for example, number of patents in the pipeline of a pharmaceutical and biotechnological company following an M&A deal. In post-merger growth due diligence investigations, the growth drivers of the acquired company should complement and improve the growth drivers of the acquiring company.

For the Deutsche Bank's competitive advantage during the economic downturn in 2008 and onwards, for instance, where it was pivotal to develop and maintain a high retail banking network, important growth drivers in the Postbank share deal was the density of the acquired branches, the number of customers, including customer churn and creditability. In the Lufthansa/Swissair deal, as another example, where productivity was important, the growth driver focus was on utilisation per seat.

Growth drivers can be measured over time and compared to the industry average. They play a significant role in reviewing the target's business historical performance and its future projections. The main questions here are: How sustainable are the growth drivers of the combined organisations? How much value will they create? What are the trends in value creation, meeting customer needs, customer loyalty/satisfaction, market share and financial performance (for example, sales, earnings, cash flow, or return on assets/

equity)? Can rivals copy them? Are they durable? Are they sustainable post-closing? In short, growth drivers represent the determining factors contributing to the growth of the combined organisation. They are the underpinning rudiments for the continuity of post-merger internal growth.

## Identify and appraise investment risks

M&A transactions should not be allowed to affect the purchaser's organic growth. To the contrary, successful deals facilitate post-merger growth through a smooth combination of the acquirer's and the acquired company's assets and capabilities. The golden rule: the deal must be halted if it is likely to erode value and significantly affect the acquirer's organic growth engine.

In a post-merger due diligence, it is vital to assess the risks affecting growth drivers. The general risk management process in a growth-oriented M&A transaction is as follows: (1) identify the potential risks affecting the post-merger growth drivers; (2) classify the potential risks by type, appraising the risks likelihood of occurrence, severity of their impact on the post-merger performance controlled by the growth drivers; and (3) prioritise the risks and quantify their probability, impact and controllability.

Post-merger growth risks can be classified into the following six key risk categories:

1. Transaction cost risks arising from forecasting errors, overruns by post-merger integration teams and scope expansion and change.
2. Schedule risks causing operational disruptions or economic failure caused by inappropriate combination of assets and capabilities; this may result in missing a window of market opportunity for a product or service. Such risks are caused by resource unavailability, including staffing delays and compressed and complex critical paths.
3. Technical risks related to a wide range of factors that can result in failure to meet post-merger growth and market performance expectations. Technical risks are typically caused by requirements changes or inherent complexity of post-merger integration.
4. Operational risks resulting in a failure to realize the benefits of the acquisition. Such risks are characterized by an inability to implement large-scale synergies towards post-merger growth effectively. Typical causes are inadequate resolution of post-merger integration priority conflicts, failure to clarify and resolve responsibility or authority conflicts, poor or inadequate communication, incomplete human resources planning, poor or inadequate training of staff, insufficient or unsuitable physical resources of the target and purchaser and inability of the post-merger company to deal confidently with the overall transformation associated with the post-merger integration.
5. Programmatic risks due to endogenous events outside the control of the acquirer, such as changes in legal and regulatory frameworks, industry developments or deal funding barriers.
6. Cultural risks as a result of cultural misfit and diversity between the combined organisations and a lack of employees' identification with the post-merger company's brand, shared values and culture.

In performing a post-merger growth due diligence, the following types of questions on risks should be asked: Are the post-merger growth requirements consistent with the strategic objectives and goals of the acquisition? Are the requirements technically feasible? Are the post-merger growth requirements subject to significant change based upon macroeconomic developments and drivers? Will sufficiently skilled and capable personnel be retained during the M&A? Are management and all resource-providing organizational units committed to making the needed resources available? Is there latitude for deviation from the expected post-merger integration costs and timeline of the post-merger growth? Do the acquisition's milestones depend on other internal initiatives or outside events? Are sufficient funds committed for the combination of capabilities and assets? How stable is the commitment of funds? Is the new management results-oriented and willing to grant internal growth mergers a level of authority commensurate with their level of responsibility? Does the post-merger culture help building effective teams? Does the culture of the post-merger organisation utilize collaboration and cooperation among employees with diversity?

## Due diligence report and closure

Ex post, after conducting the analysis of the data and information gathered in the post-merger growth due diligence, a report on the insights gained during the investigations must be prepared and delivered. The objective is to secure the evidence found and estimate the scope and cost of post-merger integration efforts (transaction costs).

When significant issues arise that may affect the purchaser's organic growth engine, the deal is not justified to consummate. And this is true even if there is a bold strategic rationale. In extreme cases, the deal must simply be halted until all doubts are removed from the transaction. Theoretically, a post-merger growth due diligence may trigger other examinations of the aspects of the target business. Maybe, it will require a more focused accounting approach to the financial results testified in annual reports including the balance sheet and income statement. In an ideal world, as with other due diligence investigations, post-merger growth due diligence teams are supposed to provide interim reports during the due diligence assignment.

The report should be designed to provide results to stakeholders with divergent interests. Buy-side or sell-side, such reports must develop a clear view of whether the deal is a good investment. It is recommended providing the results together with the commercial and financial due diligence conclusions and end results. Once integrated and combined, they can become a sound grounding guidance for deal makers, executives and financial investors.

# Growth Driven M&A Deals

Extensive review of the M&A market and extant research suggests that achieving sustainable internal growth after the post-merger integration phase tends to be completely ignored in the acquisition. It is fair to assume that post-merger growth has often been overlooked in almost all transactions. Figure 12.4 shows a more complete M&A chain of activities and work streams extended by the post-merger growth considerations.

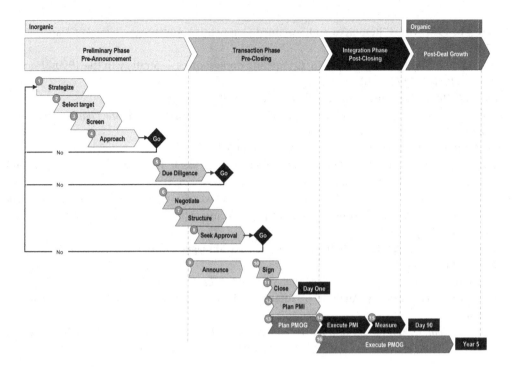

**Figure 12.4 Alternative Approach to Design an M&A**

## Conclusion

Top line growth has now become a cornerstone for most companies. Executives going through an M&A transaction face a costly and time consuming chain of activities with potentially high legal impact. From a managerial perspective, executives must always be concerned about their organic growth even if they plan growth inorganically. The challenge of M&A ought not to be solely associated with synergies. Companies that achieve post-merger growth have paid attention to the assets and capabilities they have successfully acquired and combined them with the purchaser's pre-deal resources and competences. Superior growth following an M&A deal is best achieved when the companies involved focus deliberate attention on the integration and exploitation of their pooled resources. Purposeful post-merger growth due diligence enables companies to capture the ultimate strategic benefits of organic growth in the post-deal phase.

## References

Adolph, G., Gillies, S. and Krings, J. 2006. Strategic Due Diligence: A Foundation for M&A Success. *strategy+business enews*. Booz Allen Hamilton.

Amit, R. and Schoemaker, P.J. H. 1993. Strategic Assets and Organizational Rent. *Strategic Management Journal*, 14 (1), 33.

Ansoff, I. 1957. Strategies for Diversification. *Harvard Business Review*, 35 (5), 113–24.

Barney, J.B. 1991. Firms' Resources and Sustained Competitive Advantage. *Journal of Management*, 17, 99–120.

Collis, D.J. and Montgomery C.A. 1995. Competing on Resources — Strategy in the 1990s. *Harvard Business Review*, 73 (4), 118–28.

Cook,. W.J. 1998. Maximum Merger. *U.S. News & World Rep*, 124 (19), 45–7.

Danzon, P.M., Epstein, A. and Nicholson, S. 2007. *Mergers and Acquisitions in the Pharmaceutical and Biotech Industries*. The Wharton School.

Data Monitor. 2007. Procter & Gamble Company Profile.

Farhadi, M. and Tovstiga, G. 2008a. Kommunikation in M&A Transaktionen, Ereignisse und Herausforderungen. *M&A Review*, 4, 186–93.

Farhadi, M. and Tovstiga, G. 2008b. Structural Anti-takeover Strategies in Germany. *Management Online Review* [online]. Available at: http://www.morexpertise.com/download.php?id=108. [Accessed: 20 April 2009]

Farhadi, M. and Tovstiga, G. 2009. Intellectual Property Management in M&A-Transaktionen. *M&A Review*, 3 (1), 60–8.

Grant, R.M. 1991. *Contemporary Strategy Analysis*. Cambridge: Blackwell Publishers.

Hall, R. 1992. The Strategy Analysis of Intangible Resources. *Strategic Management Journal*, 13, 135–44.

*Handelsblatt.com.* (2003, Januar 03). Retrieved May 10, 2010, from Limousine soll englisch bleiben – BMW baut jetzt Rolls Royce: http://www.handelsblatt.com/archiv/bmw-baut-jetzt-rolls-royce;594038

Hess, E.D. 2007. The Quest for Organic Growth. *Corporate Finance Review*, 12 (1), 28.

Kay, J.A. 1994. *Foundations of Corporate Success*. Oxford: Oxford University Press.

Koller, T., Goedhart, M. and Wessels, D. 2005. *Valuation: Measuring and Managing the Value of Companies*. 4th Edition. New York: John Wiley & Sons, Inc.

Lamb, R.B. 2006. *The Role of Intellectual Property and Intangible Assets in Mergers and Acquisitions*, New York University, Stern Graduate School of Business.

Lee, S. 2004. Growth Strategy: *A Conceptual Framework*. Working Paper 04-10. KDI School of Public Policy and Management Working Paper Series Index. Available at: htp://library.kdischool.ac.kr/publication/paper.aspt

Louis, H. 2004. Earnings Management and the Market Performance of Acquiring Firms. *Journal of Financial Economics*, 74 (1), 121–48.

Mahoney, J. and Pandian, J.R. 1992. The Resource-based View within the Conversation of Strategic Management. *Strategic Management Journal*, 13, 363–80.

Marks, M. and Mirvis, P. 2001. Making Mergers and Acquisitions Work: Strategic and Psychological Preparation. *Academy of Management Executives*, 80–94.

Meyer, R., Rukstad, M.G., Coughlan, P.J. and Jansen, S.A. 2005. *DaimlerChrysler Post-Merger Integration (A)*. Harvard Business School. Case study: 9-703-417.

Penrose, E. 1959, *The Theory of the Growth of the Firm*. New York: John Wiley and Sons.

Peteraf, M.A. 1993. The Cornerstones of Competitive Advantage: A Resource Based View. *Strategic Management Journal*, 14, 179–91.

Porter, M.E. 1991. Towards a Dynamic Theory of Strategy. *Strategic Management Journal*, 12, 95–117.

Porter, M.E. 2004. *Competitive Strategy* (First Free Press Export Edition ed.). New York: Free Press.

Prahalad, C.K. and Hamel, G. 1990. The Core Competence of The Corporation. *Harvard Business Review*, 68 (3), 79–91.

Raisch, S. and von Krogh, G. 2007. Navigating a Path to Smart Growth. *MIT Sloan Management Review*, 48 (3), 65–72.

Rothenbuecher, J. and Schrottke, J. 2008. To Get Value From a Merger, Grow Sales. *Harvard Business Review*, 86 (5), 24–25.

Rynbrandt, J.C. and Bruner, R. 2000. *Exercises in the Strategy of Post-Merger Integration.* Darden Business Publishing.

Sirower, M. and O'Byrne, S. 1998. The Measurement of Post-acquisition Performance Towards a Value-based Benchmarking Methodology. *Journal of Applied Corporate Finance*, 11 (2), 107–21.

Smith, G. V. 2002. *Intellectual Property Assets in Mergers and Acquisitions: Intangible Assets and Intellectual Property Accompanying Mergers and Acquisitions* (1st Edition ed.). New York, NY, US: John Wiley & Sons.

Stalk, G., Evans, P. and Shulman, L.E. 1992. Competing on Capabilities: The New Rules of Corporate Strategy. *Harvard Business Review*, 70 (2), 57–69.

Thompson, J. and Martin, F. 2005. *Strategic Management.* 5th Edition. Virginia: Thomas Learning.

Weston, F.J., Mitchell, M.L. and Mulherin, J.H. 2004. *Takeovers, Restructuring and Corporate Governance.* 4th Edition, New Jersey: Pearson Prentice Hall.

Zahra, S.A. and Das, S.R. 1993. Building Competitive Advantage on Manufacturing Resources. *Long Range Planning*, 26 (2), 57–69.

# *Index*

Printed in the United States

by Baker & Taylor Publisher Services

Printed in the United States
by Baker & Taylor Publisher Services